Environmental econo

Environmental economics

An elementary introduction

R. Kerry Turner, David Pearce and Ian Bateman

Centre for Social and Economic Research on the Global Environment
University of East Anglia and University College London

HARVESTER
WHEATSHEAF

New York London Toronto Sydney Tokyo Singapore

First published 1994 by
Prentice Hall/Harvester Wheatsheaf
Campus 400, Maylands Avenue
Hemel Hempstead
Hertfordshire, HP2 7EZ
A division of
Simon & Schuster International Group

Typeset in 9½/12pt Palatino
by Keyset Composition, Colchester

Printed and bound in Great Britain by
T.J. Press (Padstow) Ltd, Cornwall

British Library Cataloguing in Publication Data

A catalogue record for this book is available from
the British Library

ISBN 0-7450-1083-0 (pbk)

8 9 10   01 00 99

CONTENTS

v

Contents

PREFACE

Environmental economics has at last come into its own, some twenty years perhaps since the main writings that have served as its foundation. Its essence lies in a sequence of logical steps: assessing the *economic* importance of environmental degradation; looking for the *economic* causes of degradation; and designing *economic* incentives to slow, halt and reverse that degradation. The fundamental presumption of environmental economics, now almost universally accepted, is that the environment is not a separate entity from the economy. Changes in one affect the other. No economic decision can be made that does not affect our natural and built environments. No environmental change can occur that does not have an economic impact.

Environmental economists are at pains to point out that for them, as for most economists, 'economic' does not just mean what happens to the flow of money in the economy. Changes in *human wellbeing* are economic effects. So, if burning another hectare of Amazonian rainforest causes anguish and upset for individuals who care about conserving such areas, then the economic act of burning in order to clear the land for, say, cattle ranching has given rise to an environmental impact which has an economic effect (the loss of wellbeing to those who care). In other words, economics is not just about money. Indeed, we would argue that environmental economics is a fascinating and important area of study precisely because it is *not* generally about money. But money comes into it, as we show in several chapters. It comes into it partly because money is a convenient measuring rod of what people want and don't want with respect to the environment. The distinction is quite hard to accommodate initially, but we urge readers to persevere.

What we are interested in is human wellbeing, not money. If we talk about money we are not talking immoral economics; we are not reducing the importance of the environment. Quite the contrary, we argue that thinking the economic way brings insights into a powerful array of economic weapons that we can use to protect the environment; weapons we have only just started to use. We do not, therefore, deny the moral case for the

vii

environment. For example, we agree that frequently it simply isn't *right* to drain this wetland or burn that forest. But the moral argument is only one argument for protecting the environment. We think the economic argument is often more powerful, and especially so when, as is frequently the case, the 'right thing' by nature contradicts other rights such as the right to develop economically and the right to have food and shelter.

The current book has been motivated by two factors.

First, the immense success of several of our previous publications and the resulting mail led us to realize that a great many people simply want to know more about environmental economics. Our textbook *Economics of Natural Resources and the Environment* (Pearce and Turner, 1990) which has been reprinted numerous times with a new edition planned soon, is for under-graduate students, not the wider audience. Other volumes (*Blueprint for a Green Economy* by Pearce, Markandya and Barbier (1989) and *Blueprint II* edited by Pearce (1991)) have enjoyed a similar success. Whereas these were aimed at a wider audience, they still did not explain the groundwork of environmental economics, the economic way of thinking. That is the aim of this book which is targeted at non-specialists whether they are students or not. Students interested in economics will probably want to spend more time on the introductory chapter and suggested reading than the general reader. The latter can skim this chapter as succeeding chapters contain more detail and general explanations.

Second, we have become deeply conscious that academics spend too little time explaining their subject. Academic professions tend to frown on textbooks, especially those aimed at the wider audience. We think that view is fundamentally mistaken and in contradiction to one of the very rationales for academia: teaching. We accept that in making things simple many caveats and complications are glossed over. But everyone has to start somewhere and it is best to get the message across first and make things complicated later on, rather than create a sea of confusion at the outset and hope that some people will swim through it.

We hope you enjoy this book and we welcome your comments. We have tried to explain what is often a difficult subject as simply as possible. We shall be especially interested to hear from readers who feel we have not been clear enough and who, perhaps themselves, have ways of making things more simple still.

RKT
DWP
IB
Norwich and London, 1993

INTRODUCTION

A very brief economic history lesson

This book's primary objective is to introduce to a general audience the basic concepts and principles of what has become known as environmental economics. For all practical purposes, the origins of environmental economics lie in the 1960s at the time of the first wave of modern popular 'green' thinking and policy perceptions within developed countries, known as **environmentalism** (O'Riordan, 1983). This is not to say, of course, that the foundations of environmental economics appeared *de novo* during the 1960s. It is a branch of economics and shares with its parent discipline a common history. Some of the fundamental ideas that provide a framework for environmental economics go back at least to the eighteenth century.

A minority of citizens have always worried about the state of, and rate of use of, the natural environment whether locally, nationally or internationally, and have usually been ignored by their contemporaries. But elements of their message may be more relevant today than ever before.

While seemingly obvious, it is of crucial importance for an understanding of environmental economics, that we recognize that our economic system (which provides us with all the material goods and services necessary for a 'modern' standard of living) is underpinned by and cannot operate without the support of ecological systems of plants and animals and their interrelationships (collectively known as the biosphere), and *not* vice versa.

Thus environmental economics views the real economy in which we all live and work as an **open system**. What this means is that in order to function (i.e. provide goods and services or wealth for its human operators) the economy must extract resources (raw material and fuel) from the environment, process these resources (turning them into end-products for consumption) and dispose of large amounts of dissipated and/or chemically transformed resources (wastes) back into the environment. This so-called **materials balance** perspective on the economy is fundamental to environmental

1

economics analysis. We expand on the **materials balance model** of the economy in Chapter 1, but the crucial idea is that the economic system is *not a closed system*. As more resources are sucked into the economy from the environment so more wastes are pushed back into the environment. This puts pressure on its limited capacity to handle the waste without harm to humans, animals and plants.

Ecological limits on the economy

There is a very real but ultimate sense in which economic activity is 'limited' or 'bounded' by the capacities of natural environments. Now the 'limits' concept has its origins in the work of thinkers such as Malthus (1798), Ricardo (1817) and Marx (1867). Malthus worried about *absolute limits* or scarcity. He believed that as the economy developed, population growth would always tend to outgrow the means of subsistence (food produced by agriculture) and a state of misery, 'the stationary state', would be the inevitable end result. Ricardo took a more sophisticated and slightly more optimistic perspective when he argued that *relative limits* or scarcity was the real problem for a growing economy. In Ricardian analysis, limits are set by rising costs as the highest grade resources (i.e. best agricultural land, purest deposits of minerals, etc.), which are exploited first, become exhausted and have to be substituted for by successively lower grade resources. The costs of exploitation (including pollution costs, see Chapters 1 and 3) escalate as the 'grade profile' of resources declines.

Later in the nineteenth century, Marx highlighted the possibilities that economic growth might be limited because of social and political unrest within the national economy and associated society (this was later expanded by his followers into an international, global economic context). The 'social limits' to growth theme was picked up again by some economists during the development of environmental economics in the 1970s. In the early 1970s, opinion poll evidence in the developed countries, for example, seemed to indicate that despite huge absolute increases in the material standard of living, people on average said they did not feel much happier with their lives, the Easterlin paradox (Easterlin, 1974). It turned out that the 'feel good factor' was a complex phenomenon influenced as much by *relative* income and social status as by absolute quantities.

The 'social limits' theme was also further extended and elaborated on during the 1970s with the addition of *moral concerns* connected with economic growth and development. Ethical issues (i.e. questions of right and wrong) surfaced on the potentially negative impact of the fast growth modern economic system, the prospects of future human generations and non-human nature, as well as on exacerbating declining moral standards in contemporary society (see Chapter 2).

2

Our very brief historical survey should also include mention of one other influential nineteenth century thinker, J. S. Mill (1857). Mill, like previous political economists, believed that the economic growth process would end in the 'stationary state'. At this point there would be a static population level serviced by a fixed amount of housing, infrastructure, farms and other industrial plants. In economic terms, there would be a **constant stock of human capital** (people) and a **constant stock of physical capital** (machines, buildings, etc.). Incidentally, Mill argued that it was quite possible to conceive of this stationary state society as socially desirable, giving people the time and space to enjoy the spiritual, artistic and educational aspects of the human condition.

The 'constant stock' idea was another notion that reemerged during the 1970s, when it was popularized by Daly (1973) in a book advocating the deliberate creation of a no-growth **steady-state economy**. For Daly, the key policy question becomes, how big (i.e. physical scale or size of the human presence in the ecosystem) should the economy become (given that it is a subsystem of the environment) relative to the overall system (i.e. the biosphere, economies plus ecosystems and all their interrelationships)? He is critical of conventional economics because, as he sees it, the discipline fails to provide a proper analysis of the economic 'scale' issue (population x per capita resource use).

A significant caveat is in order at this point in the introductory discussion of the evolution of environmental economics. While the 'limits' and 'constant stock' (steady-state) concepts have been and remain important foci for analysis and debate, a belief in them is not a necessary feature of modern environmental economics. Indeed our position is that it is not necessary to totally embrace the steady-state philosophy (we set out the reasons why in Chapter 3) in order to adequately safeguard the environment on which we all depend.

It is also the case that environmental economics is not a static body of knowledge but an ongoing process of change, refinement and debate. Most recently, over the last five years or so, a split has occurred which has led some analysts to comment that a potentially separate subdiscipline called **'ecological economics'** has begun to emerge. There is, however, no clear consensus on what ecological economics embraces or how it differs from environmental economics. We will not in this introductory text attempt to set out in any rigorous way the possible differences between the two approaches. At the risk of great oversimplification, it is, we suppose, possible to argue that ecological economics can be viewed as a reaction to, and rejection or modification of, certain of the assumptions that tend to characterize environmental economics. Daly's advocacy of the steady-state economy and the vital importance of the 'scale' issue, is an example of how ecological economics might diverge from environmental economics. We will flag some other potential points of divergence in succeeding chapters (see in particular

Chapters 2, 4 and 8) but will stop well short of any comprehensive position. The bulk of the analysis in this text is devoted to an elementary exposition of the principles and policy perceptions of environmental economics.

Before we outline the basic structure and organization of the succeeding chapters we return to our historical survey in order to highlight a number of other important concepts which have been assimilated into modern environmental economics thinking.

Environmental pollution as an external cost

Because the economy is an open system its three basic processes (extraction, processing/fabrication and consumption) all involve the generation of waste products that eventually find their way back into the environment (the air, water or onto land). Too much waste in the wrong place at the wrong time (or over too long a time) will cause biological and other changes in the environment (known as **contamination**) which themselves may then cause harm or damage to animals/plants and their ecosystems (**pollution**). If these environmental damage effects then serve to harm human health or negatively affect human wellbeing in some other way (i.e. reduce the pleasure of outdoor recreation, etc.) economists would recognize the existence of **economic pollution**.

The economic definition of pollution is dependent upon both some physical effect of waste on the environment and a human reaction to that physical effect. In economic parlance, there has been an uncompensated loss of human welfare (wellbeing) due to the imposition of an **external cost** (i.e. health damage, morbidity or mortality increases, less pleasurable recreation experiences, etc.) related to the emission to the air or discharge to water or onto land of waste substances. So the physical presence of pollution does not mean that 'economic pollution' exists. Further, even if economic pollution was present, it is far from always being the case that it should be eliminated. We expand on this argument in Chapters 5 and 10.

It was Pigou (1920) who first formalized the impact of pollution on the working of the economy. His analysis distinguished between the *private costs* of production and consumption activities (encapsulated in fuel, raw material, labour costs, etc.) and the full *social costs* (i.e. on society as a whole) of such activities. What he saw was that pollution gives rise to external costs, which drive a wedge between private and social costs. So the social costs of production or consumption are made up of private costs plus any external costs that may be present. The socially optimal level of external costs is unlikely to be zero (zero pollution) because of the natural capacity of the environment to absorb some waste and the cost of controlling pollution. Zero pollution is desirable, however, when the predicted damage from the disposal of certain toxic and hazardous substances is thought to be

4

catastrophic in some sense. Unfortunately, real world pollution situations are often beset by a lack of data and/or understanding over just how dangerous some released substances will turn out to be over the long run. Making decisions under uncertainty is a complex task and we outline some of the issues involved in Chapters 9 and 14.

Non-renewable and renewable resource use

On the basis of the materials balance model of the economy/environment interface, resource extraction (and harvesting) activities start off the process of economic activity. Resources may be simplistically classified as **exhaustible** (or more properly **non-renewable**) or as **renewable**. The former are fixed in overall quantity, so that use of them in a given time period means that there is less of them available for other time periods. The basis of the economics of non-renewable resources was formulated by Gray (1914) and Hotelling (1931). Their analysis was developed in the context of the underlying historical concern that the world's exhaustible resources (minerals, forests and other resources – renewable and non-renewable) might be being extracted too rapidly and sold too cheaply.

Most of the non-renewable resource theory relating to the activities of mineral extracting firms is primarily concerned with the best ('optimal') *rate* at which resource deposits or fields should be extracted, and also with the optimal *amount* of the resource that should be extracted. What Gray and Hotelling showed was that in the case of, for example, the minerals-extraction industry, the production in any given period is not independent of production in any other period. They proved that because the current rate of extraction of a mineral actually affects the amount of that mineral that may be extracted in future periods, the current costs of extraction (and rates of extraction) are subject to a set of quite complicated forces. Thus, current extraction costs depend on current input costs (fuel, labour, etc.), and also on past rates of extraction and on the effect of current extraction on the future profitability of the mineral deposit. The owner of the mineral deposit will try to maximize total profits over a given time horizon (known as the 'net worth') rather than simply maximize profit in any given period.

Because of the assumption of a fixed amount of a given mineral resource, Gray reasoned that extraction costs (usually analyzed in terms of marginal cost, i.e. costs per unit of additional output) would include an additional element. He developed a concept that we now call **user cost**, the notion that possible future use of a non-renewable resource is necessarily sacrificed if units of the resource stock are exploited and used today. So in strict economic terms the cost of using a non-renewable resource (e.g. coal, gas, oil and other mineral deposits) is therefore made up of the sum of its extraction costs (e.g. cost of mines, drilling rigs, etc.) and the user cost element.

It was noted that the owner of a mineral deposit might well maximize total profits by postponing extraction (conserving resources for the future) if, for example, it was expected that the price of the mineral would increase substantially in the future (i.e. increase in user costs); or if extraction costs due to a new technology were thought likely to fall in the future. On the other hand, if current interest rates paid out on financial investments were to increase then this would serve to increase current rates of mineral extraction in known deposits. The owner could now invest any current profits derived from extraction and gain the higher rates of interest. Profits now have been made more valuable relative to future profits, with the latter now being more heavily **discounted** by the owner. Discounting is a very important general concept in economic analysis and it reflects the fact that we tend to regard costs and benefits in the future as being of less importance than costs and benefits now (see Chapter 7). It turns out that the discount rate (how much less valuable future costs and benefits are) is of prime importance in determining the rate at which non-renewable and renewable resources are used (see Chapters 15 and 16). Hotelling (1931) showed that under certain conditions the **rent** or **royalty** on a resource (the price net of extraction costs) would increase over time at a percentage rate equal to the resource owner's discount rate.

Changes in the rate of interest in the real world will affect not just the value of profits, but also the level of effort that mineral firms will put into exploring for and developing new sites for future extraction. They also influence investment in new capital equipment, both in deposits already being worked and at new deposits. There can therefore be a number of offsetting forces to the increased rates of extraction of known deposits.

Carlisle (1954) brought the question of the **optimal amount** of the total resource deposit to extract to the fore. He emphasized the point that no mining/drilling firm would ever extract the entire amount of a deposit. Carlisle's analysis showed that the optimal rate of extraction varies with the level of extraction and vice versa, and that the existence of uncertainty complicates the problem even further. Modern economic optimal resource use analysis reflects these complications and we deal with it in outline form only in Chapter 16 (the published literature is technically very demanding).

Hotelling's work served to highlight another important set of factors in environmental economics analysis. He showed that in situations related to free or easy access/entry to the resource deposit (or for that matter to a renewable resource such as a forest or a fishery) too rapid a rate of extraction would result. **Open access** is possible because either **property rights** do not exist or are easily challenged. So if many firms can drill an oil field, for example, no firm is induced to hold back and the field is exploited too rapidly; oil and gas are also lost. The open access problem has, unfortunately, been confused in the environmental economics literature by frequent references to the **common property problem** and the **tragedy of the commons**

problem. In fact common property is property owned by a community and is often subject to usage rules or social norms (see Chapter 15). We therefore prefer the term the 'tragedy of open access' and link it not just to the problem of the best rate of resource exploitation, but to the problem of pollution and the rate at which the environment's **assimilative capacity** (i.e. its ability to 'absorb' wastes produced by the economy without exhibiting signs of excessive change and stress and therefore physical and economic pollution) could itself be depleted or destroyed (see Chapters 10 to 14).

In the case of renewable resources (e.g. fisheries, forests or livestock, and rangeland), the rules for optimal use over time were first comprehensively formulated by Gordon (1954). He compared the utilization of a fishery under open access and single ownership conditions and showed that under the former regime, resource rents would be exhausted and the resource itself would be pushed close to extinction. In the renewable resource case, decisions about the optimal amount of the resource to harvest and when to harvest it are interdependent. This is because the resource itself (strictly its biomass stock) grows through time and this increases the potential harvest yield the longer is the delay in harvesting.

From 'cowboy economy' to 'Spaceship Earth'

In 1966 Boulding wrote an essay on 'Spaceship Earth' which combined economics and some science in order to bring together the view of the economy as a circular resource flow system, and of the environment as a set of limits, resource stocks (or **sources**) and natural assimilative capacities (or **sinks**) for wastes. Boulding argued that we must cease to behave as if we lived in a 'cowboy economy', with unlimited new territory (i.e. resources, sources and sinks) to be conquered and learn to treat planet earth as a 'spaceship'. The spaceship is a circular system in which every effort has to be made to recycle materials, reduce wastes, conserve exhaustible energy sources and tap into potentially limitless energy sources such as solar power.

Boulding's synthesis work was formalized in the materials balance models of Ayres and Kneese (1969) and Kneese *et al.* (1970). Their additional contribution was to show that wastes are pervasive throughout the economic system. Since the discharge and emission of wastes into the environment is inevitable, pollution externality effects are also potentially pervasive. Some form of government intervention to 'control' the rate and extent of pollution is therefore required. Control could be exercised via regulations and laws and/or via economic incentive instruments such as taxes and permits (see Chapters 10 to 14). Government intervention is, however, no panacea for environmental degradation problems and uncoordinated policies (intervention failure) can make matters worse (see Chapter 6).

Because environmental economics has accepted the hypothesis that there is an extensive interdependence between the economy and the environment, some of its analysts have also pointed out that the design of economies (free market, planned or mixed) offers no guarantee that the **life support functions** of natural environments will persist. The materials balance model shows clearly that the environment provides three basic functions: it supplies resources (renewable and non-renewable); it assimilates waste products; and it provides humans with natural services such as aesthetic enjoyment, recreation and even spiritual fulfilment. These three functions can also be regarded as components of one general function of natural environments – the function of life support.

All these environmental functions are economic functions because they all have a **positive economic value**: if we bought and sold these functions in the market-place they would all have **positive prices**. Mistreatment of natural environments often arises because we do not recognize the positive prices for these economic functions, as there are no markets and therefore no market prices for many environmental goods and services (**market failure**, see Chapter 5).

We lack information and analysis that could demonstrate whether any particular economy is consistent with the natural environments, which are necessarily linked to that economy. We do not have what we could call an **existence theorem** that relates the scale and components of an economy to the set of environment–economy interrelationships underlying that economy. Without this theorem we run the risk of degrading and perhaps destroying environmental functions. If we are interested in sustaining our economy over time, it becomes important to establish some principles and then practical rules for **sustainable economic development** (see Chapter 4).

The **valuation** of environmental functions, which are generally unpriced, is an important task in order to help correct economic decisions which treat natural environments as if they were free goods and services, and therefore lead to overuse. Some of the methods and techniques that have been developed in order to value these environmental assets in monetary terms are reviewed in Chapter 8. Economists generally advocate what they call **cost–benefit thinking**, which can be applied to individual projects (new dams, roads, power plants, etc.) or to policies or even wider courses of action. Simply put, the idea is to compare all the relevant benefits from, say, the building of a new water supply reservoir with the costs (construction and running costs) of such a project (including the environmental effects). Both costs and benefits are translated, as far as is feasible, into monetary terms and discounted over a given time horizon. Only projects with benefits greater than costs are acceptable (see Chapter 7).

Environmental economics merely deploys cost–benefit thinking in the context of environmental problems and issues. So 'benefits assessment', i.e. the monetary evaluation of the environmental benefits of environmental policy, or its obverse 'damage cost assessment', has had two main uses: first, to integrate the unpriced but valuable functions of natural environments into cost–benefit analysis of real world projects, and, second, to illustrate the kinds of economic damage done to national economies by resource depletion and pollution (see Chapter 3).

Once society has decided on an 'acceptable' level of environmental quality assisted by, among other factors, economic cost–benefit analysis, there are still further problems to be resolved. To transform the decision into reality requires a change of behaviour on the part of producers and consumers. Again a continuing debate exists in environmental economics concerning the relative merits of **command and control regulations** (CAC) and **market-based incentives** to control pollution.

Norton (1984) has summarized the position as follows. In choosing a pollution control policy, we need to determine:

(a) what policy instruments and technologies for abatement of pollution are available;
(b) what the objectives of the pollution control policy are, with particular reference to the type of pollution and the degree of environmental risk posed, the extent and reliability of pollution control methods, the full social costs of pollution control, and the social incidence of the costs and benefits (i.e. distributional effects);
(c) how cost-effective are the different policy instruments with respect to these objectives.

The **regulatory approach** (CAC) is based on the issuing of orders by some central government agency to do or not to so something (i.e. install and operate a piece of equipment or new process), known in the United Kingdom as the application of **Best Practicable Means** (BPM) and **Best Available Technology Not Entailing Excessive Cost** (BATNEEC), or in the United States as **Best Available Control Technology** (BACT) (see Chapter 14). The regulations may also cover the following issues:

(a) limits in terms of maximum rate of discharge from a pollution source;
(b) pollution discharge bans related to pollution concentration measures or damage costs;
(c) specification of inputs or outputs from a given production process.

Economic incentives require not action but payments, and, in principle, encourage the economically rational polluter to change behaviour by balancing reduced payments (of say a pollution tax) against increased costs incurred in reducing pollution discharges. Early economic work in the field of pollution control stressed the desirability of the economic incentive approach (Kneese, 1964). Given certain assumptions it can be shown that the most efficient (strictly the most cost-effective) way of achieving some predetermined level of environmental quality is via the imposition of a pollution tax or related economic incentive instrument. However, when some of these assumptions are relaxed and criteria such as distributional equity and ethical considerations are introduced, the case in favour of the incentive approach is much less clear cut (Bohm and Russell, 1985).

The rest of this book is organized in the following way:

- Part I (Chapters 1 to 4) covers a range of basic issues ending up with a discussion of the concept of sustainable economic development.
- Part II (Chapters 5 and 6) deals with the causes of environmental problems which are analyzed in terms of two interrelated 'failures' concepts, market failure and government policy failure.
- Part III (Chapters 7 to 9) covers cost–benefit analysis and its application to environmental issues. The methods and techniques that have been applied, in the absence of market-based price/value data, in order to value environmental assets in monetary terms are reviewed, and the section ends with a discussion of the problems caused by uncertainty.
- Part IV (Chapters 10 to 14) deals with various forms of government intervention that are possible in order to protect environmental quality. A range of policy instruments, taxes, charges, permits and regulations are appraised in terms of their economic efficiency and other criteria.
- Part V (Chapters 15 and 16) cover the basic analytics of natural resource usage and sustainable management.
- Part VI (Chapters 17 to 23) is composed of a series of mini case study chapters on various 'local' and 'global' scale environmental management topics.

References

R. Ayres and A. Kneese, 'Production, consumption and externalities', *American Economic Review* **59**: 282–97, 1969.

P. Bohm and C. Russell, 'Comparative analysis of alternative policy instruments', in A. Kneese and J. Sweeney (eds), *Handbook of Natural Resource and Energy Economics*, North Holland, Amsterdam, 1985.

K. Boulding, 'The economics of the coming Spaceship Earth', in H. Jarrett (ed.), *Environmental Quality in a Growing Economy*, Johns Hopkins University Press, Baltimore, 1966.

D. Carlisle, 'The economics of a fund resource with particular reference to mining', *American Economic Review* **44**: 595-616, 1954.

H. Daly, *Steady State Economics*, Freeman, San Francisco, 1977; second edition, Island Press, New York, 1991.

R. A. Easterlin, 'Does economic growth improve the human lot?', in P. David and R. Weber (eds), *Nations and Households in Economic Growth*, Academic Press, New York, 1974.

H. S. Gordon, 'Economic theory of a common-property resource: the fishery', *Journal of Political Economy* **62**: 124–42, 1954.

L. Gray, 'Rent under the assumption of exhaustibility', *Quarterly Journal of Economics* **28**: 466–89, 1914.

H. Hotelling, 'The economics of exhaustible resources', *Journal of Political Economy* **39**, 137–75, 1931.

A. Kneese, *The Economics of Regional Water Quality Management*, Resources for the Future, Johns Hopkins University Press, Baltimore, 1964.

A. Kneese, R. Ayres and R. d'Arge, *Economics and the Environment: A Materials Balance Approach*, Resources for the Future, Washington DC, 1970.

T. Malthus, *An Essay on the Principle of Population*, first published in 1798, reprinted by Macmillan, London, 1909.

K. Marx, *Capital*, Vols I, II and III, Lawrence and Wishart, London, 1970, 1970 and 1972; but see R. Freeman (ed.), *Marx on Economics*, Penguin, Harmondsworth, 1962.

J. S. Mill, *Principles of Political Economy*, Parker, London, 1857.

G. A. Norton, *Resource Economics*, Edward Arnold, London, 1984.

T. O'Riordan, *Environmentalism*, 2nd edition, Pion Press, London, 1983.

A. C. Pigou, *The Economics of Welfare*, Macmillan, London, 1920.

D. Ricardo, *Principles of Political Economy and Taxation*, Everyman, London, 1926.

PART I

Economics and the environment

CHAPTER 1

The big economy

According to the authors of a recent non-conventional economics text it is important to recognize that human communities are part of a larger community that encompasses both them and non-human nature (Daly and Cobb, 1990). From this perspective, 'the industrial economy is only part of the "Great Economy" – the economy that sustains the total web of life and everything that depends on the land' (Daly and Cobb, 1990, p. 18). It is this big economy that is of ultimate importance.

Conventional economics textbooks often convey a very misleading picture of the relationship between an economic system (a set of institutions and activities designed to efficiently allocate scarce resources among things that provide benefits, thereby satisfying human wants and desires) and the environment (made up of ecosystems or interrelationships between living species themselves and with non-living or abiotic structure) that surrounds and underpins it. Basically, simple economic models have ignored the economy–environment interrelationships altogether. The economy is portrayed as a **closed and linear system** shown in Box 1.1. This, of course, is physically impossible and the implications of how an economy does in fact sustain itself over time lies at the core of environmental economic thought. In reality the opposite is the case. The economy is an open and circular system which is only able to function because of the support of its ecological foundations. A working economy must extract, process and discard large amounts of physical materials. This means that the economy is subject to physical constraints.

The materials balance perspective

Environmental economics takes as its starting point, the lessons to be drawn from the 'laws' of thermodynamics. The economy–environment interactions are best portrayed via the **materials balance model**, based on the First and

15

Box 1.1 Conventional economic model

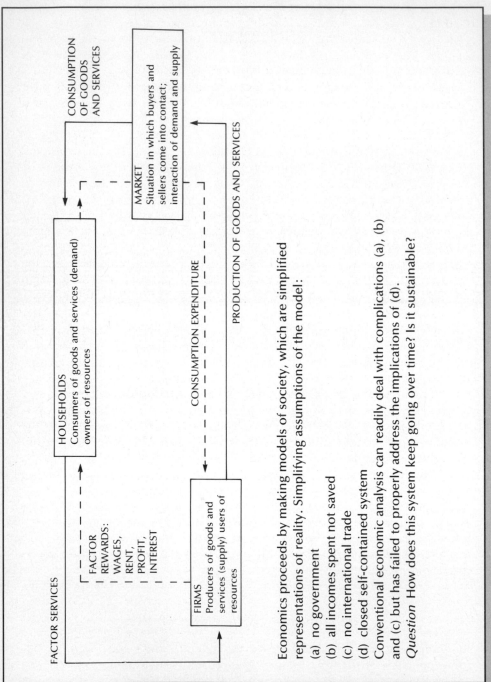

Economics proceeds by making models of society, which are simplified representations of reality. Simplifying assumptions of the model:

(a) no government
(b) all incomes spent not saved
(c) no international trade
(d) closed self-contained system

Conventional economic analysis can readily deal with complications (a), (b) and (c) but has failed to properly address the implications of (d).

Question How does this system keep going over time? Is it sustainable?

Second Laws of Thermodynamics, as shown in Box 1.2. The model represents the economy as a materials processing and product transformation system. 'Useful' materials are drawn into the economic system (e.g. non-renewable resources such as fossil fuels can be extracted until their stocks are exhausted and renewable resources such as fisheries and forests can be harvested) and then undergo a series of changes in their energy and entropy (i.e. usefulness) states. Eventually after a time lag, the non-product output of the system can be partially recycled with the residual 'useless' materials (wastes) returned to the environment from various points in the economic process, see Box 1.3.

The materials that first enter the economic system are not destroyed by production and consumption activities; they are, however, dispersed and chemically transformed. In particular, they enter in a state of low entropy (as 'useful' materials) and leave in a state of high entropy (as 'useless' materials, such as low temperature heat emissions, exhaust gases, mixed municipal wastes, etc.). At first sight, the entropy concept seems counter-intuitive and it is not used formally or defined rigorously in this discussion. In lay terms, entropy is a certain property of systems which increases in any irreversible process. When entropy increases, the energy in the system becomes less available to do 'useful work'. No material recycling processes can therefore ever be 100 per cent efficient (Ayres and Kneese, 1989). Once the materials balance perspective is adopted, it is easy to see that the way humans manage their economies impacts on the environment and, in the reverse direction, environmental quality impacts on the efficient working of the economy.

The multifunctional nature of environmental resources

Environmental economists are seeking to expound the principle that natural systems are multifunctional assets in the sense that the environment provides humans with a wide range of economically valuable functions and services:

- a natural resource base (renewable and non-renewable resources);
- a set of natural goods (landscape and amenity resources);
- a waste assimilation capacity;
- a life support system.

The principles of scarcity and opportunity cost, as well as the objective of an efficient allocation of scarce resources, can now be applied to the complete collection of environmental goods and services: waste assimilation functions, peace and quiet, clear air and water, unspoilt landscapes, etc. If environmental resources are becoming more scarce then economic analysis can play a role in devising strategies to mitigate some of the consequences of that process. A balance will be required between the interests of people wishing to use the environment now in a direct way (e.g. as a source of raw materials or a **waste sink**) and those wishing to enjoy it now in an indirect use sense (e.g. to

Box 1.2   Simplified materials balance

In this model, the economy is portrayed as an open system pulling in materials and energy from the environment and eventually releasing an equivalent amount of waste back into the environment. Too much waste in the wrong place at the wrong time causes pollution and so-called external costs (externalities).

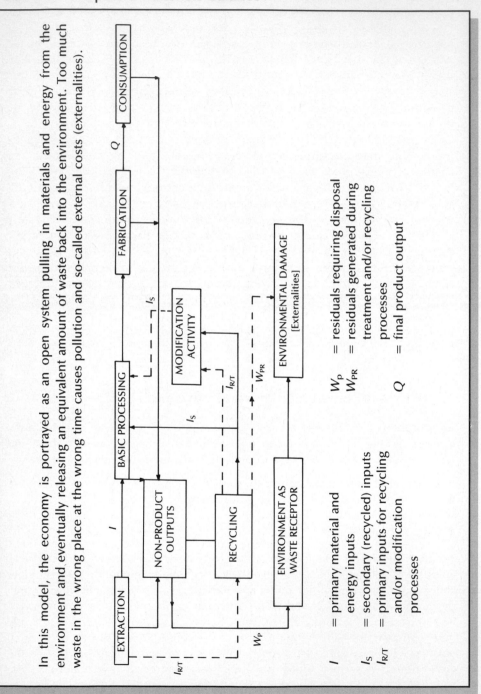

I = primary material and energy inputs

I_S = secondary (recycled) inputs

$I_{R/T}$ = primary inputs for recycling and/or modification processes

W_P = residuals requiring disposal

W_{PR} = residuals generated during treatment and/or recycling processes

Q = final product output

Box 1.3   Simplified materials flow chart

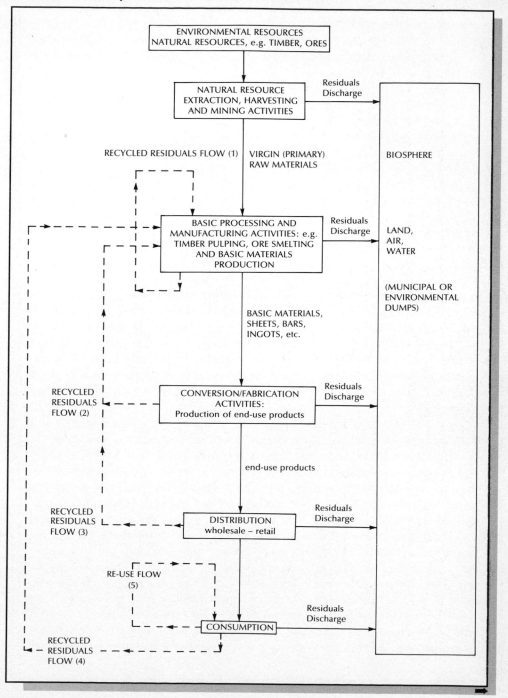

The laws of thermodynamics lead to two propositions that are important in environmental economics:

1. All resource extraction, production and consumption eventually result in waste products (residuals) equal in matter/energy terms to the resources flowing into these sectors.

2. There is no possibility of the 100 per cent return (recycling) of these waste products to enter the resource flow again because of the second (entropy) law of thermodynamics.

All economic systems contain a number of recycling flows, although the level of recycling effort and activity varies between national economies. *Recycling flow (1)* is known as the 'home scrap' flow because the recycled 'secondary' material never leaves the processing plant. Home scrap recycling rates are very high. *Recycling flow (2)*, 'prompt scrap' flow also has a high activity rate, but does require the intervention of a secondary material merchant firm to facilitate the collection of scrap and its redirection back into basic processing. *Recycling flow (3)*, 'commercial scrap' is composed of packaging waste and is the staple business of the recycling merchant firms. *Recycling flow (4)*, 'post-consumer scrap' is the potentially recyclable components of the household and small commercial premises waste stream (municipal solid waste, MSW). Activity rates associated with this type of recycling have historically been low in all industrialized economies (typically less than 10 per cent of the total MSW until quite recently, with the spread of bottle, can, paper and even plastics recycling banks). *Recycling flow (5)*, 're-use' is a practice that has all but disappeared in modern economies and is now restricted to returnable bottles and a limited number of other examples.

Why is it that type 1, 2 and to a lesser extent 3, recycling operates at a high activity rate, while types 4 and 5 remain at relatively low levels of activity? Much of the answer is due to four physical factors (characteristics) and the influence of thermodynamics. The four factors are *mass* (volume of recyclable materials), *homogeneity* (the level and consistency in quality terms (known as grade) of the recyclable materials), *contamination* (the degree to which different materials and other substances are mixed together), and *location* (the number of points at which the materials are first discarded as waste). Compare home scrap (flow (1)) and post-consumer scrap (flow (4)). The former is characterized by large mass, high homogeneity, low contamination and single location. The latter is characterized by small mass, low homogeneity, high contamination and multiple locations. In financial (private cost) terms the profitability of recycling flows 1, 2 and 3 will be much higher than flow 4; indeed the latter will often incur net financial costs. All this is not to say that recycling of MSW may not yield net social benefits sufficient to outweigh the private costs and therefore represent an economically efficient activity. Nevertheless, the message is clear, 100 per cent recycling is not feasible and very high overall rates of recycling may not necessarily be socially desirable (we expand on this argument in Chapter 18).

The extent of recycling in a national economy will also be determined by

Table 1 Britain's place in EEC recycling league (1989)

	Paper	Glass (tonnes)	Aluminium
Belgium	691 000	208 000	n.a.
Denmark	311 000	58 000	n.a.
France	2 881 000	760 000	2 331 000
Germany (FRG)	5 627 000	1 538 000	527 000
Great Britain	2 975 000	310 000	220 000
Greece	n.a.	14 000	n.a.
Ireland	n.a.	11 000	n.a.
Italy	1 733 000	670 000	390 000
Netherlands	1 488 000	279 000	129 000
Portugal	273 000	34 000	n.a.
Spain	1 591 000	287 000	77 600
		(tonnes/head)	
Belgium	0.0671	0.021 00	n.a.
Denmark	0.0610	0.011 40	n.a.
France	0.0522	0.013 00	0.0040
Germany (FRG)	0.0922	0.024 70	0.0086
Great Britain	0.0526	0.005 60	0.0040
Greece	n.a.	0.001 40	n.a.
Ireland	n.a.	0.003 10	n.a.
Italy	0.0304	0.011 75	0.0068
Netherlands	0.1026	0.018 80	0.0087
Portugal	0.0268	0.003 30	n.a.
Spain	0.0412	0.007 40	0.0020

Note: On tonnage/capita basis, however, Britain fares less well. It was fifth out of nine countries in paper recycling, eighth out of eleven for glass, and joint fourth out of six for aluminium.

Overall, the best recycling performance was turned in by West Germany and the Netherlands. Their recycling rates on a per capita basis were about twice as good as Britain's for paper and aluminium, and three to five times as good for glass.

Source: Ends Data Services (1990)

other factors, such as the *relative prices* of secondary (recycled) and primary raw materials as inputs into production processes; the *end-use structure* (number of uses and the grade of material required) for any given secondary material: typically lower grade secondary materials, e.g. mixed waste papers and mixed colour glass, and the small number of uses that are available; *technical progress* in both secondary and primary materials industries; historical and cultural factors which condition the degree of 'environmental awareness' in society – see Table 1.

The basic idea of a national recycling rate is given by the ratio:

$$R = \frac{\text{tonnage recycled annually}}{\text{annual tonnage available for recycling}}$$

But matters are made more complicated by, among other things, the existence of international trade in secondary materials. If imports of secondary material are included in the calculation, then a recycling activity rate (the 'utilization rate') has been calculated. If imports are not included, then a recycling effort rate (the 'recovery rate') has been calculated. These two rates are often confused in debates about recycling between different materials and countries. Taking the example of waste paper, the UK recovery rate in 1990 was 30.4 per cent, while its utilization rate was 53 per cent.

In 1989, Britain was in the lower half of the European Community recycling league for paper, glass and aluminium. The figures in Table 1 show that, on a tonnage basis, Britain performed reasonably well. It was second out of nine countries in the paper recycling league, third out of eleven for glass, and fourth out of six for aluminium.

appreciate a scenic landscape or tropical forest kept in as natural a state as possible). Further, the needs of the present generation of people will have to be balanced against future generations' needs.

The question of how, and under what conditions, free markets can help achieve this balance has spawned a long and extensive literature (Norton, 1984; Pearce *et al.*, 1989). Economic theory demonstrates that given certain assumptions the market mechanism is capable of achieving efficient resource allocations, provided that **externalities** are not present (see Box 1.4). When externalities are present and/or when **public-type goods** (to be defined below) require allocation, markets can fail the efficiency test (see Chapter 5).

Box 1.4   Market mechanism

Buyers (demand) and sellers (supply) coming into contact via a voluntary decentralized exchange process can, given the right conditions determine an equilibrium price and an efficient allocation of resources (i.e. there is no alternative allocation that leaves everyone at least as well off and makes some people better off).

Panel (a) Demand and supply relationship.

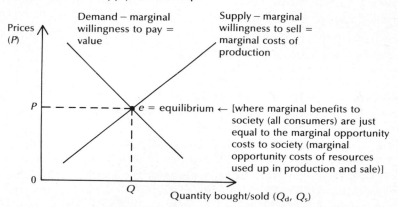

Panel (a) illustrates a situation in which the price of a good is taken to be of primary importance in determining just how much of a good people are prepared to buy, and conversely how much of the good firms are prepared to offer sale. All other factors which could influence demand and supply are assumed constant (i.e. income, price of substitute goods, etc.). So

$$Q_d = f(P)$$
$$Q_s = f(P)$$

At position e, $Q_d = Q_s$ given a market price P.

At e, the marginal willingness of consumers to pay (their valuation of the good) is just equal to the marginal costs (labour, raw materials, energy, etc.) of producing that good and efficiency is maximized as long as the structural conditions for perfect competition are satisfied:

(a) large numbers of buyers and sellers;
(b) perfect information;
(c) goods being exchanged can, in principle, be individually owned;
(d) the full costs of production and consumption are reflected in market prices.

Price has adjusted until at e the amount that people demand of something is equal to the amount that is supplied. Resources are allocated sufficient to produce an amount $0Q$. There is no alternative allocation that leaves everyone at least as well off and makes some people better off.

Pollution externality: the case of a recycled paper production plant

Market failure is related to the absence of structural condition (d) listed above.

Panel (b) The true cost of recycling paper.

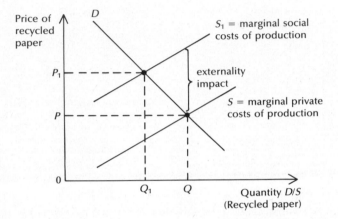

In the real world, all markets are not freely competitive and the structural conditions necessary for perfect competition are not present. In the case of the recycled paper plant Panel (b), the price that would operate, if there were no government controls (laws, regulations or taxes) on pollution, would be *P* and the amount of the good bought and sold would be 0*Q*. Now this position would not represent an efficient allocation of scarce resources if externalities also existed. It is likely that a pollution externality (social costs) would exist in this situation. Unfortunately, recycling paper and board plants produce a potentially damaging liquid waste as well as the 'environmentally friendly' paper products.

In the absence of pollution control regulations or some other official control instrument, let us assume the plant discharges its liquid effluent straight into the local river. Assume further, that downstream of the recycling plant another plant takes water out of the river in order to process food products, and further downstream again a nature reserve and re-creational swimming and boating area also exist. The downstream users (e.g. the food plant and the birdwatchers and recreationalists) suffer costs due to the water pollution caused by the recycling plant. The food plant has to install more expensive water purification equipment, and the boating and swimming enthusiasts have to put up with a poorer quality experience or may even have to give up swimming in that location altogether. If the pollution is particularly severe, wildlife may disappear altogether from the nature reserve areas.

The full costs of producing and consuming the recycled goods were not reflected properly in the price level P. The recycling plant's private costs of production should be augmented by the extra social costs (in monetary terms) involved, shifting S to S_1. Once the social costs have been internalized and the supply curve shifted to S_1, a new price is determined at P_1. The efficient allocation of resources (properly reflecting the waste assimilation service of the environment) required a higher price of P_1 and a lower output level of Q_1.

Correcting for externalities in practice requires a set of government interventions in the market system via some combination of regulations and pollution taxes (Pearce *et al.*, 1989).

Externalities and public-type goods

Externalities are usually defined as unintentional side-effects of production and consumption that affect a third party either positively or negatively. For example, the factor that pollutes the surrounding local atmosphere to such an extent that the local incidence of some respiratory illnesses increases, has created a negative externality (external cost). An activity by one agent (the production plant) has caused a loss of welfare to another agent (the people made ill) and the loss of welfare is involuntary and not compensated for. Identifying and assessing the significance of pollution externalities in practice is often a very difficult task. Particularly troublesome issues are raised in situations where people have been exposed to a pollutant in very small doses over prolonged periods of time. Identifying and measuring the risks involved is far from easy, and very often decisions have to be taken on the best available evidence, which may not be very substantial.

The crucial feature of externalities is that there are goods people care about (e.g. clean air and water, landscapes, etc.) that are not sold on markets. The majority of environmental goods fall into a category in which market values are not available (public-type goods). Public goods generally have the characteristics of **joint consumption** and **non-exclusion**. What this means is that when the good is consumed by one person, it does not diminish the amount consumed by another person. So, for example, one person's consumption of clean air does not diminish any other person's consumption. Non-exclusion means that one person could not prevent ('exclude') another from consuming the resource.

The very characteristics of many environmental goods have meant that their 'true' value (total economic value) has been underestimated or ignored altogether. They have remained unmeasured and unpriced, and have therefore been inefficiently exploited. It is also the case, however, that by no means all negative externalities are due to market failure. Think about the damage (loss of habitats and landscapes, and water pollution due to fertilizers and pesticides) done by agricultural practices to the environment. In this context, it is **intervention** failure that is significant. The Common Agricultural Policy has involved governments in the European Community intervening in agricultural markets to control prices and support farmer incomes. One of the consequences has been massive overproduction and related unintended but significant pollution run-off problems (see Chapter 6).

Many environmental goods are also **common property** and/or **open access** resources. The combination of weak property right (legal) protection against overuse (or complete open access) together with free or cheap usage of these resources has inevitably led to overexploitation, sometimes to the point of destruction of the stock. Tropical rainforests, marine fisheries and the waste assimilation capacity of seas are all examples of such overexploited resources (see Chapter 15).

Conclusions

To summarize the discussion so far, we have argued that environmental economists have been at pains to emphasize that at least one class of negative externalities – those associated with the disposal of wastes generated by economic systems – are not isolated and rare events but inevitable and commonplace. Further, their economic significance tends to increase as economies develop (industrialize and support larger populations), and the ability of the environment to receive and assimilate them is reduced (increasing scarcity) thereby increasing the value of such natural resource capacities.

From a theoretical viewpoint, it has also been shown that if the capacity of the environment to assimilate wastes is scarce, the market mechanism cannot be free of externality effects (and therefore does not represent an efficient resource allocation mechanism) unless:

(a) the material and energy drawn into an economy via production activities produce no waste (100 per cent recycling efficiency) and all final outputs are eventually totally destroyed by consumption;

(b) property rights cover all relevant environmental goods, placing them in private ownership and allowing them to be exchanged in competitive markets.

Condition (a) contravenes the fundamental physical (thermodynamic) law of conservation of mass/energy and condition (b) is impossible or impracticable given the characteristics of many environmental goods.

Since the essence of environmental issues is that they inevitably involve, among other things, externalities and public-type goods, the market mechanism cannot be relied upon to provide efficient levels of environmental goods and services. But this leaves us with a fundamental question: How can and how should society decide what amount of environmental quality it should purchase? One possible approach which has received most support from economists is to rely on cost–benefit analysis (see Chapter 7).

Bibliography

Ends Data Services, *HC Written Answers*, 22 October 1990, Cols 39–40.

For a recent restatement of the materials balance model see:

R. U. Ayres and A. V. Kneese, 'Externalities: economies and thermodynamics', in F. Archibugi and P. Nijkamp (eds), *Economy and Ecology: Towards Sustainable Development*, Kluwer, Dordrecht, 1989.

Good introductory analysis of market failure and the valuation of environmental goods and services can be found in:

H. Daly and J. Cobb, *For the Common Good*, Greenprint Press, London, 1990.

G. A. Norton, *Resource Economics*, Edward Arnold, London, 1984.

D. W. Pearce, A. Markandya and E. B. Barbier, *Blueprint for a Green Economy*, Earthscan, London, 1989.

CHAPTER 2

Environment and ethics

Introduction

Many environmentalists feel that modern academic economics is somehow not addressing the 'real' problems of the day, and that a 'new' or 'alternative' economics is required (Daly and Cobb, 1990). This view is not endorsed in this chapter, instead it will be argued that the environmental economics that has been developed since the 1960s has a great deal to offer anyone who wants to understand environmental problems. The principle of opportunity cost, for example, emphasizes that nothing, including environmental resources, is free. Using the environment to produce boating marinas in place of wetlands, for example, means forgoing all the benefits (opportunities) that such natural systems can provide, such as pollution buffering zones, storm protection zones, wildlife habitat, etc.

Nevertheless, the conventional economic approach tends, in practice, to be rather narrow and dominated by the economic efficiency objective (i.e. using scarce resources in such a way as to get maximum benefits net of any costs). By their very nature, environmental issues raise a broad set of scientific, political, ethical and economic questions. Thus, while it is important to investigate ways of using our environmental resources as efficiently as possible, it is also vital, for example, to monitor the fairness of the resulting distribution of benefits and costs (economic equity objective).

Questions concerning 'fair' distributions of resources can quickly become complicated and, in the environmental context, will involve fairness not just between individual people alive now but also between them and future generations yet to come. To take just one illustrative example, the exploitation of resources such as fossil fuels and minerals like iron ore and bauxite (non-renewables) today means less of a stock left for future generations. Other resources (renewables) like fisheries and forests may also be over-exploited and not given enough time to regenerate. Again the stocks of such assets for future generations will be reduced. The question can then be posed, Is this fair? Is it 'right' that those of us alive now should essentially destroy assets (and the economic opportunities that they yield) gaining benefits in the process, while passing on the costs to people not yet alive and who have had no say in the matter? Now, this argument has been deliberately set up in a simple way in order to provoke the reader into thinking about a number of important and tricky problems that are involved in the use and abuse of our environment.

The position taken in the analysis that follows is that economic efficiency – getting the most 'welfare' (benefits net of costs) out of a given collection of resources – is vitally important. But the very nature of environmental issues requires an extension (a 'greening') of the conventional economic approach to encompass, among others, distributional equity and environmental quality objectives.

However, there are a variety of green positions on offer and **environmentalism** (a social and political movement that encompasses how we feel about the natural world, and how we feel we ought to behave towards all living and inanimate objects (O'Riordan, 1991)) manifests itself in various ways especially in the green politics of Europe. In the next section, we will survey the various forms ('shades') of greenness with particular reference to their economic dimensions, as well as trying to discern some common features.

Shades of green economics

The different *environmental ideologies* that make up environmentalism are complex and dynamic phenomena, and it may even be the case that individuals can experience, to a greater or lesser extent, a number of 'shades' or levels of greenness. But in terms of the economic dimension there seem to be three common features:

1. A rejection of the idea that economic systems should be deliberately designed to satisfy the unlimited wants of 'rational economic person' (*homo economicus*) – the archetypal selfish (greedy) inhabitant of the unfettered market economy. We need to think more about people's (collective) needs and less about their individual wants. Human behaviour must be modified to some extent and *greed constrained* (Pearce, 1992).
2. A green economy is also one that has the capability of replicating itself on a sustainable basis. We will take a detailed look at **sustainability** and **sustainable economic development** in Chapter 4. Many definitions of sustainable development have been put forward but for now we will limit ourselves to thinking about this concept simply in terms of economic development that endures over the long run.
3. A green economy must, over time, evolve in such a way as to **decouple** the growth in economic output (activity) from the environmental impacts of that activity. On the basis of the materials balance principle, decoupling

will involve technical changes such that our use of resources is made more efficient and our output of pollution becomes less and less damaging. Total decoupling is thermodynamically impossible and some environmentalists argue that decoupling is a necessary but not sufficient condition for a green economy. They would go further and either freeze the **scale** (i.e. size of economic output, its rate of change and the level and rate of change in population) of the economy, or actually reduce it.

At the risk of oversimplification, we can distinguish two broad ideological camps in environmentalism: **technocentrism** and **ecocentrism** (see Box 2.1). Supporters of an extreme technocentrist position would not wish to see constraints placed on individual consumers or on markets. They would support an 'unfettered free market' philosophy and combine this with a strong faith in the power of technology to overcome any 'environmental limits' problems (extensive decoupling possibilities). We label this position 'cornucopian technocentrism' and the resulting system *the anti-green economy* in Box 2.1.

A less extreme position, 'accommodating technocentrism' accepts that free markets have beneficial effects on the environment but only if individuals think and act green. The green consumer, green investor, green citizen and green employee are therefore powerful agents for a *green economy*. From this perspective, decoupling possibilities will be relevant, but also some environmental limits (e.g. life support system maintenance and waste assimilation capacity maintenance) will become binding and will require some scale changes if the economy is to be sustainable. Some environmental resources (known as 'critical natural capital') will have to be strictly conserved (and development activities forgone) to be handed over to future generations undiminished. Other environmental resources ('other natural capital') can be exploited because of substitution possibilities – between different categories of natural capital, or between natural capital and physical capital (i.e. man-made, machines, etc.) and human capital (i.e. human skills, knowledge and ingenuity). This 'constant capital' rule is an important feature of what we mean by sustainable economic development (see Chapter 4).

In reality, these categories are overlapping and as we pointed out at the start of this chapter several levels of greenness can coexist within one individual depending on the situation and context under study. Thus crossing the ideological divide into ecocentrism we can distinguish a position called 'communalist ecocentrism' which supports the idea of a *deep green economy*. Supporters of this position argue that absolute levels of scale should not decline, but neither should they increase. Limits thinking is now dominant and translates into calls for zero economic growth and zero population growth in order to establish the **steady-state economy**. Decoupling is supported but must be buttressed by moves to eliminate any increase in the future scale of the economy.

Box 2.1 Environmentalism

Technocentric (overlapping categories)		Ecocentric		
'Cornucopian'	'Accommodating'	'Communalist'	'Deep Ecology'	
Resource exploitative, growth-orientated position	Resource conservationist and 'managerial' position	Resource preservationist position	Extreme preservationist position	GREEN LABELS
Anti-green economy, unfettered free markets	Green economy, Green markets guided by economic incentive instruments (EIs) (e.g. pollution charges, etc.)	Deep green economy, steady-state economy regulated by macroenvironmental standards and supplemented by EIs	Very deep green economy, heavily regulated to minimize 'resource-take'	TYPE OF ECONOMY
Primary economic policy objective, maximize economic growth (max Gross National Product [GNP])	Modified economic growth (adjusted green accounting to measure GNP)	Zero economic growth; zero population growth	Reduced scale of economy and population	MANAGEMENT STRATEGIES
Taken as axiomatic that unfettered free markets in conjunction with technical progress will ensure infinite substitution possibilities capable of mitigating all 'scarcity/limits' constraints (environmental sources and sinks)	Decoupling important but infinite substitution rejected. Sustainability rules: constant capital rule. Therefore some scale changes	Decoupling plus no increase in scale. 'Systems' perspective – 'health' of whole ecosystem very important; Gaia hypothesis and implications	Scale reduction imperative; at the extreme for some there is a literal interpretation of Gaia as a personalized agent to which moral obligations are owed	
Support for traditional ethical reasoning: rights and interests of contemporary individual humans; instrumental value (i.e. of recognized value to humans) in nature	Extension of ethical reasoning: 'caring for others' motive – intragenerational and intergenerational equity (i.e. contemporary poor and future people); instrumental value in nature	Further extension of ethical reasoning: interests of the collective take precedence over those of the individual; primary value of ecosystems and secondary value of component functions and services	Acceptance of bioethics (i.e. moral rights/interests conferred on all non-human species and even the abiotic parts of the environment); intrinsic value in nature (i.e. valuable in its own right regardless of human experience)	ETHICS
VERY WEAK SUSTAINABILITY	WEAK SUSTAINABILITY	STRONG SUSTAINABILITY	VERY STRONG SUSTAINABILITY	SUSTAINABILITY LABELS

Finally, we come to extreme ecocentrism which we have labelled the 'deep ecology' position supportive of a very deep green economy. Economic systems must as quickly as is feasible, be transformed into 'minimum resource-take' systems (i.e. minimum environmental impacts on sources and sinks). This transformation can only be accomplished by reductions in the absolute level of economy activity, negative change in economic output and reduced population levels (scale reduction). The deep ecology proponents also support a radically different set of *ethical/moral principles* (**bioethics**). We now turn to examine a little more closely the ethical arguments that underlie green economics and politics.

We have also fitted different versions of 'sustainability thinking' into the typology in Box 2.1, but we leave a proper discussion of sustainable development to Chapter 4.

Environmental ethics: opening up the 'moral reference class'

Ecological economists would argue that once one adopts the 'systems perspective' then the requirements of the system (the economy and its supporting ecosystems) can take precedence over those of the individual. This argument has important ethical implications for the role and rights of present individual humans compared with the system's survival and therefore the welfare of future generations. The constant capital rule for sustainable economic development requires us to adopt an explicit position on *equity (justice) and asset transfers across people and through time*. The ethical argument is that future generations have a right to expect an inheritance (in the form of natural capital/physical capital/human capital bequests) sufficient to allow them the capacity to generate for themselves a level of welfare (wellbeing) no less than that enjoyed by the current generation. In more formal language, the requirement is for an **intergenerational social contract** that guarantees the future the same 'opportunities' that were open to the past ('justice as opportunity' (Page, 1982)).

All this implies that the current generation has *obligations* to future people. This, in turn, requires that traditional forms of ethical reasoning (which are confined to questions relating to contemporary individual humans) must be broadened, or even abandoned. Philosophers refer to this as an 'extension of the moral reference class'. Green economics supports this extension beyond current individuals to cover the rights and interests of future generations of humans (the **intergenerational equity criterion**). But deep ecology goes much further and opens up the reference class to cover the interests and rights of non-human nature (animal rights, plants, species and even ecosystem rights). Such radical ethical thinking is necessary, they argue, because non-human nature (conscious and non-conscious) is capable of being inherently valuable (i.e. possesses **intrinsic value**).

So 'concern for others' is an important ethical issue in the green economics/politics and sustainability debate. To be ethically consistent, sustainable development seems to require us to increase the wellbeing of the least advantaged people in societies today, while at the same time ensuring that the prospects of future generations are not seriously impaired (**intragenerational and intergenerational equity objectives**). Clearly this is a tall order and will require (among other things) a strong moral commitment. Given that individuals are, to a greater or lesser extent, self-interested and greedy, sustainability analysts are exploring the extent to which such behaviour could be modified and how to achieve the modification. We devote much of Part III and Part IV of this book to an examination of the ways in which such a modification ('greening') could be stimulated. Box 2.2 summarizes very briefly some of the main *ethical rules* which can guide resource allocation.

Some analysts have argued that a 'stewardship ethic' is sufficient for sustainability, i.e. people should be less greedy because other people (especially the world's poor and future generations) matter and greed imposes costs on these other people. If humans are the stewards of nature, it is in their interests to protect and maintain nature because of the **instrumental value** that it represents. The protection given brings with it conservation of habitats and other non-human species (which may or may not be morally significant and possess intrinsic value).

Since bioethicists go further and argue that since all living things and even systems matter (i.e. have moral significance) then individual greed must be constrained because greed imposes costs on these elements of non-human nature. This latter position would be stewardship on behalf of the planet itself (known as **Gaianism**) in various forms up to deep ecology. Gaianism is linked to the scientific *Gaia hypothesis* (first published in 1972) which seeks to explain the survival of life on Earth for billions of years by treating life and the global environment as two parts of a single system (Lovelock, 1988; Watson, 1991). The system ('Gaia') has developed so that it can regulate and repair itself. Regulation means *life actively keeps* the global environment comfortable for life to continue. If Gaia is knocked dangerously off balance (by human activity and waste disposal), it can repair itself. But the process of repair only guarantees the system's survival and *not* the survival of any one (including humans) individual species. Thus Gaianism supports the systems' perspective and the need for pre-emptive environmental 'standards' (e.g. covering key species and processes (known as 'keystones') but also conservation zones like national parks, green belts and air, water and solid waste disposal practices, etc.).

The anchor point for most positions that advocate the moral significance of systems and not just individuals is Leopold's 'Land Ethic' (Leopold, 1949). According to Norton (1990, 1992), Leopold's ideas can be viewed as an argument for a two-level criterion of ecosystem health and two-stage policy process. In the first stage, limits inherent in ecological systems (need for

Box 2.2   Ethical rules

Teleology

This involves weighing up goods and bads, and aims to maximize what is good. Goods and bads are broadly interpreted. So, for example, maximizing the economist's notion of wellbeing ('utility' or preference satisfaction) would be a particular form of teleology known as **utilitarianism**. The essence of teleology is that it permits a balancing of goods and bads or of one good against another – equality against utility, for example. The cost–benefit approach (see Chapter 7) is teleological, being a form of utilitarianism based on preference satisfaction as a 'good thing'.

On the teleological approach it would be consistent to adopt a policy that made future generations worse off compared to present generations, if the gains to the present are deemed to be greater than the costs to the future. Thus we may decide *not* to cut back very drastically on our emissions of CO_2 (carbon dioxide) and other so-called greenhouse gases because of the benefits we derive from the economic activity that is the cause of the emissions and/or because of the costs of abatement. It now seems fairly clear that atmospheric concentrations of the greenhouse gases are rising rapidly due to human activities and this does imply warmer temperatures and possibly other climate changes. But great uncertainty surrounds the scale and extent of climate change and the likely damage costs. So we might reason that the impacts of climate change will be gradual and easily managed by adaptive behaviour (helped by technical progress) in the future. Overall, on this reasoning the cost burden on the future will be positive but not very significant.

But teleology is not consistent, therefore, with the *sustainability* criterion which can be interpreted as ruling out policy programmes that impose substantial risk with regard to future welfare, and mandates above all that we provide for flexibility as future generations adapt to unforeseen and unforeseeable events (Howarth and Monahan, 1992). On this basis we should be cutting back now on greenhouse gas emissions and also making investments to reduce the vulnerability of certain geographical areas (e.g. low-lying coasts at risk from climate-induced sea level rise) and social groups (e.g. poor people in developing countries suffering from food insecurity).

Theories of justice

There are several theories of justice, some have been applied to the issue of how to account for the intergenerational distribution of goods and bads.

Contractualism

Contractualists argue that people will come together to determine rules of social behaviour because it is to their mutual advantage to do so. But this doctrine of mutual advantage will arise only in social contexts where the parties to the 'contract' are of roughly equal power. But future generations not yet born have no power at all, so the requirement of roughly equal power is not met. Future generations cannot hurt us no matter how much we neglect their interests; they are vulnerable. Despite a large amount of literature trying to link the contractarian approach to the intergenerational equity criterion (based on variations of John Rawls' work in 1971) none of the efforts are entirely satisfactory. These efforts are also inconsistent with teleology: justice would take precedence over the good.

Rights

On this approach, justice implies a duty to behave in a certain way, and confers a right on the person who is the subject of the duty to expect that behaviour. The rights approach is also inconsistent with teleology because what is right takes precedence over what is good. The 'constant capital' rule (the capital bequest over time) fits this approach since it is predicated on the view that future generations have a right to at least the same level of wellbeing as current generations.

But a problem arises because of the 'contingency' of *future people*, i.e. the fact that they may not exist at all; from the viewpoint of the present they are only 'possible' people, and the number and type of people depend in large measure upon current actions and decisions. It may not now be clear, therefore, who holds the rights. Take a resource allocation policy which has two alternative variants – fast growth and resource depletion over the next 200 years; or low growth and conservation. Depending on which choice was made, two sets of possible people can be envisaged, but only one set will become actual people. Actual people will depend on the chosen policy variant and that policy will be the desirable one since the actual people owe their existence to it, providing that their life is not so miserable as to be not worth living. Our intuition, of course, says conservation policy is desirable because its set of actual people would have been relatively better off. Assuming this 'person-affecting view', it is not clear to whom rights will belong in the future – called the 'non-identity problem'.

Resourcism

On this approach each generation should have the same level of resources or productive capacity as each other. Their wellbeing may then differ, depending on what each generation makes of this stock of resources. But their capability to generate wellbeing would be the same. The 'justice as opportunity' argument (Page, 1982) fits into this category, as does the 'Lockean standard' view, i.e. each generation should leave 'enough and as good for others' (Pasek, 1992).

Strict egalitarianism

Here the insistence is on equality of some characteristic for each generation. It might be resource endowments (as with resourcism), or wellbeing itself. Or the rigidity may relate to the wellbeing of a target group, say the least advantaged groups or societies (the poor). No change would be permitted if the wellbeing of this poorest group was reduced, regardless of gains to other groups (Rawls called this the 'difference principle'). Again such approaches are inconsistent with the teleological view since none of them allows gains and losses to be weighed up independently of to whom they accrue.

Simplifying the literature a great deal we can group arguments against giving the same consideration to the future as to the present around the following notions:

(a) because of the very temporal location of future individual people – possible *vs.* actual people, 'circumstances for justice' are not present, and future people are vulnerable not equal to current generation;
(b) ignorance of future individual people's wants and needs;
(c) because of the contingency of future people there is a 'non-identity' problem.

Philosophers who support the intergenerational equity idea put up the following counter-arguments:

1. As long as some people will exist and will be in no relevant way unlike current right-holders, they are worthy of equal consideration.
2. Whatever the uncertainty about the extent of future preferences, it is clear that basic needs will exist and will not be substantially different from contemporary ones. The satisfaction of these basic needs will be a prerequisite of the satisfaction of most of the other desires and interests of future people regardless of their uncertainty.

3. Obligations need not be tied to actual individuals but can be viewed as 'generalized obligations' from one generation to the next. Obligations on the current generation are to maintain a stable flow of resources into the indefinite future in order to ensure ongoing human life, rather than meeting individual requirements.

4. Generations are not separate but overlap; therefore there is a 'chain of obligation' stretching across time. Since families endure over time, concern about descendants cannot be separated from concern about the welfare of those in the present generation from whom the descendant will inherit. Concern for future generations should reinforce concern for current fairness. Equally, future generations are vulnerable to our actions so we are obligated to provide for the actual children of today, who will in turn be obligated to provide for their children and so forth from generation to generation. A chain of obligation is thus defined, from the present into the indefinite future. If we do not ensure conditions favourable to the welfare of future generations we wrong our existing children in the sense that they will be unable to fulfil their obligation to children while enjoying a favourable way of life themselves (Daly and Cobb, 1990; Howarth, 1992).

Bioethics

An ethic 'of the environment', it requires two conditions: that there are non-human beings which have moral standing; and the class of those beings which have moral standing includes, but is larger than, the class of conscious beings. Moral standing can be given to a being only if society morally ought to consider how it is affected by a given action or policy. Both conditions are satisfied if non-human nature (conscious and non-conscious) is capable of being inherently valuable (i.e. possesses *intrinsic value*) – see H. Rolston (1988). The debate in this context has been over how far to extend the moral reference class: animal interests and rights, plants and ecosystems as morally considerable beings – Leopold's 'Land Ethic'. Analysts have also argued over a literal and a metaphorical interpretation of Gaian theory which pushes the 'systems' perspective further (Wallace and Norton, 1992).

stability and resilience, i.e. capacity to withstand/recover from external shocks and stress) need to be determined. Given the scientific uncertainties surrounding the fragility of systems, a 'safety margin' approach is recommended. In the second stage, subsystems (e.g. agriculture, forests, wetlands, rangelands, etc.) must be operated on the basis of resource-conservation rules derived from economic analysis, but constrained by rules for system maintenance derived from biological science.

The issue of valuation

The focus on the system also serves to highlight questions of **valuation**. To the economist, economic value arises if someone is made to feel better off in terms of their wants and desires. Positive economic value – a benefit – arises when people feel better off, and negative economic value – cost – arises when they feel worse off. What economic valuation does is to measure *human preferences* for or against changes in the state of environments. It does not 'value the environment'.

Objections to economic valuation must mean one of the following things:

1. The methods and techniques deployed by economists to measure preferences (e.g. willingness to pay for environmental quality) are unreliable and not valid. We examine these techniques and their limitations in Chapter 8 and conclude that reliable estimates of the value of a wide range of environmental goods and services are possible.
2. The fate of environments should not be determined by human wants at all. This we consider unacceptable on democratic grounds.
3. Human wants matter, but are not the only source of value. There is 'intrinsic' value in nature. The debate between instrumental and intrinsic value in nature is a sterile one. Economists do not deny the possibility of intrinsic value but choose to apply instrumental value via willingness to pay. The debate is sterile because it is not possible to show empirically what intrinsic value in nature is; it has to be accepted or rejected intuitively.

Nevertheless, there is a sense in which economic valuation of the environment will represent only a *partial value*. This is a criticism long held by scientists. Taking once again a 'systems' perspective, it is possible to argue that healthy ecosystems have to exist prior to the existence of individual functions and services such as watershed protection, storm buffering, waste assimilation, etc. Now *total economic value* (defined more fully in Chapter 8) relates to these individual functions and services (called *secondary values*). But total secondary value does *not* encompass the *primary value* of the system itself, its life-supporting functions and their 'glue value' that holds everything together and therefore has economic value. We cannot directly estimate primary value, but it serves to remind us that total economic value is an underestimate of the 'true' value of the environment. In terms of the ideological positions we reviewed at the start of this chapter, acceptance of the primary value concept gives further support to *strong sustainability* thinking.

We end this chapter by returning to the level of the individual as a consumer, investor, citizen and employee. Daly and Cobb (1990) are concerned that self-interested behaviour at the core of the market system will lead to corrosion in the system itself. They argue that self-interest corrodes the very moral context of 'community' that is presupposed by the market. The market actually depends on a community that shares such values as honesty, freedom, initiative, thrift and other virtues whose authority is diminished by the unfettered free market philosophy of value. If all value derives only from the satisfaction of individual wants, then there is nothing left over on the basis of which self-interested individualistic want satisfaction can be restrained. It could be argued then, that the market depends on the wider 'system' or 'community' to regenerate its *moral capital*, just as much as it depends on the ecosystem for its *natural capital*.

Ecological economists have highlighted the need to view individuals both as consumers (driven by self-interest, which requires modification) and as citizens (driven by ethical motives and moral arguments about what 'ought' to be done). Individuals have *needs* and not just *wants*. Needs are not substitutable as wants are, and most higher order needs relate to the wider community and its guiding principles. Sustainability may therefore represent high-order needs and values.

Conclusions

In this chapter we have argued that there are different 'shades of green' thinking within environmental economics and environmentalism in general. Much of the economic debate has centred on the need to constrain human greed, the sustainability of economic systems and the scope for decoupling economic systems from environmental constraints.

The adoption of the 'systems perspective' and the recognition of critical natural capital and the constant capital rule for sustainable economic development have ethical implications. Almost all shades of green economic thinking require support for an intergenerational social contract, i.e. the passing on over time of an adequate capital (all forms) inheritance. The strong sustainability position seeks to pass on a sufficient critical natural capital stock to future generations. Such assets have very high economic value but also in aggregate possess primary value (i.e. value over and above individual functions and services value).

Further reading

A non-technical survey of environmental ethics can be found in:
D. W. Pearce (ed.), *Blueprint 2*, Earthscan, London, 1991.

D. W. Pearce and R. K. Turner, *Economics of Natural Resources and the Environment*, Harvester Wheatsheaf, Hemel Hempstead, 1990.

R. K. Turner, 'Wetland conservation: Economics and ethics', in D. Collard, D. W. Pearce and D. Ulph (eds), *Economics, Growth and Sustainable Environments*, Macmillan, London, 1988.

References

H. Daly and J. Cobb, *For the Common Good*, Greenprint Press, London, 1990.

R. B. Howarth, 'Intergenerational justice and the chain of obligation', *Environmental Values* **1**: 133–40, 1992.

R. B. Howarth and P. A. Monahan, 'Economics, Ethics and Climate Policy', Report LBL-33230, UC-000, Lawrence Berkeley Laboratory, University of California, Berkeley, 1992.

A. Leopold, *Sand County Almanac*, Oxford University Press, Oxford, 1949.

J. Lovelock, *The Ages of Gaia: A Biography of Our Living Earth*, Oxford University Press, Oxford, 1988.

B. G. Norton, 'Context and hierarchy in Aldo Leopold's theory of environmental management', *Ecological Economics* **2**: 119–27, 1990.

G. A. Norton, *Resource Economics*, Edward Arnold, London, 1984.

T. O'Riordan, 'The new environmentalism and sustainable development', *The Science of the Total Environment* **108**: 5–15, 1991.

T. Page, 'Intergenerational justice as opportunity', in D. Maclean and P. Brown (eds), *Energy and the Future*, Rowman and Littlefield, Totowa, 1982.

J. Pasek, 'Obligations to future generations: A philosophical note', *World Development* **20**: 513–21, 1992.

D. W. Pearce, 'Green Economics', *Environmental Values* **1**: 3–13, 1992.

J. Rawls, *Theory of Justice*, Oxford University Press, Oxford, 1971.

H. Rolston, *Environmental Ethics*, Temple University Press, Philadelphia, 1988.

R. Wallace and B. Norton, 'Policy implications of Gaian theory', *Ecological Economics* **6**: 103–18, 1992.

A. Watson, 'Gaia', New Scientist Inside Science No. 48, *New Scientist*, 6 July 1991.

CHAPTER 3

Economic growth, population growth and the environment

Are there limits to growth?

Chapter 1 showed that the economy and the environment are closely linked through the materials balance principle. Economic activity can be viewed as a process of transforming materials and energy. Because we cannot destroy materials and energy in an absolute sense (the 'first law of thermodynamics'), they will reappear as waste which, eventually, will be discharged to the environment. This suggests that the bigger the economy gets, the more waste will be produced. If we think of the environments that have to handle the wastes – rivers, land dumps, the seas, the atmosphere – as having a *limited capability* to absorb them, then the real possibility emerges that there is a limit to the expansion of the economy. We tend to measure the expansion of the economy in terms of increase in its **national output**, or Gross National Product (GNP). GNP is a measure of the level of economic activity in the nation. Increases in GNP are generally known as **economic growth** (Box 3.1). It follows that there may be a limit to economic growth. As growth increases, so the volume of waste increases relative to the limited capacity of natural environments to absorb that waste. When that capacity is exceeded, severe damage may be done to the environment, so much so that human wellbeing may actually fall. We will call this first 'limit to growth' the **waste receiving limit to growth**.

But this is not the only possible limit to growth. The materials and energy that are transformed by the economic system must come from somewhere. There are basically two sources: *renewable* resources such as forests and fisheries, and **exhaustible** resources such as copper, coal and oil. If a renewable resource is used carefully it is possible to 'cream off' some of it each year and allow it to grow back again. For every tree that is cut down, for example, another can be grown. Fish can be left to regenerate their stocks naturally, and so on. So, if we use renewable resources *sustainably* there need be no 'limit to growth' from renewable resources. But we cannot say the same

Box 3.1 Economic growth

Panel (a) GNP per capita.

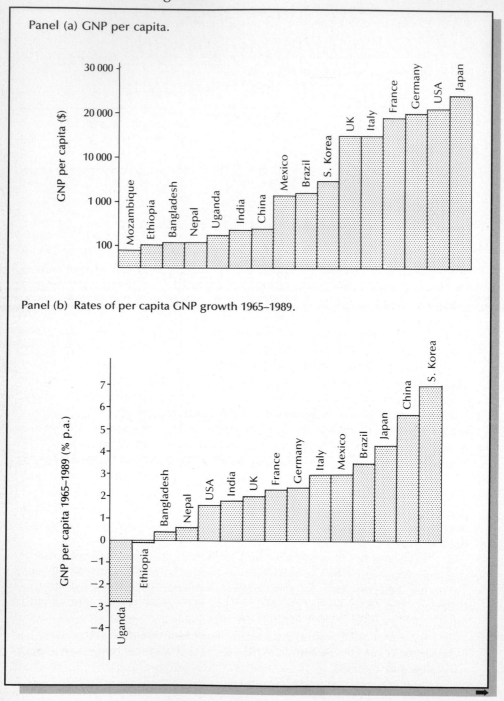

Panel (b) Rates of per capita GNP growth 1965–1989.

Panel (a) shows the absolute levels of gross national product (GNP) per capita for selected countries of the world, and Panel (b) the rate of growth of GNP per capita. In a few cases, even where GNP grows overall, some countries have population growth rates which are faster than their GNP growth – hence the GNP per capita falls.

	GNP US$000 million	GNP per capita $	Growth rates in per capita GNP 1965–1989 (% p.a.)
USA	5156	21 000	1.6
Japan	2818	24 000	4.3
Germany	1189	20 000	2.4
France	956	18 000	2.3
Italy	865	15 000	3.0
UK	718	15 000	2.0
China	418	350	5.7
Brazil	319	2 500	3.5
India	235	340	1.8
S. Korea	212	4 400	7.0
Mexico	201	2 000	3.0
Bangladesh	20	180	0.4
Ethiopia	5	120	−0.1
Uganda	4	250	−2.8
Nepal	3	180	0.6
Mozambique	1	80	n.a.

Source: World Bank (1991)

about exhaustible resources since, by definition, there is only a finite amount of them; and they cannot be regenerated. So, if economic growth means using up more and more oil, for example, perhaps there will be a limit to economic growth set by the available stocks of oil under ground. We will call this the **resource availability limit to growth**.

We have two possible candidates for limits to economic growth:

- the limited capacity of natural environments to receive the waste generated by economic systems;
- the finite nature of exhaustible resources.

A somewhat more rigorous definition of economic growth is in terms of increases in *per capita* GNP, rather than GNP itself. After all, we are unlikely to say that people are 'better off' economically if the economy grows but the *average* level of income falls. This possibility is a real one because in quite a few countries the rate of population growth is so fast that increases in economic growth are more than offset by the increased number of people. The average income falls, or at least does not rise as much as it might have done without population growth. This suggests that population growth is also a source of pressure on natural environments. This pressure takes many forms. The more people there are the more food will be needed. To get more food it becomes necessary to put more land under agriculture, displacing forests and many natural habitats. More people mean more demand for water. We tend to think of water as being plentiful, but in many countries water is a very scarce commodity. More people mean more demand for energy and hence more pollution from energy sources, and, in the developing world, more deforestation as people demand fuelwood (though this is not a major cause of deforestation in most countries). The faster is population growth, then, the quicker we are likely to approach both the waste receiving and resource availability limits to growth.

The interaction between population growth, economic growth, natural resource availability and waste receiving capacity is still regarded by many environmentalists as the reason why growth has to stop. The most celebrated expression of this view was in *The Limits to Growth*, a book by 'The Club of Rome' published in 1972 (Meadows *et al.*, 1972), but the view also has more current adherents (Daly and Cobb, 1990).

Critics of the limits to growth thesis point to a number of reasons why there may not be limits after all. Some of the reasons are given below:

- Changes in technology enable us to extract more and more economic activity from a given unit of natural resource. Put another way, the 'productivity of resources' increases over time and this makes available resources last longer and longer (Box 3.2). This is an important issue. It suggests that we can *decouple* economic activity and environmental impact by making our use of resources more and more efficient. Total decoupling is not possible: economic activity will always use *some* resources (by the laws of thermodynamics). But provided the amount used per unit of GNP goes down faster than GNP goes up, the impact on the environment can be reduced each year. One exception to this is *cumulative* pollutants: pollutants that build up over time because environments cannot break them down into harmless substances.
- We tend to discover more and more resources: the idea of a 'fixed quantity' is illusory (Box 3.3).
- We can control the amount of waste entering the environment by recycling materials and taking waste gases out before they leave the economic system.

44

Box 3.2 The productivity of resources

Energy use

Panel (a) shows that the amount of energy needed to produce one unit of GNP in the countries shown has declined substantially from the early 1970s to the present day. This shows that $1 of GNP is being produced in a more energy efficient way today than it was twenty years ago. Of course, other things besides being more energy efficient account for the decline in energy intensity – the switch from more energy intensive goods to less energy intensive ones, for example. But energy efficiency has played a major role.

For there to be true *decoupling*, however, we need to see these reductions in energy intensity translated into reductions in the *total amount* of energy used. This will happen only if GNP does not grow faster than the rate of change in energy intensity. Despite the reduced energy intensity shown in Panel (a), all the countries actually increased their energy use because of growth of GNP. But that decoupling is possible can be shown by the exception of Denmark which had slightly less energy consumption in 1989 than it did in 1970, despite having a 48 per cent increase in GNP in this

Panel (a)

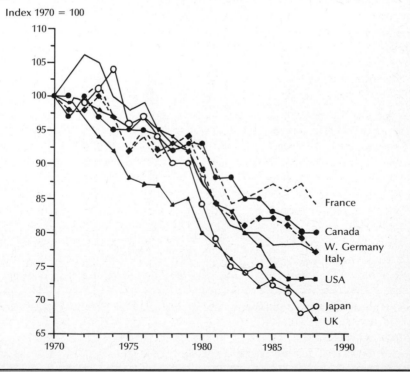

Index 1970 = 100

period. The United Kingdom also consumed only 5 per cent more energy in 1989 than it did in 1970 despite a 55 per cent increase in GNP. Clearly, if there was a bigger effort at energy conservation, decoupling would be possible.

	Energy intensity						Energy requirements	
						Change from 1970	Per capita	Total
	(TOE per 1000 US$)							
						(%)	(TOE/cap.)	(MTOE)
	1970	1975	1980	1985	1988	1970–1988	1988	1988
Canada	0.80	0.76	0.74	0.66	0.64	−20.5	9.6	249.5
USA	0.60	0.57	0.53	0.45	0.44	−27.4	7.8	1928.4
Japan	0.38	0.37	0.32	0.28	0.27	−30.9	3.3	398.8
Australia	0.54	0.53	0.53	0.48	0.47	−12.6	5.0	82.7
New Zealand	0.48	0.50	0.56	0.60	0.63	32.4	4.3	14.3
Austria	0.49	0.45	0.44	0.42	0.41	−16.4	3.8	28.8
Belgium	0.72	0.64	0.60	0.54	0.53	−26.3	4.6	45.9
Denmark	0.49	0.40	0.38	0.34	0.32	−35.5	3.7	19.0
Finland	0.58	0.54	0.56	0.50	0.49	−16.3	6.0	29.6
France	0.44	0.41	0.41	0.38	0.37	−16.3	3.7	208.9
W. Germany	0.53	0.48	0.47	0.43	0.41	−22.5	4.5	274.1
Greece	0.43	0.49	0.53	0.57	0.58	36.6	2.0	20.5
Ireland	0.61	0.53	0.52	0.49	0.48	−21.4	2.7	9.7
Italy	0.42	0.41	0.37	0.33	0.32	−23.1	2.6	151.7
Netherlands	0.55	0.57	0.55	0.49	0.48	−12.7	4.4	64.5
Norway	0.57	0.52	0.49	0.46	0.44	−21.9	6.7	28.0
Portugal	0.55	0.57	0.58	0.62	0.67	22.1	1.5	15.7
Spain	0.39	0.44	0.48	0.46	0.45	16.5	2.2	84.6
Sweden	0.58	0.55	0.52	0.55	0.52	−10.6	6.7	56.2
Switzerland	0.27	0.28	0.29	0.29	0.28	3.3	4.2	28.2
Turkey	0.49	0.76	0.80	0.78	0.79	61.0	0.9	50.3
UK	0.61	0.53	0.49	0.44	0.41	−33.1	3.7	208.5
OECD	0.54	0.52	0.48	0.43	0.41	−24.6	4.8	4002.9
World				0.38	0.41		1.6	7956.5

Note: Primary energy requirements per unit of GDP (at 1985 prices and exchange rates).
Source: OECD (1991)

Box 3.3 Discovering 'new' resources

In the physical sense, fossil fuel energy resources are, of course, finite. But new discoveries of what there actually is are made all the time. The 'proved' or 'proven' reserves therefore tend to *increase* over time as exploration and recovery technology improves (e.g. the North Sea, Alaska). Panels (a) and (b) show how the proven reserves of oil and gas have changed since 1965. In recent years the increases in oil are accounted for mainly by discoveries in the Middle East. The picture for natural gas also shows increases in proven reserves, although the picture here is one of continuous steady increases in contrast to the growth then stable reserves then growth again picture for oil.

Source: BP (1991)

Proved reserves.
Panel (a) Proved reserves of natural gas. Natural gas reserves have risen steadily for the past 25 years. This growth is particularly marked in the USSR and Middle East.

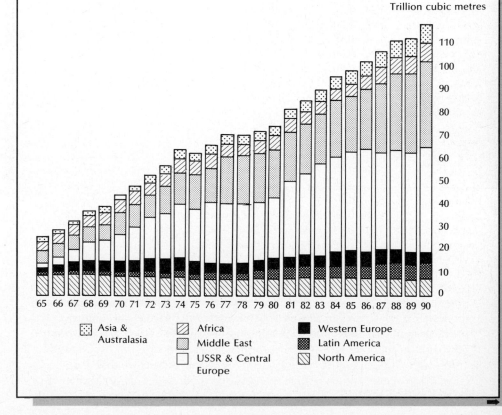

Trillion cubic metres

65 66 67 68 69 70 71 72 73 74 75 76 77 78 79 80 81 82 83 84 85 86 87 88 89 90

Asia & Australasia	Africa	Western Europe
Middle East	Latin America
USSR & Central Europe	North America

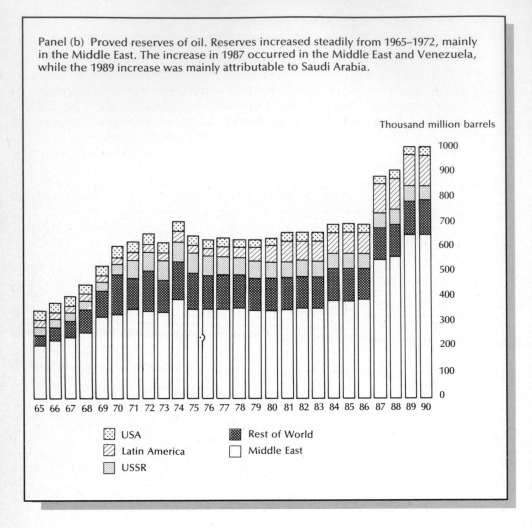

Panel (b) Proved reserves of oil. Reserves increased steadily from 1965–1972, mainly in the Middle East. The increase in 1987 occurred in the Middle East and Venezuela, while the 1989 increase was mainly attributable to Saudi Arabia.

Thousand million barrels

Legend:
- USA
- Latin America
- USSR
- Rest of World
- Middle East

- We can change polluting technologies for less polluting ones.
- If resources do get scarce then supply and demand theory tells us that their prices will rise and this will induce people to be more careful in their use (**conservation**) and to switch into other resources (**substitution**). This could be true for those resources that have market prices (coal, oil, copper, etc.) but, of course, it does not hold for those resources which are not bought and sold in market-places – the resource of the atmosphere, for example.
- Although the population is growing, in many countries that growth is slowing down as people realize the benefits of having smaller families (Box 3.4).

Box 3.4 Growth of the world's population

There are currently around 5 billion people in the world. By the end of next century there may be twice this number. In only 30 years' time the population is expected to reach 8 billion, an additional 3 billion people. But *rates* of growth are declining. Taking the years 1900–2000 and 2000–2100 as two distinct periods, the rates of change are given in Table 2.

Table 1 World population (in millions)

	1900	1950	1985	2000	2025	2100
Africa	133	224	555	872	1617	2591
Asia[a]	867	1292	2697	3419	4403	4919
Latin America	70	165	405	546	779	1238
Total: Developing World	1070	1681	3657	4837	6799	8748
Europe, USSR, Japan, Oceania	478	669	917	987	1062	1055
North America	82	166	264	297	345	382
Total: Developed World	560	835	1181	1284	1407	1437
Total: World	1630	2516	4837	6122	8206	10185

[a]Excludes Japan.
Source: T. W. Merrick (1986)

Table 2 The rates of change in population growth (% p.a.)

	1900–2000	2000–2100
Africa	1.9	1.1
Asia	1.4	0.4
Latin America	2.1	0.8
Europe, USSR, Japan, Oceania	0.7	0.1
North America	1.3	0.2

The North–South divide

All of these things happen but it would be foolish to be complacent. It may be true that the rich countries will be clever enough to invent new technologies, find more resources, recycle more waste and still enjoy the benefits of economic growth. But for the poor world the picture is much less optimistic. A number of parts of the world already have populations that are close to, even in excess of, the **carrying capacity** of their environments. Carrying capacity is a useful if not altogether very rigorous concept. It refers to the capability of a given system to support a population. For example, suppose the prevailing agricultural system produces X calories and that each person needs a minimum of $X/10$ calories to survive. Then the carrying capacity of the system is computed as:

$$\frac{X}{X/10} = \frac{10.X}{X} = 10$$

The carrying capacity of an area is categorically not the *desirable* level of population: carrying capacity is usually defined as relating to the maximum sustainable population at the minimum standard of living necessary for survival. Maintaining the maximum number of people at a minimum standard of living hardly qualifies as a desirable objective.

The most extensive analysis of the carrying capacity of the world was carried out by the Food and Agriculture Organization (FAO) of the United Nations. The FAO approach involved looking at the potential food production of each of 117 countries. Obviously, potential food production depends on the level of technology applied to agriculture. FAO categorized these as:

low level: corresponding to no fertilizers, pesticides or herbicides, with traditional crop varieties and no long-term conservation measures;
intermediate level: corresponding to use of basic fertilizers and biocides, use of some improved crop varieties and some basic conservation measures;
high level: corresponding to full use of fertilizers and biocides, use of improved crop varieties, conservation measures and the best crop mixes.

On the basis of these different technological scenarios, it was then possible to estimate the potential calorie output. By dividing this by the per capita calorie intakes recommended by FAO and the World Health Organization for each country, a sustainable population can be estimated. These estimates were made for 1975 and the year 2000.

Box 3.5 summarizes the results in a convenient form. It shows the ratio of potential sustainable population in the year 2000 to the expected population in 2000 for various regions of the world, and at the three different levels of technology. For example, for the developing world as a whole, if all cultivable land was devoted to food crops, at the lowest level of technology those lands could support 1.6 times the number of people expected in the year 2000. In

Box 3.5 Carrying capacities for world regions in the year 2000 (potentially supportable population divided by expected population)

Input level	Africa	SW Asia	South America	Central America	SE Asia	Average
Low	1.6	0.7	3.5	1.4	1.3	1.6
Intermediate	5.8	0.9	13.3	2.6	2.3	4.2
High	16.5	1.2	31.5	6.0	3.3	9.3

Source: FAO (1986) p. 16.

southwest Asia the actual expected population will exceed the carrying capacity at both low and intermediate technology levels. As the technological assumptions improve so, dramatically, does the carrying capacity of the regions.

Box 3.5 might appear to suggest a fairly optimistic picture. Certainly, it highlights the role which technological improvement can play in vastly increasing carrying capacity. However, it is important to understand why the picture is far from an optimistic one.

First, carrying capacity relates to the maximum number of people that can be sustained with the given resource, not to the desirable level. Second, the carrying capacity figures relate to a minimum calorie intake, so that even for a single person the approach makes no allowance for increasing nutritional levels. Third, the time horizon of 2000 does not permit much change to take place in levels of applied technology so that at least the high technology input scenario is of limited relevance to what will actually be the case. Fourth, the approach assumes *all* cultivable land will come under food production or livestock pasture, which is a clear exaggeration of what is feasible. Allowing for non-food crops, the ratio of 1.6 in Box 3.5 becomes 1.07, i.e. at low technology the carrying capacity of the developing countries is only 7 per cent more than the actual population.

In fact the situation may be worse still than is suggested in Box 3.5. The FAO study was concerned with carrying capacity in terms of *food*. But other resource scarcities may begin to exert an influence before cultivable land. A notable example is the availability of fuelwood. A study of the Sahelian and Sudanian zones of West Africa computed the carrying capacity of various zones according to the limits set by crops, livestock and fuelwood. The results are shown in Box 3.6. It will be observed that the carrying capacity of natural forest cover – the main source of fuelwood – is very much lower than that of

51

Box 3.6 Carrying capacities in Sahelian/Sudanian zones of West Africa (in people/km²)

Zone	Sustainable population			Actual rural population	Sustainable population: fuelwood	Actual total population
	Crops	Livestock	Sum			
Saharan	—	0.3	0.3	0.3	—	0.3
Sahelo–Saharan	—	0.3	0.3	2	—	2
Sahelian	5	2	7	7	1	7
Sahelo–Sudanian	10	5	15	20	10	23
Sudanian	15	7	22	17	20	21
Sudano–Guinean	25	10	35	9	20	10

Source D. Steeds (1985) p. 13.

crops using traditional technologies. Moreover, in five of the six regions (underlined) fuelwood carrying capacity is already exceeded, compared to two regions where food and livestock carrying capacity is exceeded. The general picture on world zone carrying capacities may therefore understate the problem of resource carrying capacity generally. What matters is which resource scarcity 'bites' first.

Conclusions

While we have shown that a great many of the criticisms of the original *Limits to Growth* book were justified, it does not follow that there are *no* limits to economic and population growth. Man's ingenuity has found many ways of making resources last longer, of getting more from less, and of preventing many potential pollutants from reaching the environment. But the benefits of a great many of those achievements have accrued to people who are already relatively wealthy. Breaching the limits in the rich world may well mean more ill health, more nuisance, more inconvenience. In the poor world breaching the limits may well mean starvation.

Even if we are not sure that there are limits to growth it would be prudent to behave *as if* there were. Provided we make no major sacrifices, this 'precautionary approach' serves to make people about as well off as they would have been without taking anticipatory action, while protecting them against major environmental damage that could seriously affect human wellbeing. As we shall see in later chapters, the world does tend to operate on this basis in respect of some environmental threats – the depletion of the ozone layer, for example. For others, it tends to react rather too slowly, as may be the case with global warming (see Chapter 19), and for still others it reacts hardly at all.

Further reading

BP, *BP Statistical Review of World Energy 1991*, BP, London, 1991.

FAO, *Land, Food and People*, FAO, Rome, 1986.

T. W. Merrick, 'World population in transition', *Population Bulletin* **42**(2), 1986.

OECD, *Environmental Indicators: A Preliminary Set*, OECD, Paris, 1991.

D. Steeds, *Desertification in the Sahelian and Sudanian Zones of West Africa*, World Bank, Washington DC, 1985.

World Bank, *World Development Report 1991*, Oxford University Press, Oxford, 1991.

The book that did most to advance the idea that economic and population growth would eventually bring about ecological disaster was:

D. Meadows *et al.*, *The Limits to Growth*, Earth Island, New York, 1972.

A modern statement is:

H. Daly and J. Cobb, *For the Common Good*, Greenprint Press, London, 1990.

Modern academic debates tend not to be conducted in terms of 'growth versus the environment'. Major critiques of limits to growth arguments therefore tend to be found in books and articles published in the 1970s. A good example is:

W. Beckerman, *In Defence of Economic Growth*, Cape, London, 1974.

The idea of 'decoupling' the economy from its environmental impact is explored in:

D. W. Pearce, A. Markandya and E. B. Barbier, *Blueprint for a Green Economy*, Earthscan, London, 1989.

CHAPTER 4

Sustainable development

Definitions

Many definitions of sustainable development (SD) (often incompatible with each other) have been suggested and debated in the literature. What this suggests is that the debate has exposed a range of approaches which differ because they are linked to alternative environmental ideologies (see Box 2.1). From the ecocentric perspective, the extreme deep ecologists seem to come close to rejecting even a policy of 'modified' development based on the sustainable use of nature's assets. For them only a minimalist development strategy is morally supportable. From the opposite technocentric perspective, other analysts argue that the concept of sustainability contributes little new to conventional economic theory and policy. Given this worldview, the mainte-nance of a sustainable economic growth strategy over the long run merely depends on the adequacy of investment expenditure. Investment in natural capital is not irrelevant but it is not of overriding importance either. A key assumption of this position is that there will continue to be a *very high degree of substitutability between all forms of capital* (physical, human and natural capital). The classification scheme set out in Box 2.1 labelled these two positions as *very weak sustainability* and *very strong sustainability* respectively.

The most publicized definition of sustainability is that of the World Commission on Environment and Development (WCED) (the 'Brundtland Commission', 1987). The Commission defined SD as: 'development that meets the needs of the present without compromising the ability of future generations to meet their own needs' (WCED, 1987, p. 43).

On the basis of this SD definition both *intergenerational equity* and *intragenerational equity* concerns must be met before any society can attain the goal of sustainability. Social and economic development must be undertaken in such a way as to minimize the effects of economic activity (on resource sources and waste assimilation sinks – see Chapter 1) whenever the costs are borne by future generations. When currently vital activities impose costs on the future (e.g. mining of non-renewable minerals – see Chapter 16) *full compensation* must be paid (e.g. performance or assurance bonds yielding financial aid, or new technologies allowing resource switching say from fossil fuels to solar power, etc. – see Chapter 11).

The Commission also highlighted 'the essential needs of the world's poor, to which overriding priority should be given'. In other words, SD must allow for an increase in people's standard of living (broadly defined) with particular emphasis on the wellbeing of poor people, while at the same time avoiding uncompensated and significant costs on future people.

The Commission also took a fairly optimistic view of the possibilities for decoupling economic activity and environmental impact (see Chapter 3) and in terms of our classification system has put itself into the *weak sustainability* camp. Recall that the *strong sustainability* supporters, while not dismissing decoupling, argue that modifications to the scale of the economy (the throughput of matter and energy) will also be required. The amount of scale reduction is debated within the strong sustainability camp (which is a fairly 'broad church').

SD, it is generally agreed, is therefore economic development that endures over the long run. Economic development can be measured in terms of Gross National Product (i.e. the annual output of goods and services adjusted for exports and imports) per capita, or real consumption of goods and services per capita. In a later section we will argue that, in fact, the traditional GNP measure needs to be modified and extended if it is to measure SD. But for the moment SD is defined as at least non-declining consumption, GNP, or some other agreed welfare indicator.

The conditions for sustainable development

A more difficult task is to determine the necessary and sufficient conditions for achieving SD. Fundamentally, how do we compensate the future for damage that our activities today might cause? The answer is through the transfer of **capital bequests**. What this means is that this generation makes sure that it leaves the next generation a stock of capital no less than this generation has now. Capital provides the capability to generate wellbeing ('justice as opportunity' and the 'Lockean Standard' notions are relevant in this context – see Chapter 2) through the creation of goods and services upon which human wellbeing depends.

Weak sustainability (WS)

Under this interpretation of SD, it is not thought necessary to single out the environment (natural capital) for special treatment, it is simply another form of capital. Therefore, what is required for SD is the transfer of an *aggregate capital stock* no less than the one that exists now (this then is the **weak sustainability constant capital rule**). We can pass on less environment so long as we offset this loss by increasing the stock of roads and machinery, or other man-made (physical) capital. Alternatively, we can have fewer roads and factories so long as we compensate by having more wetlands or mixed woodlands or more education. WS is, as we pointed out in Chapter 2, based on a very strong assumption, **perfect substitutability** between the different forms of capital.

Strong sustainability (SS)

Under this interpretation of SD, perfect substitution between different forms of capital is not a valid assumption to make. Some elements of the natural capital stock cannot be substituted for (except on a very limited basis) by man-made capital. Some of the functions and services of ecosystems are essential to human survival, they are life support services (biogeochemical cycling) and cannot be replaced. Other ecological assets are at least essential to human wellbeing, if not exactly essential for human survival – landscape, space, and relative peace and quiet. These assets are **critical natural capital** and since they are not easily substitutable, if at all, the SS rule requires that we protect them.

Measuring sustainable development

Another way of looking at the idea that SD means generating human wellbeing now without impairing the wellbeing of future generations is to think about a *sustainable flow of income*. This is a level of income that the nation can afford to receive without depreciating the overall capital stock of the nation. The danger is that a failure to adequately account for natural capital and the contribution it makes to economic welfare and income will lead to misperceptions about how well an economy is really performing. This danger is real because the current system of national accounts used in many countries fails, in almost all cases, to treat natural capital as assets which play a vital part in providing a flow of output/income over time. Extended national accounts (i.e. not restricted to market-based outputs, incomes and expenditure, as measured in the Gross National Product concept) are required in order to improve policy signals relating to SD.

Two adjustments are required, one for the depreciation of natural capital (changes in quantity) and the other for degradation of the natural capital stock (changes in quality). A framework to reflect the use of natural resources at the national level is in the process of being agreed by the United Nations

Statistical Office. However, the theory and practice of making these adjustments is complex and they are not discussed further here (we provide some suggested reading at the end of the chapter). Instead we present a simple test for SD which yields data which is at least indicative of national sustainability. The test is, however, far from a definitive sustainability indicator, but it is based on modified national accounting information.

Simple indicator of sustainable development

One SD rule states that an economy must save at least as much as the sum of the depreciation on the value of man-made and natural capital (Pearce and Atkinson, 1992). An analogy with a business is useful in this context. If our business consistently failed to save enough money to plough back into the business, to replace machinery and buildings as they wear out (depreciate), we might stay afloat for a while but not long term – our business would be unsustainable. The same is true for any economy, its national savings ratio (savings over some measure of income like Gross Domestic Product (GDP)) must be greater than or equal to depreciation in the natural capital and man-made capital stock, if it is to pass our simple sustainability test. Box 4.1 illustrates some sustainability indicators for a selection of countries. Nothing definitive is being claimed since the data available is not always comprehensive and the test itself is 'static' and ignores factors such as technological change, population growth and international trade.

Precautionary principle and safe minimum standards

For some analysts supportive of the strong sustainability position, sustainability constraints (such as the critical natural capital protection rule) should be seen as expressions of the so-called **precautionary principle** and one similar to the notion of **safe minimum standard** (SMS). The SMS concept is one way of giving shape to the intergenerational social contract idea we discussed in Chapter 2. Somehow we have to trade off using resources to produce economic benefits and conservation of resource stocks and flows to guarantee sustainable benefit flows. The trade-off decisions have to be taken within a context of *uncertainty* and possible **irreversibilities** (i.e. decisions once taken result in changes that are physically impossible to reverse or prohibitively expensive to reverse, e.g. loss of tropical forests and complex wetlands). To satisfy the *intergenerational social contract* (via the constant capital rule and capital bequests), the current generation could rule out in advance, depending on the costs (strictly known as the social opportunity costs, i.e. what society has to give up or forgo), development activities that could result in natural capital depreciation beyond a certain threshold of damage cost and

Box 4.1 Test for weak sustainable development

An economy is sustainable if it saves more than the depreciation on its human-made and natural capital.

Country	Gross savings ratio (S/Y)	Depreciation of human-made capital (d_M/Y)	Depreciation of natural capital (d_N/Y)	Sustainability indicator (Z)
Finland	28	15	2	+11
Germany	26	12	4	+10
Japan	33	14	2	+17
UK	18	12	6?	0?
USA	18	12	4	+2

Notes and sources:
Y denotes that the values are expressed as a percentage of GDP.
S/Y is taken from World Bank, *World Development Reports* –
d_M/Y is taken from the UN *System of National Accounts* (UNSO, 1990).
The test takes the form,

$$Z >= S/Y - d_M/Y - d_N/Y$$

Z must be greater than or equal to zero for sustainability.

irreversibility (i.e. loss of critical natural capital, life support services, keystone species and processes) – see Box 4.2. The compatibility between SMS and strong sustainability is not, however, quite complete. SMS says conserve unless the benefits forgone are very large. SS says that, whatever the benefits forgone, loss of critical natural capital is unacceptable.

Sustainable livelihoods

Any sustainable strategy for the future will have to confront the question of how a much larger total global population can gain at least a basic livelihood in a manner which can be sustained. For the people of the South, many of their livelihoods will have to endure in environments which are fragile, marginal and vulnerable. Sustainable livelihoods can only be promoted via policies which reduce vulnerability – e.g. flood protection to guard against sea-level rise induced by climate change due to global warming (see Chapter 19); measures to improve food security and to offset market and intervention failures such as inappropriate resource pricing and uncoordinated development policies (see Chapters 5, 6 and 23).

Box 4.2 Safe minimum standards approach to sustainability

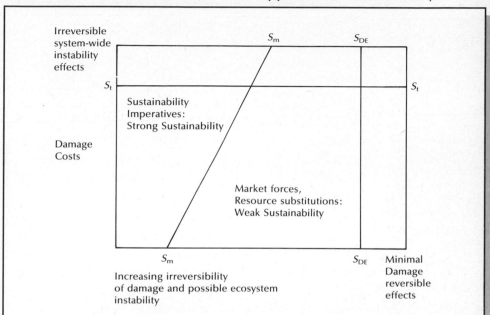

The line S_m–S_m represents some hypothetical safe minimum standard trade-off decision. Supporters of the weak sustainability (technocentric) position(s) might favour a line such as S_t–S_t; while very strong sustainability advocates, such as the deep ecologists, might favour a line such as S_{DE}–S_{DE}.

Source: Adapted from B. Norton, Georgia Institute of Technology, quoted in Toman (1992).

Sustainable development: operational principles

A number of rules (which fall some way short of a blueprint) for the sustainable utilization of the natural capital stock can now be outlined (roughly ordered to fit the VWS to VSS progression):

1. Market and intervention failures related to resource pricing and property rights should be corrected.
2. Maintenance of the regenerative capacity of renewable natural capital (RNC) – i.e. harvesting rates should not exceed regeneration rates – and avoidance of excessive pollution which could threaten waste assimilation capacities and life support systems.
3. Technological changes should be steered via an indicative planning system such that, switches from non-renewable (NRNC) to RNC are fostered; and

Box 4.3 Sustainability practice

Sustainability mode (overlapping categories)	Management strategy (as applied to projects, policy or course of action)	Policy instruments (most favoured)		
		Pollution Control and Waste Management	Raw Materials Policy	Conservation and Amenity Management
VWS	Conventional Cost–Benefit Approach: Correction of market and intervention failures via efficiency pricing; potential Pareto criterion (hypothetical compensation); consumer sovereignty; infinite substitution	e.g. pollution taxes, elimination of subsidies, imposition of property rights		
WS	Modified Cost–Benefit Approach: Extended application of monetary valuation methods; actual compensation, shadow projects, etc.; systems approach, 'weak' version of safe minimum standard	e.g. pollution taxes, permits, deposit-refunds; ambient targets		
SS	Fixed Standards Approach: Precautionary principle, primary and secondary value of natural capital; constant natural capital rule; dual self-conception, social preference value; 'strong' version of safe minimum standard	e.g. ambient standards; conservation zoning; process technology-based effluent standards; permits; severance taxes; assurance bonds		
VSS	Abandonment of Cost–Benefit Analysis: or severely constrained cost-effectiveness analysis; bioethics	standards and regulation; birth licences		

Source: R. K. Turner (1993)

efficiency-increasing technical progress should dominate throughput-increasing technology.

4. RNC should be exploited, but at a rate equal to the creation of RNC substitutes (including recycling).

5. The overall scale of economic activity must be limited so that it remains within the carrying capacity of the remaining natural capital. Given the uncertainties present, a precautionary approach should be adopted with a built-in safety margin.

Box 4.3 summarizes some of the measures and enabling policy instruments that would be involved in any application of an SD strategy. Succeeding chapters in this book cover these various elements in greater detail.

Conclusions

Although it has been defined in many different, and sometimes contradictory, ways the concept of sustainable development does have both relevance and meaning. Weak and strong versions of the concept can be distinguished, and a rudimentary measure of sustainability can be calibrated. How precisely sustainability principles can be translated into operational practice remains more uncertain. But the framework for general sustainability rules has been set out and will require adaptation to specific economic and environmental circumstances.

Further reading

The basic idea of sustainable development and the constant capital rule are covered in:

D. W. Pearce, A. Markandya and E. B. Barbier, *Blueprint for a Green Economy*, Earthscan, London, 1989

and in the context of developing countries by

D. W. Pearce, E. B. Barbier and A. Markandya, *Sustainable Development*: *Economics and Environment in the Third World*, Earthscan, London, 1990.

The strong sustainability position is set out in:

R. Costanza and H. Daly, 'Natural capital and sustainable development', *Conservation Biology* **6**: 37–46, 1992.

Modified national income accounting is discussed in:

P. Bartelmus *et al.*, 'Integrated environmental and economic accounting: framework for a SNA satellite system', *Review of Income and Wealth* **37**: 111–48, 1991.

C. Bryant and P. Cook, 'Environmental issues and the national accounts', *Income Trends*, No. 469: 99–122, HMSO, London, 1992.

H. Daly and J. Cobb, *For the Common Good*, Greenprint, London, 1990.

On the safe minimum standard see:

R. C. Bishop, 'Economics of endangered species', *American Journal of Agricultural Economics* **60**: 10–18, 1978.

References

D. W. Pearce and G. Atkinson, 'Are National Economies Sustainable? Measuring Sustainable Development', CSERGE GEC Working Paper 92–11, University College London and University of East Anglia, 1992.

M. A. Toman, 'The difficulty of defining sustainability', *Resources* **106**: 3–6, 1992.

R. K. Turner (ed.) *Sustainable Environmental Economics and Management: Principles and Practice*, Belhaven, London, 1993, Chapter 1.

World Commission on Environment and Development, *Our Common Future*, Oxford University Press, Oxford, 1987.

PART II

The causes of environmental degradation

CHAPTER 5

How markets work and why they 'fail'

The importance of markets and market efficiency

The world's economies can be classified into two polar types: market economies where producers decide which goods they will make and sell to consumers; and centrally planned economies where it is the government who generally decides who will produce what and in which quantities. Many real economies are mixed systems. Market-type economies have always been more prevalent than centrally planned systems, a trend reinforced by the recent breakup of such systems in Eastern Europe and the former USSR. The vast majority of the world's resources are therefore used in market-type economies, which are thereby also responsible for a significant proportion of the world's pollution. It is therefore important that we understand the process by which market forces determine how much of any one resource a producer will use in the manufacturing process and similarly why the operation of markets affects the types and quantities of pollution produced. Understanding how the market operates and the types of signals which it gives to producers also helps us to understand how we might best modify markets to ensure that producers do not overexploit scarce environmental resources and are given incentives to reduce the amount of pollution they produce.

The producer's objective – profit

Why do producers produce? The production of goods is not an end in itself, rather it allows the producer to exchange the goods produced for money and so create an income. However, the production of an item is not a costless exercise, the producer must buy in resources (raw materials, labour, etc.). Therefore the producer must ensure that the amount of money received for the goods produced (the firm's revenue) exceeds costs so that a profit can be made (the difference between revenue and costs) and the firm can continue in business. Clearly there will always be a strong incentive for the firm to reduce any costs and thereby maximize profits. Although firms can have other objectives, the goal of profit maximization is still a relevant one.

Revenues and costs

We can now consider in turn the separate elements of revenue and cost, which together determine profit. Let us consider the example of a paper mill producing boxes of paper. The revenue which the paper mill receives from selling one box of paper is given by the market price of that good. This price is in turn determined by how much paper people demand and how much producers as a whole (i.e. all paper mills) supply of that good; factors which are generally out of the control of the single firm. It was established in Box 1.4 that people generally would wish to increase their consumption of a good when its price falls while they decrease their consumption when price increases, i.e. there is a 'negative' relationship between the price of an item and quantity demanded of it. Therefore we get the downward sloping 'demand for paper' curve shown as line D in Panel (a) of Box 5.1. On the other side of the market if the price of a good falls, firms reduce their production of it, while if prices rise, they increase their supply of the good, i.e. there is a 'positive' relationship between the price of an item and the quantity which producers will supply. Therefore we get the upward sloping 'supply of paper' curve shown as line S in Panel (a) of Box 5.1. As discussed previously, there is only one price (P_e, the market equilibrium price) at which the quantity of paper that producers wish to supply is equal to the amount of paper which consumers wish to buy (quantity Q in Box 5.1). Therefore, for any price of paper other than P_e the price will move towards P_e, i.e. the system is self-equilibrating.

The marginal amount is a central concept in economics and so it is important that it is clearly understood. A marginal amount pertains to a single unit, thus **marginal revenue** is the amount of revenue (or payment) which a firm receives from selling one particular unit of output. This is, of course, likely to be the same for all units of output, i.e. the marginal revenue of say the first box of paper sold is the same as the marginal revenue of the 10,000th box sold. However, this is not always the case for all marginal amounts. For example, the costs of producing the first unit of output (the **marginal cost** of the first box of paper) may not be the same as the costs of producing the 10,000th unit of output (the marginal costs of the 10,000th unit). It is important not to confuse marginal amounts with total amounts; for example, while the marginal revenue (extra revenue earned on each extra unit produced) is constant as production rises, the total revenue (i.e. the total amount received by the firm for all its goods) obviously increases as production rises.

Box 5.1   Determining marginal revenue

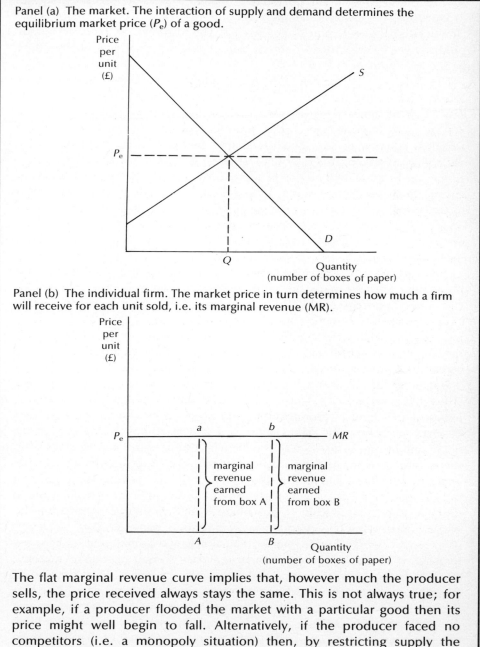

Panel (a) The market. The interaction of supply and demand determines the equilibrium market price (P_e) of a good.

Price per unit (£)

S

P_e

D

Q

Quantity (number of boxes of paper)

Panel (b) The individual firm. The market price in turn determines how much a firm will receive for each unit sold, i.e. its marginal revenue (MR).

Price per unit (£)

a b

P_e ———————————————— MR

marginal revenue earned from box A

marginal revenue earned from box B

A B

Quantity (number of boxes of paper)

The flat marginal revenue curve implies that, however much the producer sells, the price received always stays the same. This is not always true; for example, if a producer flooded the market with a particular good then its price might well begin to fall. Alternatively, if the producer faced no competitors (i.e. a monopoly situation) then, by restricting supply the monopolist might force up price. These are important real world problems but we shall, for the purpose of this introduction, ignore such issues.

Because our producer receives the same amount of money for the first box sold as for the one hundredth or one millionth box sold, we say that the producer has a constant marginal revenue (MR). This MR curve is therefore shown as a flat line in Panel (b) of Box 5.1. The total revenue received by our producer can be calculated by simply multiplying marginal revenue (per box) by the total number of boxes sold.

This analysis determines how much money our paper manufacturer receives for selling its goods. However, in order to determine how much profit it makes on each box of paper produced, the firm will also have to take into account how much each box costs to make, i.e. its costs per unit or marginal costs. Costs can be divided into two categories; **fixed costs** and **variable costs**. Fixed costs refer to those items which are essential for our firm to pay for before even one box of paper can be produced but which do not change thereafter; for example, the costs of the buildings and land which form the physical structure of the paper mill will be the same whether one or a very large number of boxes are produced. Fixed costs do not change as the output of boxes of paper changes. In contrast, variable costs refer to those items which must be bought in afresh whenever a new batch of paper is made, such as wood pulp or labour. These costs rise with the level of production, i.e. to increase the amount of paper produced the firm will have to increase its purchases of wood pulp and hire more workers, i.e. its variable costs increase. To simplify our analysis, let us ignore fixed costs for the moment on the grounds that these have to be paid irrespective of how much the company chooses to produce. Instead let us concentrate upon the variable cost of each unit produced, i.e. the **marginal variable costs** (MVC).

Unlike marginal revenue, the marginal variable cost of producing any good is not likely to be a constant irrespective of the amount produced. This is because of changes in **productivity**. Productivity is essentially a measure of how cheaply a firm can manufacture each unit of output. In the case of the paper mill, a simple measure of productivity can be calculated by examining the number of extra workers which must be hired to increase production of paper by successive amounts. If the owner of the paper mill only hired one worker then that worker would have to do all the tasks of the mill, moving the raw paper from machine to machine. In such an inefficient situation the single worker might only produce, say, ten boxes of paper per day. However, if a second worker were hired they could now divide tasks between themselves in a more efficient manner, e.g. one worker operates a machine while the other moves the raw paper between machines. This 'division of labour' encourages specialized expertise to evolve so that it is very likely that the two workers working together would produce *more than twice* the amount the single worker produced; say thirty boxes of paper per day. We term this an increase in productivity, or an efficiency gain. Now notice that, when we move from one worker to two workers, while our variable costs (their wages) have doubled, the amount of paper produced has tripled. Therefore the cost

Box 5.2 The marginal variable cost (MVC) curve

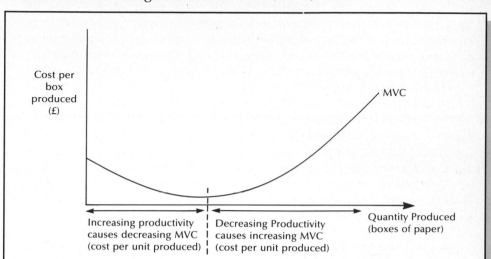

The paper mill can increase its output by hiring more workers. The first few workers hired have plenty to do and this results in a large increase in output, i.e. costs per box of paper produced fall (declining marginal variable costs). However, as all the machines in the mill become fully manned, then hiring extra workers only results in a relatively small increase in output, i.e. cost per box of paper produced begins to rise (increasing marginal variable costs). The consequent shape of the MVC curve applies to most cost items (inputs); for example, the paper mill can also increase its output by raising the temperature of its pulping vats, i.e. increase its input of fuel. Initially a small increase in temperature (small increase in variable costs) causes a large increase in paper production, i.e. costs per unit produced (marginal variable costs) fall. However, eventually as the pulping process becomes pushed to its limits, it requires a large increase in temperature (large increase in variable costs) to produce a comparatively small increase in paper production, i.e. costs per unit produced (marginal variable costs) rise.

per box of paper produced (the marginal variable cost), has fallen. Therefore, whenever increasing output is synonymous with increasing productivity, we get a fall in marginal variable costs.

This trend of increasing productivity (decreasing marginal variable costs) often occurs when firms initially expand their output, see Box 5.2. However, now consider what happens if we go on increasing output and hiring more and more workers. The increase in productivity (decrease in marginal variable costs) continues up to a point (say when each machine has its own operator and person transferring its output to the next machine) but declines thereafter. To continue hiring more labour increases wage costs but does not add much to the amount of paper being produced. As productivity per employee begins to decline, so costs now begin to rise faster than the quantity of paper produced, i.e. the cost of producing each extra box of paper rises (increasing marginal variable costs).

This phenomenon of eventually declining productivity (increasing MVC) is well recognized and applies not only to labour but to almost all the resources which a manufacturer uses. For example, consider the most fundamental resource of energy. Suppose the paper-making process requires heated vats of chemicals which break down the wood fibers to make paper. Starting from a vat temperature of, say, 0°C, if the manufacturer increased the temperature to 100°C, paper production might double while further increasing temperature to 200°C might increase output tenfold, i.e. increasing productivity (decreasing MVC of energy). However, raising the temperature by a further 100 degrees to 300°C might only increase output by one-quarter while raising temperature to 400°C might make no difference to output (increasing MVC of energy). Here we have increasing productivity up to 200°C and decreasing productivity thereafter. The important result is that all these resources exhibit similar MVC characteristics so that, when we consider all variable costs together, we get an MVC curve which initially declines and then rises.

Maximizing profits: the market optimum level of output

The amount of profit which the paper mill makes on a single box of paper (the **marginal profit**) is simply the difference between the amount of money it receives for selling that box (marginal revenue) and the amount of money it cost to produce that box (marginal variable cost). While marginal revenue is the same for each box sold, we know that, as the paper mill increases the amount it produces, so its marginal variable costs change. Therefore we need to consider each box in turn calculating the marginal profit made on that box by subtracting marginal variable cost from marginal revenue – this is shown graphically in Box 5.3

Over time, as the paper mill increases its production of paper, productivity initially rises, marginal variable costs fall and the marginal profit increases. Once productivity begins to fall, marginal variable costs rise and marginal profit declines. However, the firm will produce each and every box of paper on which it makes at least some marginal profit. At this point, known as the market optimum level of output, its total profit (the sum of marginal profit made on each box) will be at a maximum. If it expands its output by say one box more then the marginal variable cost of producing this last box will exceed its marginal revenue, i.e. the firm makes a loss on the box. The free

Box 5.3 The market optimum level of output

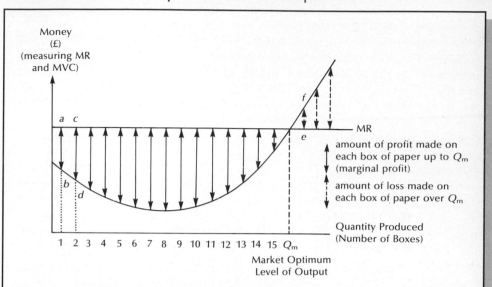

Here we have superimposed our MR curve (Box 5.1) onto our MVC curve (Box 5.2). We can now see the profit made on the first box of paper as the difference between the marginal revenue of that box (distance 1*a* as measured on the vertical money axis) and the marginal variable cost of that box (distance 1*b* measured on the vertical axis), i.e. the marginal profit of producing the first box of paper will be the amount *ab* as measured on the vertical axis. Similarly the marginal profit of producing the second box is the difference between its MR and its MVC, i.e. the distance *cd*. Therefore profit per unit (marginal profit) is shown as the unbroken arrow headed lines.

The firm will produce each unit of output where the marginal revenue it receives for that unit exceeds the marginal variable cost of producing that unit. Consequently the firm produces all units up to the output level Q_m. This is the market optimum level of output. In order to stay in business in the long term, the total profit made at output Q_m must at least cover all fixed costs, e.g. cost of buildings, ground rent, etc.

market profit incentive therefore leads firms operating in a market to expand their output until marginal variable costs equal marginal revenues as this point coincides with the firm earning its maximum possible profit.

We can now bring the firm fixed costs (building, land, etc.) back into consideration. These must now be subtracted from the total profits figure. Of course, if total profits do not exceed fixed costs then the net profit figure will be negative and the firm risks bankruptcy and closure.

Since a firm will always fix its production where marginal variable cost is rising, economists often simplify their drawings of the MVC curve by ignoring its initial downward sloping section and instead draw it as a simple upward sloping line. As this is a common convention we will now change to this approach too – see Box 5.4. However, it is useful to know that, in reality, productivity almost always rises before it falls, i.e. MVC in reality falls before it rises.

How markets use priced and unpriced (environmental) resources

We have now seen that, in a free market, firms take two factors into account when determining what level of output to produce:

1. How much they can sell each unit of output for.
2. How much it will cost to produce each unit of output.

We have seen that the cost of making each successive unit (the marginal variable cost, MVC) eventually rises as the firm expands the number of units of output produced. Furthermore, when MVC equals the amount each unit is sold for (the marginal revenue, MR) then the firm stops expansion and fixes its total output. What implication does this have for how a firm will use its resources? Remember that in our paper mill example the MVC of producing each extra box of paper included items such as the amount of extra labour which has to be hired, the amount of extra wood pulp which will be bought in and the cost of the extra energy needed to heat the paper making vats. What our market analysis has shown is that the firm will only increase its output when the price received for the extra paper produced exceeds the cost of the extra resources used. This means that the firm will be very careful not to squander those resources which it has to pay for.

This leads us to an important conclusion; that free markets give firms a strong incentive to conserve rather than overexploit all those resources for which they have to pay. They will only use such resources up to the point where their cost equals the revenue they generate and will not overuse these resources beyond this point. This conclusion appears encouraging, indicating that markets are somehow efficient users of resources. However, such a conclusion becomes less comforting when we move to consider those resources provided free of charge by the environment.

Consider the hidden assumption behind the statement that markets only use resources where their value is less than that of the finished good that their use will produce. This assumes that the cost of these resources is an accurate indicator of the resources' value. But consider again the extra energy which the paper mill used to boost output. This energy will almost certainly ultimately depend upon the use of either fossil (coal, gas, oil, etc.) or nuclear

72

Box 5.4 The simplified MVC curve and the marginal net private benefit (MNPB) curve

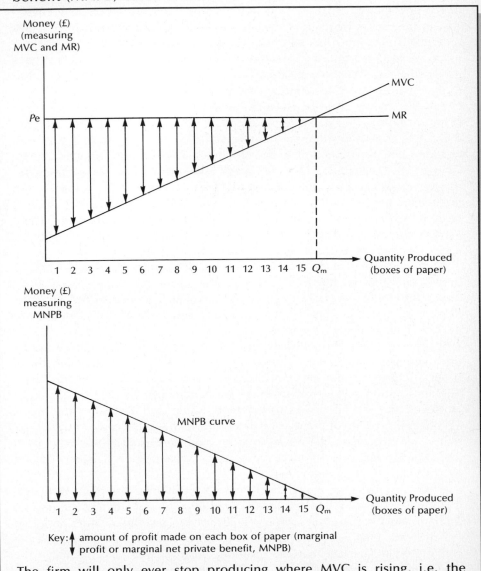

Key: ↑ amount of profit made on each box of paper (marginal
     ↓ profit or marginal net private benefit, MNPB)

The firm will only ever stop producing where MVC is rising, i.e. the simplified MVC curve is an upward sloping line. The difference between MR and MVC gives the producers marginal net private benefit (MNPB) curve (previously referred to as marginal profit). The firm will produce all units of output which yield at least some positive MNPB, i.e. MR > MVC, resulting in output being fixed at Q_m.

fuel. Suppose in this example, that our paper mill's energy strategy is to heat its vats electrically and that this electricity is generated by burning coal (any of the possible combinations will give the same general result). The energy cost to the firm is therefore simply its electricity bill. However, this bill will only reflect how much the electricity company itself pays for coal, employing its power station workforce, maintaining pylons, etc. and how much it pays its stockholders. What the electricity bill will not reflect is the damage caused to the environment by generating electricity in this manner.

Burning coal to generate electricity in turn generates nitrous oxides and sulphur dioxide (together responsible for increased respiratory disease, damage to crops and trees, and acidification of waterways) as well as carbon dioxide (a major contributor to the 'greenhouse' effect and possible climate change). In the absence of government regulation, none of the pollution damage caused by these emissions is paid for by the generating company and is therefore not reflected in the paper mill's electricity bill. Therefore the cost faced by the paper mill for increasing its use of energy will not reflect these extra environmental damages. Instead these costs are ultimately paid for by society in terms of ill health and environmental degradation.

While some market prices, such as those for electricity, may be only a partial reflection of the true cost of using certain resources, an equally important problem is posed by those environmental services which are used directly by companies but which, while they may be vital to the production process, have in effect no market price at all.

Suppose that our paper mill discovers that it can raise its output either by increasing the temperature in the pulping vats or by increasing its use of water in those vats and then discharging its liquid waste into a nearby river. The first option will involve increased energy bills, i.e. increased MVC. However, the second option (using more water and thereafter the waste assimilative capacity of the river) will only raise the firm's costs to the extent that water abstraction charges have to be paid (historically these have been low). Clearly if the firm's objective is profit maximization it is this second option which the firm will prefer.

While such a strategy of resource use is clearly of benefit to the private firm it can have costly implications for the environment and thereby for society. Again in the absence of regulation, the firm releases polluted water back into the river but pays no price for the vital waste assimilation services of the water, despite the fact that the resulting polluted water may damage the environment in numerous ways. For example, if as a result of this pollution certain fish species in the river are killed off, fishermen will lose a valuable resource. Similarly, water companies may have to fit purification equipment to ensure that public water supplies are of drinkable quality. The damage associated with such environmental degradation does not affect the private company (i.e. it is not an **internal cost** as reflected in the firm's MVC) but instead affects society as a whole. Such damages are known as **external costs**.

Note that any such environmental damage not rectified by the polluter will involve an external cost whether society pays for it directly in money terms (as in fitting the water purification equipment) or not (as in the loss of fish species).

The firm is actually using unpriced resources in the same manner as any priced resource in that it will always increase its use of any resource where the cost of doing so is less than the revenue of extra output produced. Unfortunately, the cost to the firm of using unpriced environmental resources is of course zero and so the firm increases its use until no more output can be obtained from that use.

Output, pollution and external costs (the social optimum level of output)

While the market system appears to be highly efficient at using priced resources, it fails to correctly guide firms towards the efficient use of unpriced environmental resources. This **market failure** arises because firms only take account of the market price of a resource when deciding how much of that resource to use. When a firm uses and degrades an unpriced environmental resource (such as the waste assimilation function of water), this incurs no internal cost upon the firm (i.e. the firm's MVC curve does not rise) but it does create an external cost upon society. Box 5.5 shows how the production

Box 5.5 External costs and the socially optimal level of output

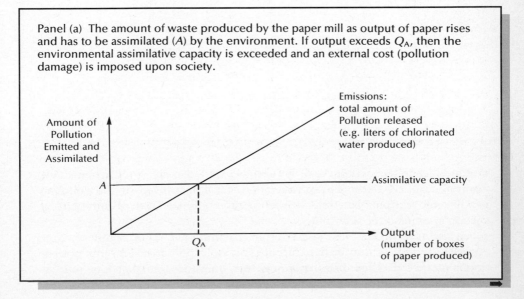

Panel (a) The amount of waste produced by the paper mill as output of paper rises and has to be assimilated (A) by the environment. If output exceeds Q_A, then the environmental assimilative capacity is exceeded and an external cost (pollution damage) is imposed upon society.

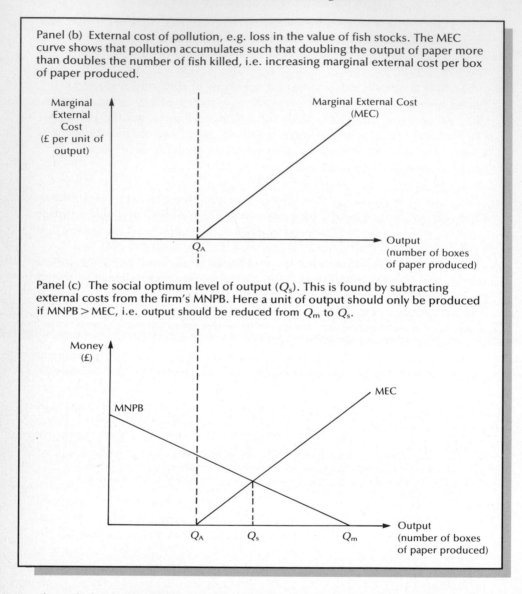

Panel (b) External cost of pollution, e.g. loss in the value of fish stocks. The MEC curve shows that pollution accumulates such that doubling the output of paper more than doubles the number of fish killed, i.e. increasing marginal external cost per box of paper produced.

Marginal
External
Cost
(£ per unit of
output)

Marginal External Cost
(MEC)

Q_A

Output
(number of boxes
of paper produced)

Panel (c) The social optimum level of output (Q_s). This is found by subtracting external costs from the firm's MNPB. Here a unit of output should only be produced if MNPB > MEC, i.e. output should be reduced from Q_m to Q_s.

Money
(£)

MEC

MNPB

Q_A Q_s Q_m

Output
(number of boxes
of paper produced)

of goods leads to pollution and thereby to external costs. Only when these external costs are taken into consideration (i.e. internalized by the polluter) will we move from the profit driven market optimal level of output to a socially optimal level of output.

We can now incorporate these external costs into a decision about whether a particular unit of output (box of paper) should be produced. Our private firm's **market decision rule** regarding this question was that any unit of output should be produced if it resulted in the firm gaining a positive MNPB (i.e. if MR > MVC), up to the point where MR = MVC, the market optimum production level. We can now state a **social decision rule** that external costs (MEC) must also be taken into consideration, i.e. polluters should be compelled to pay for the pollution they emit (known as the 'Polluter Pays Principle'). We examine this principle further in Chapter 10.

Public-type goods

Markets work best when allocating private goods which are characterized by **exclusivity** (i.e. anyone who is unwilling to pay the market price for the private good in question is excluded from its use) and by **rivalness in consumption** (sometimes referred to as divisibility). This latter characteristic ensures that a resource can be subdivided such that each individual who is willing to pay for it can exclude all others (rivals) from its benefits.

Environmental goods tend to be non-exclusive and divisible (e.g. migratory fish shoals and groundwater reserves), exclusive and indivisible (e.g. closed access nature reserves and private beaches up to some maximum use level) or non-exclusive and indivisible (e.g. scenic views and clean air and water) – see Box 5.6.

Conclusions

The free market takes into account the price of resources when deciding how much of that resource to use in the production of goods. Where those prices accurately reflect the true value of resources, the free market encourages conservation. However, we have seen that the prices of many resources often do not reflect the full costs involved in their use (the price of electricity does not reflect the environmental damage caused by its generation). Furthermore, we have noted that many environmental resources, though extremely valuable, often have effectively no price attached to their use (e.g. the waste assimilation capacity of the environment). The use of environmental resources and pollution of the environment may be incorrectly (i.e. under-) costed by the firm concerned. However, they do impose costs upon the rest of society. Consequently, market failure situations arise where a firm produces units of output which create private profits but also impose large external costs upon society. Only when these external costs are brought into consideration (for example, by forcing the firm to pay for the external costs it causes, in line with the Polluter Pays Principle) will firms act so as to prevent market failures occurring and move from a market optimal to a socially optimal level of output.

We have also seen that an additional complication is that many environmental goods do not act like goods in the market-place: they are 'public'-type

Box 5.6 Private and public-type goods spectrum

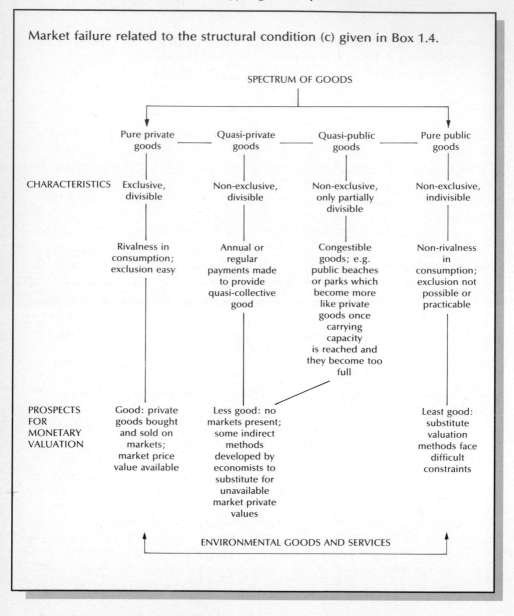

Market failure related to the structural condition (c) given in Box 1.4.

SPECTRUM OF GOODS

	Pure private goods	Quasi-private goods	Quasi-public goods	Pure public goods
CHARACTERISTICS	Exclusive, divisible	Non-exclusive, divisible	Non-exclusive, only partially divisible	Non-exclusive, indivisible
	Rivalness in consumption; exclusion easy	Annual or regular payments made to provide quasi-collective good	Congestible goods; e.g. public beaches or parks which become more like private goods once carrying capacity is reached and they become too full	Non-rivalness in consumption; exclusion not possible or practicable
PROSPECTS FOR MONETARY VALUATION	Good: private goods bought and sold on markets; market price value available	Less good: no markets present; some indirect methods developed by economists to substitute for unavailable market private values		Least good: substitute valuation methods face difficult constraints

ENVIRONMENTAL GOODS AND SERVICES

rather than 'private' goods. This 'publicness' is one of the reasons why markets do not evolve naturally in environmental goods and services.

CHAPTER 6

How governments fail the environment

Why governments intervene

Chapter 5 showed that freely functioning markets cannot be relied upon to look after the environment. They 'fail' because they are very unlikely to establish markets in environmental goods and services. The phenomenon of an *externality* provided one main reason for this: the actions of one individual or firm affect the wellbeing of others, but there is frequently no incentive for the generator of this effect to take account of it in its decision-making. On the face of it, this would seem to suggest that there is a need for *government* to intervene in the market-place to protect those who suffer from externalities. This is exactly what governments do in many cases. They may set regulations on aircraft noise, for example, since airlines are unlikely *voluntarily* to offer noise insulation to householders in the vicinity of an airport. They set river quality standards because upstream users of rivers are very unlikely to take account of the loss of wellbeing to downstream users from pollution. Governments also intervene when the action that is needed is *international* in scope. The citizens of mainland Europe, for example, are unlikely voluntarily to reduce acid rain emissions which land in Scandinavia. Governments have to act together.

Another important reason for intervening, which is especially important for environmental issues, arises when the damage being done occurs because no-one effectively *owns* a resource. If we think of the atmosphere as a resource – which it is because it acts as a 'sink' for gaseous emissions such as carbon dioxide, methane and so on – then it is fairly obvious that no-one owns it. We say it is an *open access* resource. But because no-one owns it, no individual has any incentive to restrict their own contribution to the pollutants that we put into the atmosphere. Each individual stands to gain from a self-interested point of view by not curbing emissions. But as long as *everyone* thinks that way, the resource will be in danger of being overused. This is exactly why the phenomenon of global warming has come about and

79

it is an example of what has come to be known – not very accurately – as 'the tragedy of the commons'. (Not very accurately, because 'the commons' refers to common property resources owned by a fairly well-defined group of individuals, whereas the real tragedy of overuse is much more likely to occur when the resource is not owned at all: open access resources – see Chapter 15.) In such circumstances, it is necessary for governments to intervene and manage the resource. They do this by issuing regulations which say that certain pollutants cannot be emitted beyond a certain level.

Why governments fail

Although there are good reasons why governments intervene, unfortunately they are often no better at managing natural resources than the free market. There are many reasons for this, some of which are given below.

First, we tend to think, as citizens, that the duty and purpose of government is to act in our interests *as a community* rather than as individuals. This is why we have laws, police forces, a judiciary, public health regulations and so on; but this image of 'benign' governments can be false. At one extreme, governments may be despotic and interested only in favouring the interests of some part of the community rather than the community as a whole. Even in democratic countries, governments may act to please a particular pressure group rather than the community as a whole. This means that governments may well *not* act to protect the environment, especially if they think that environmental protection will impose costs on members of powerful pressure groups. Since environmental legislation *does* tend to impose costs on industry and agriculture, as well as on the ordinary citizen, it is often resisted by many interested groups.

Second, governments may not be very good at getting the right *information* which enables them to trace through the full consequences of a particular action. Even where a government is well intentioned, what actually happens may not be what it intended simply because the process of being informed becomes very complicated. As we shall see, this is important in the environmental context because politicians often do not see that actions that are, ostensibly, *not* about the environment, will have an effect on the environment. The very interrelatedness of environment and economy that we stressed in Chapter 1 can work to the disadvantage of the environment simply because politicians tend to 'compartmentalize' issues. We cannot have an 'environment policy' that is distinct from an energy policy, or a regional development policy, and so on. They all interact.

Third, government, in the form of politicians, may have good intentions and frame a good environmental law in principle. However, it has to be translated into practice and this involves using experts who are part of a government bureaucracy. The bureaucrats become very important and can easily influence the nature of the regulation in practice. Since bureaucrats are very often not elected officials and, unlike many workers, they tend not to be paid by results, they therefore have little explicit incentive to behave in the best interests of the community unless closely scrutinized by politicians – and that can be very difficult.

Illustrating government failure

We can illustrate government failure with several examples.

The Common Agricultural Policy

In the European Community, the agricultural sector is subject to the Common Agricultural Policy (CAP) which was formulated in 1958. The aims of the CAP were to raise the incomes of the farming community, to stabilize agricultural markets, to ensure that food supplies were always available (against the threat of international interruptions in supply) and to ensure reasonable consumer prices. In reality, the policy reflected the power of the agricultural lobby that had, since the Second World War, secured quite extensive national protection from individual governments. Box 6.1 shows, in broad outline, how the CAP works. Rather than let the forces of supply and demand for food operate freely, there is an agreed 'intervention price' which is above the market price that would otherwise rule. The market price, if it prevailed, would be set by the price – the 'world price' – at which *imported food* would enter the European Community (EC). But this imported food is subject to a tariff which is equal to the difference between the world price and the intervention price. The effect of the intervention price is therefore to restrict cheaper imports, and to guarantee farmers prices for their products.

The CAP is an instance of 'government failure' because it protects one group, the farmers, at the expense of a larger group – consumers and taxpayers – at a net cost to society as a whole. Consumers end up paying higher prices than they would have done if the market was free – so they are worse off. Taxpayers also pay some of the cost because other means, such as production quotas, are used to protect EC agriculture. Even if there was an argument for protecting farmers' incomes at the expense of others' incomes, it turns out that this form of protection is very expensive: consumers and taxpayers have to give up more than £1 in order to pay £1 to farmers. Expenditure under the CAP in the United Kingdom alone was some £1.7 billion in 1990/1991.

How is the CAP linked to environmental loss? Box 6.1 shows that one effect of the CAP is to stimulate overproduction. The incentive to produce too much arises because farmers can sell however much they produce at the

Box 6.1 Overproduction under the Common Agricultural Policy and the effect on the environment

Panels (a) and (b) Supply and demand for agricultural produce in the EC.

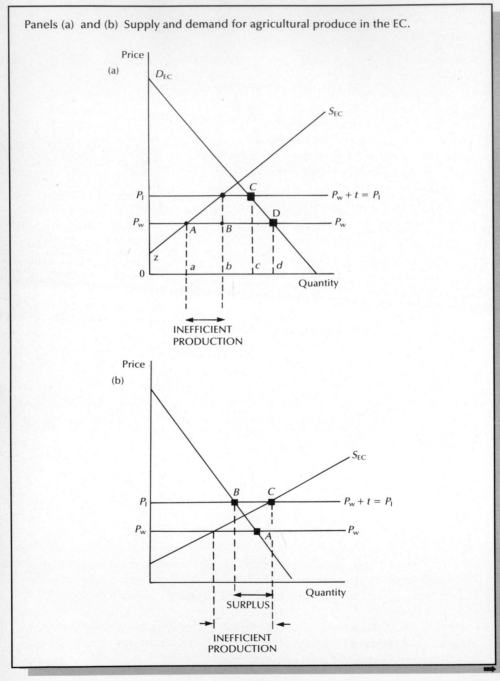

Panels (a) and (b) show the supply and demand for agricultural produce in the EC. Two cases are distinguished. In Panel (a) the EC demand for food is shown as D_{EC}, and the amounts that EC farmers would be willing to supply are shown by S_{EC}; but the rest of the world produce food more cheaply, and their supply curve is shown by P_w. *If the free market prevailed* then the actual supply curve would be *ZABD* and the EC would consume at *D*. EC farmers would supply 0*a* and the rest of the world *ac* (note that the overall supply curve is 'kinked' because, beyond 0*a* the rest of the world can produce more cheaply than the EC). But the EC does not allow this. Not only does it guarantee an 'intervention price' (P_I) to its farmers, but it protects them from world imports by putting a tariff, *t*, on world supplies so that they too are priced at the intervention price. The effect is to encourage EC farmers to produce 0*b*, for imports to be *bc*, and for demand to be at 0*c*. But the EC output *ab* is inefficient production (because the rest of the world could have produced it more cheaply).

Panel (b) shows a situation in which imports can be excluded altogether and EC farmers can produce so much that the market cannot accommodate supplies. Here the intervention price has risen so high that the EC farmers meet all the demand for food (point *B*) and in fact overproduce (point *C*). The level of inefficient production has expanded compared to Panel (a) and there is an actual surplus which has to be stored ('wine lakes', 'butter mountains') or sold for export. But, in the case of exports, EC produce would fetch only the world price P_w which is below the price farmers have been guaranteed. Hence the difference appears as an export subsidy (called a 'restitution' payment). Notice that in this case there are no imports at all. In practice, the market can move from situation (a) to situation (b) depending on domestic supplies and world market conditions. Imports and excess supply can also exist simultaneously once allowance is made for quality differences and market imperfections.

The environment of the EC countries suffers under the CAP because of the level of inefficient production. The higher production is achieved by expanding the area cultivated (removing hedgerows and establishing mechanized monoculture), by the intensive application of fertilizers and pesticides – leading to high runoff into rivers and groundwaters – and through intensive stocking of livestock, giving rise to overgrazing and the creation of animal slurry which can pollute rivers.

The effect on hedgerows

Panel (c) shows the length of hedgerows in (W) Germany and England and Wales per hectare of agricultural land. The effect of the CAP can be

Panel (c) The lengths of hedgerows in England and Wales and West Germany.

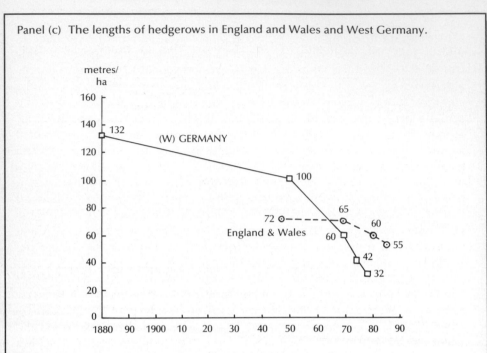

discerned despite the very limited data. In Germany and England and Wales, the sharpest decline in length occurs from about the early and mid-1960s (the chart for Germany shows a decline earlier than this because of the limited number of observations between 1950 and 1960).

Sources: Authors' calculations based on data in Department of the Environment, *Digest of Environmental Protection and Water Statistics 1990* and US Environmental Protection Agency (1990).

Fertilizer use

Since the extent of agricultural land tends to be limited in developed countries, the main way of increasing output is through *intensification* – applying more fertilizers and pesticides to crops. Fertilizer use has tended to increase in all countries, regardless of the EC. But it is significant that in 1988, and compared to the OECD *average* application rate, nitrogenous fertilizers were applied most heavily in EC countries. Thus, compared to the average of 5.7 tonnes/km^2, the situation was that shown in Table 1.

Table 1 Use of fertilizers in the EC (countries in brackets are not members of the EC)

In excess of 10 tonnes/km² over the OECD average	From 5–10 tonnes/km² over the OECD average
Belgium	(Japan)
Germany	Denmark
Netherlands	France
UK	(Norway)
(Switzerland)	

Source: OECD (1991)

intervention price (unless, as in some cases, there are production quotas). Production is increased in two ways: by expanding the area farmed and by farming more intensively.

One of the ways of expanding the land under cultivation in countries where there is not much 'spare' land is to remove hedgerows. Box 6.1 shows that hedgerow removal accelerated in Germany and the United Kingdom during the period in which CAP was introduced.

The other way of expanding output is through intensification. This tends to mean more fertilizer and pesticide use, and the existence of guaranteed prices for output is one of the reasons why overuse is encouraged. Box 6.1 shows some evidence to the effect that fertilizer application rates in the EC countries are above those in other countries.

Government failure in developing countries

In the developing world, free markets are very often not allowed to function. Governments intervene and control prices, but unlike the EC case they tend to keep prices down *below* their market equilibrium. They do this usually from well-meaning motives. For example, they wish to keep food prices low so as to subsidize food costs to the poor; or they wish to stimulate industrial development and this leads them to keep energy prices down. Unfortunately, such interventions often cause more problems than they solve. The negative effects are:

- governments use up substantial tax revenues and other income in subsidies for price control, even though government revenues are at a premium because of the need to use them to develop the economy;

- the subsidies encourage overuse of the resources that are subsidized. While we tend to think that poor countries will use scarce resources wisely, the effect of keeping prices down is to encourage wasteful use;
- the subsidies make the economic activity in question appear artificially attractive. This tends to attract more people into that industry or sector because profits, or 'rents', are high. (This is known as **rent-seeking**.) This diverts resources away from more important activities in the economy.

The impact on the environment can be illustrated in the context of the pricing of irrigation water and energy.

Irrigation water

In many countries the prices charged for water that is used for irrigating crops are generally below costs of supply, and often there is a lack of incentives to conserve water, e.g. charges are often set on the basis of irrigated acreage regardless of water quantity consumed. One of the effects of such low charges is overwatering with the result that the irrigated land becomes waterlogged. Applications of irrigation water often exceed design levels by a factor of three. In India 10 million hectares of land have been lost to cultivation through waterlogging and 25 million hectares are threatened by salinization. In Pakistan some 12 million hectares of the Indus Basin canal system is waterlogged and 40 per cent is saline. Worldwide, maybe some 40 per cent of the world's irrigation capacity is affected by salinization. Irrigation from river impoundments has resulted in other environmental effects. Large dams produce downstream pollution and upstream siltation as the land round the reservoir is deforested. Indigenous peoples are moved from their traditional homelands when the dammed area is flooded. Clearly, not all damage done by irrigation is due to low pricing, nor, by any means, can the environmental costs of large dams be debited to inefficient pricing. But there is an association between wrong pricing and environmental damage. By adopting prices that are too low more irrigation water than is needed is demanded, exaggerating the requirement for major irrigation schemes such as dams and for other schemes as well. Even if the scheme is justified, the amounts of water that are used are likely to be excessive because of the failure to price the resource closer to its true cost of supply.

Box 6.2 shows the ratio of actual revenues obtained from selected irrigation schemes to operating and maintenance costs (O + M) and to moderate estimates of capital plus O + M costs. While some countries succeed in recovering most or all of the O + M costs, the highest recovery rate of total costs is around 20 per cent only.

The underpricing encourages a wasteful attitude so that systems are kept in a poor state of repair. Inefficient irrigation negatively affects agricultural output. As charges are low, there is excess demand giving a premium to

Box 6.2   Cost recovery in irrigation schemes (per cent)

Country	Actual Revenues	
	O + M Costs	Capital + O + M Costs
Indonesia	78	14
Korea	91	18
Nepal	57	7
Philippines	120	22
Thailand	28	5
Bangladesh	18	neg

Notes: neg = negligible. Capital costs are 'moderate' estimates only.
Source: R. Repetto (1986) p. 5.

those who can secure water rights, e.g. by being the first in line to receive water. This can be achieved by ensuring that the system irrigates particular parcels of land first, leaving the poorer farmer to secure whatever is left over after wasteful prior uses. Moreover, water tends to be allocated according to acreage, not by crop requirements. This results in the phenomenon of *rent-seeking*: the interest is in securing control of the allocation system. The high rents get capitalized in higher land values, making the incentive to compete for the allocation more intense. But the competition does not take place in the market-place. It manifests itself as bribery to officials, corruption, expenditures on lobbying, political contributions, and so on. The allocators of rights similarly expand their own bureaucracies and secure benefits for themselves. Rent-seeking obviously favours the already rich and powerful, and discriminates against the poor and unorganized. And because it encourages wasteful use of the resources, rent-seeking harms the environment, adding to the social costs of policy failures in the price-setting sphere.

Energy

Commercial energy – coal, oil, gas, electricity – is widely subsidized in developing countries. As with irrigation water, the effects of the subsidy are to encourage wasteful uses of energy, and hence, in environmental terms, add to air pollution and problems of waste disposal. The economic impacts of the subsidies tend to be more dramatic, since they are a drain on government revenues and thereby divert valuable resources away from productive sectors; they tend to reduce exports of any indigenous energy, thereby adding to external debt, and encourage energy intensive industry at the expense of more efficient industry.

There are two measures of subsidy. The *financial* measure indicates the difference between prices charged and costs of production. An *economic* subsidy measures the difference between the value of the energy source in its most productive use (the 'opportunity cost value') and its actual price. A convenient measure of the opportunity cost value, or 'shadow price', is either:

(a) the price the fuel would fetch if it was exported, or the price that would have to be paid if it was imported (the 'world' price), or

(b) if the fuel is not tradeable (as with most electricity, for example), the **long-run marginal cost of supply**. The long-run marginal cost of supply is the cost of providing an additional supply in the long term. Financial subsidies measure the direct financial cost to the nation of subsidizing energy, but the economic measure is more appropriate as an indicator of the 'true cost' of subsidies, since it measures what the country could secure if it adopted a full shadow-pricing approach.

Box 6.3 shows the size of the economic subsidy for selected oil-exporting countries. Here the subsidies have an additional distortion in that they divert potentially exportable energy to the home market, thus adding to balance-of-payments difficulties and hence to international indebtedness. The scale of

Box 6.3 Economic subsidies to energy in selected countries

	Size of subsidy ($m)	Subsidy as %	
		All exports	Energy exports
Bolivia	224	29	68
China	5400	20	82
Egypt	4000	88	200
Ecuador	370	12	19
Indonesia	600	5	7
Mexico	5000	23	33
Nigeria	5000	21	23
Peru	301	15	73
Tunisia	70	4	10
Venezuela	1900	14	15

Source: M. Kosmo (1989)

the distortion can be gauged by looking at the subsidies as a percentage of energy exports and as a percentage of all exports. In Egypt, for example, the subsidies are equal to 88 per cent of all exports and are twice the value of oil exports.

Conclusions

Governments are very often themselves the cause of environmental degradation. While we are all used to the idea that governments should put things right, we are less familiar with the idea that government policies that ostensibly have nothing to do with the environment can, and often do, damage the environment. This is 'government failure'. Clearly, since markets fail too, the issue for policy is to find the proper balance between markets and intervention. This is addressed in Part IV.

Further reading

The role that governments play in giving incentives to degrade the environment is the subject of several publications from the World Resources Institute in Washington DC. See in particular:

M. Kosmo, *Money to Burn? The High Cost of Energy Subsidies*, World Resources Institute, Washington DC, October 1987.

R. Repetto, *Paying the Price: Pesticide Subsidies in Developing Countries*, World Resources Institute, Washington DC, December 1985.

R. Repetto, *Skimming the Water: Rent Seeking and the Performance of Public Irrigation Systems*, World Resources Institute, Washington DC, December 1986.

See also:

D. W. Pearce (ed.), *Blueprint 2*, Earthscan, London, 1991.

D. W. Pearce and J. Warford, *World Without End: Economics, Environment and Sustainable Development*, Oxford University Press, Oxford, 1992.

References

Department of the Environment, *Digest of Environmental Protection and Water Statistics 1990*, HMSO, London, 1990.

M. Kosmo, 'Commercial energy subsidies in developing countries', *Energy Policy* **4**: 244–53, 1989.

US Environmental Protection Agency, *Agriculture and the Environment: OECD Policy Experiences and American Opportunities*, Washington DC, January 1990.

PART III

Decision-making and the environment

CHAPTER 7

Cost–benefit thinking

The idea of cost–benefit analysis

Meeting individuals' preferences

Everyone is used to making decisions on the basis of a balance of gains and losses, advantages and disadvantages. The idea behind such a weighing up is that we only do those things that yield us *net* gains, and that, where we have to choose between alternatives, we choose that one which offers the *greatest net gain*. Instead of speaking of gains we could speak of benefits, and instead of losses we can talk of costs. This is the simple foundation of **cost–benefit analysis** (or, in the United States, benefit–cost analysis). However, cost–benefit analysis (CBA) defines costs and benefits in a particular way, and it goes beyond the idea of an *individual*'s balancing of costs and benefits to *society*'s balancing of costs and benefits.

Costs and benefits are defined according to the satisfaction of wants, or preferences. If something meets a want, then it is a benefit. If it detracts from wants, it is a cost. Put more formally, anything is a benefit that increases human wellbeing, and anything is a cost that reduces human wellbeing. For the economist, whether wellbeing has increased or not is to be discovered by looking at people's preferences. If an individual states a preference for situation A to the present condition, then the net benefits of moving to A must be positive for that individual. *Why* A is preferred is not the immediate concern, although no-one would argue that the individual should be allowed to get to situation A if it involves some immoral or illegal act. Subject to the wider considerations about the 'morality' of giving people what they want, CBA functions on the basis that a 'better' allocation of resources is one that meets people's preferences (wants). For the individual, i, we could write that i should accept a proposal to move to situation A if

$$[B_A - C_A] > 0 \qquad (7.1)$$

93

where *B* is benefit and *C* is cost, and benefits and costs are measured in terms of people's wellbeing.

Getting a social decision rule

To make this a *social* decision rule for accepting the move we need to know what everyone else prefers. If everyone prefers the move to A, we have no problem. If many people prefer the move and the rest simply don't care (they are indifferent) we also have no problem. In this latter case, those who prefer the move are 'better off' (by definition) and those who are indifferent are neither better off nor worse off. But what happens if some people are made better off (they prefer to move) and some worse off (they prefer being where they are)? In order to decide whether society as a whole is better or worse off we need to compare individuals' gains and losses. Many economists believe that this is not possible. They say it is not possible to compare individuals' wellbeing (in the jargon, they say 'interpersonal comparisons of utility' are impossible – utility is just another word for wellbeing here). But we do in fact make such comparisons on a regular basis. We do judge how other people feel – by how they look, how they behave and what they say. We might add that all policy decisions actually *do* involve such comparisons because it is virtually impossible to find a policy that makes *everyone* better off – someone always loses. If such comparisons can be made, then we could develop some rules for comparing the extent to which the wellbeing of individuals will change because of a given policy.

Willingness to pay (WTP)

In order to pursue the idea of aggregating individual preferences, we should first ask how we might *measure* the gains and losses in wellbeing. One way to do this would be to observe how people vote in a referendum, but this will not tell us about the strength of the preference for or against something. Another way is to look at what people are *willing to pay* for something. A measure of an individual's preference for a good in the market-place is revealed by their willingness to pay (WTP) for that good. A somewhat less familiar idea is that people are WTP to *avoid* something they do not like, or that they might be willing to accept (WTA) compensation for tolerating something they do not like. Chapter 8 looks more closely at these concepts: for now it is necessary only to get an intuitive idea of the link between WTP and human wellbeing.

By looking at what people are WTP *for* a benefit, or WTA to tolerate a cost, we have found a way of measuring the strength of individuals' preferences. Box 7.1 investigates the idea of WTP in a little more detail. The WTP concept

94

Box 7.1   Willingness to pay

Panel (a) Demand curve.

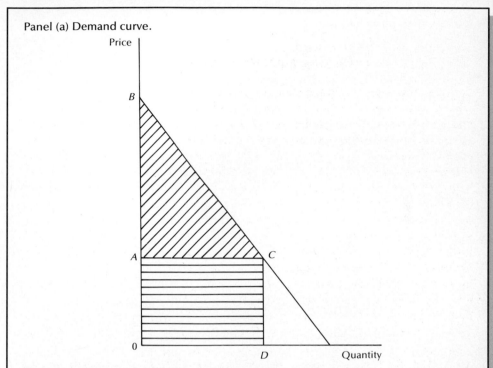

Panel (a) shows a demand curve for a product. This could be a product sold in the market-place (a marketed good) or it could be one which does not have a market (a non-marketed good). In the latter case, it is necessary to find out the demand curve by special means (see Chapter 8).

Suppose the price that we observe is 0A. The quantity demanded is then 0D. We can think of the demand curve as a 'willingness to pay curve': it shows the WTP for extra units of the good and is therefore a *marginal willingness to pay* curve. The amount that individuals actually pay in the market-place (or the amount they would pay if there was a market-place) is given by the amount of expenditure 0ACD. But there are WTP higher prices for the first units, e.g. WTP is 0B for the first unit, down to DC for the last unit bought. So WTP exceeds *actual* payment. If we add the excess of WTP over 0A (the price paid) for each unit, we get the shaded triangle ABC. This is known as the *consumer's surplus*: it is the benefit received over and above the amount actually paid. The *gross* WTP is 0ACD + ABC = 0BCD, and this is made up of the actual payment made and the consumer surplus. Alternatively, we could call 0BCD the gross WTP and ABC the net WTP. The important concept here is the *net* WTP, since this is a measure of the net gain that consumers secure.

is what we need to solve the problem of aggregating across individuals when some prefer a situation like A above, and some do not. For example, the picture may be as follows:

Individual 1:   WTP to move to A =   £10
Individual 2:   WTP to move to A =   £8
Individual 3:   WTA to tolerate a move to A = £6
Individual 4:   WTA to tolerate a move to A = £5

Individuals 1 and 2 are gainers, and 3 and 4 are losers. Is society as a whole better or worse off from the move to A? The rule we could use is:

$$(WTP_1 + WTP_2) - (WTA_3 + WTA_4) > 0 \qquad (7.2)$$

which would give us the result:

$$(10 + 8) - (6 + 5)$$

which comes to +7 which is >0, so the move is socially worthwhile.

Hypothetical compensation

Using this rule to declare the move to A to be socially worthwhile may seem odd. After all, two people are better off and two are worse off. This hardly seems like a good criterion for saying things have improved overall. But to see that there is a net social gain, suppose individuals 1 and 2 are required to compensate individuals 3 and 4 for their losses. Then, individual 1 could give 8 to individual 3, leaving him with 3. Individual 1 would be better off than he was without the move, and individual 3 would be no worse off, having been compensated for the loss. Individual 2 could compensate individual 4 and the same situation would arise. Now it turns out that individuals 3 and 4 are no worse off, and 1 and 2 are better off. This is known technically as a **Pareto improvement**[1]. Or at least, it is an *actual* Pareto improvement if the compensation is actually paid, and a *potential* Pareto improvement if the compensation is 'hypothetically' paid[2].

The social cost–benefit rule embodied in Equation (7.2) provides the foundation of CBA. Instead of WTP we can write B for benefit, and instead of WTA we can write C for cost. Then Equation (7.2) looks just like Equation (7.1), but it is for the *aggregate* of individuals that make up society, rather than for one individual. So, (7.2) can be rewritten as:

$$\Sigma_i[B_i - C_i] > 0 \qquad (7.3)$$

where Σ means 'sum of', and the subscript refers to each individual. We now need to modify this rule for the introduction of time.

Introducing time

Discounting

Equation (7.3) is timeless. It does not indicate the time period over which costs and benefits are being added up. But, as we all know, changes in a situation could involve costs and benefits occurring over long periods of time, or occurring immediately, after which they disappear, or occurring later on. We need to add up benefits in each time period. The simplest way to do this would be to say that a benefit of £1 to individual 1 in year 1 should be added to a £1 benefit in year 2, and so on. This would be correct *if the individual concerned did not care when benefits and costs occurred*. But typically people do care. They prefer to have benefits now rather than later, and costs later rather than now. They have what we call **time preference**. Since the very rationale of CBA is that preferences count, it is essential to take account of the preferences for time in the same way as we do with the measures of WTA and WTP. This brings us to the phenomenon of **discounting**.

The process of discounting can best be understood by looking at the mechanism of compound interest. It we invest £1 at 5 per cent annually compounded, it will be worth £1.63 in ten years' time. Conversely, 61 pence invested now, at the same rate of interest, will be worth £1 in ten years' time. We would then refer to 0.61 as the **present value factor** for a ten-year period when the **discount rate** is 5 per cent. Given this direct relationship between discounting and compound interest, it is evident that the higher is the discount rate, the lower will be the discount factor, and the faster will the discount factor fall, as the time horizon is extended. From this we can see that discounting is really only compound interest back-to-front. If £1 now is worth:

$$£1 \ (1 + r)^5$$

in five years' time at a rate of interest of r per cent, then £1 in five years' time must be worth *now*:

$$\frac{£1}{(1 + r)^5}$$

This is the *present value* of £1 in five years' time. If we invest this sum at r per cent compound interest for five years it will come to:

$$\frac{£1}{(1 + r)^5} \ \cdot \ \frac{(1 + r)^5}{1} = £1$$

Box 7.2 provides some worked examples of calculations of present value. More generally, the present value of £1 in year t is:

$$\frac{£1}{(1 + r)^t}$$

97

Box 7.2 Computing present values

The basic formula for computing a present value is:

$$\frac{B_t}{(1+r)^t}$$

where B_t is the benefit in year t and r is the discount rate. The same formula would hold for costs – simply substituting C for B. The general formula for computing a present value of a set of benefits *and* costs that occur through time, known as a **net present value** (NPV) would be:

$$\Sigma_t \frac{B_t - C_t}{(1+r)^t}$$

The CBA rule then, is that for any policy or project, the NPV should be positive.

To illustrate the above rule, consider a project that has the following sequence of costs and benefits:

	Year 1	Year 2	Year 3	Year 4	Year 5
Cost	30	10	0	0	0
Benefit	0	5	15	15	15
Net benefit	−30	−5	15	15	15

Note that costs appear as minuses and benefits as pluses. Suppose the discount rate, r, is 10 per cent (which is written as 0.1). Then the computation is:

$$-30/1.1 - 5/(1.1)^2 + 15/(1.1)^3 + 15/(1.1)^4 + 15(1.1)^5$$

Typically this would be done with a discounted cash flow computer program, but in this case the calculations are simple:

$$-27.3 - 4.1 + 11.3 + 10.3 + 9.3 = -0.5$$

The NPV is negative and therefore the project is not worthwhile. Notice that without the discounting procedure, benefits of 45 exceed costs of 35. Discounting can therefore make a big difference to the ultimate decision to accept or reject a project.

The choice faced by a decision-maker may be a simple 'accept/reject' decision like the one above, but it may also be one of choosing between competing alternatives, e.g. a hydroelectric power plant or a coal-fired plant

➡

---

or a nuclear power station. If each option has a positive NPV, the choice should be made on the basis of the highest NPV. Yet another decision context arises where a number of projects can be chosen but the budget available is limited. The rule then is to *rank* the projects according to the *ratio* of the PV of benefits to the PV of costs (the 'benefit–cost ratio') and work down the ranked list until the budget is exhausted.

The practice of *discounting* arises because individuals attach less weight to a benefit or cost in the future than they do to a benefit or cost now. Impatience, or 'time preference', is one reason why the present is preferred to the future. The second reason is that, since capital is productive, £1's worth of resources now will generate more than a £1's worth of goods and services in the future. Hence an entrepreneur would be willing to pay more than £1 in the future to acquire £1's worth of these resources now. This argument for discounting is referred to as the 'marginal productivity of capital' argument, the use of the word 'marginal' indicating that it is the productivity of additional units of capital that is relevant.

Time and the cost–benefit rule

We can now modify the CBA rule in Equation (7.3). With time incorporated into the approach, we have as our decision rule that any move is potentially worthwhile if:

$$\Sigma_t (B_t - C_t)\,(1+r)^{-t} > 0 \tag{7.4}$$

where the subscript t now refers to time and we take it for granted that B and C are now aggregated across individuals. In order to highlight the environment, we need to remind ourselves that both B and C in Equation (7.4) *include* environmental costs and benefits. That is, if there is a change in environmental quality that people like (their preferences for the change are positive), then we need to find their WTP for it. This WTP will appear as part of the benefit of any policy that includes the change in environmental quality. Equally, if the change in the environment is for the worse, then we seek the WTP to avoid that change, or the WTA to put up with it. This value will appear as part of C in Equation (7.4).

Environment and the cost–benefit rule

To highlight environmental costs and benefits, we will write them separately as E. Equation (7.4) then becomes:

$$\Sigma_t\,(B_t - C_t \pm E_t)\,(1+r)^{-t} > 0 \tag{7.5}$$

Equation (7.5) is the fundamental equation of cost–benefit analysis: it tells us that for any project or policy to be regarded as potentially worthwhile, its non-environmental benefits (*B*) less its non-environmental costs (*C*) plus or minus the value of the environmental change (*E*), all discounted to a present value, must be positive.

Box 7.3 illustrates an actual cost–benefit study.

Box 7.3   Cost–benefit in practice: case study of lead in gasoline

Under Executive Order 12291 of 1981 in the United States, government agencies were required to use 'Regulatory Impact Analysis' (RIA) and to adopt regulatory processes that would maximize 'the net benefits to society'. The Order was the first to establish the net benefit objective as the criterion for adopting regulatory processes, although its adoption has been circumscribed by existing laws relating to other objectives.

Benefit–cost analysis played an important role in the adoption of regulations concerning lead in gasoline. Ambient lead concentrations were thought to be linked to serious health effects, including retardation, kidney disease and even death. The Environmental Protection Agency (EPA) conducted a benefit–cost study with the results shown in Table 1.

The regulation involved reducing lead in gasoline from 1.1 grams per gallon (g.p.g.) to 0.1 g.p.g. The costs of the rule are shown as 'total refining costs'. Refinery costs increase because lead has traditionally been used to boost octane levels in fuel, and other means would have to be found to achieve this. The benefits included:

(a) improved children's health;
(b) improved blood pressure in adults;
(c) reduced damages from misfuelled vehicles, arising from hydrocarbon, NO_x and CO emissions; and
(d) impacts on maintenance and fuel economy.

Children's health

The EPA study found that blood lead levels closely tracked trends in gasoline lead. Medical costs for the care of children would be reduced by reducing lead concentrations, and there would be less need for compensatory education for IQ-impaired children. These savings are shown as 'children's health effects' in Table 1.

Table 1 Year-by-year costs and monetized benefits of final rule, assuming partial misfuelling (milliions of 1983 dollars)

	1985	1986	1987	1988	1989	1990	1991	1992
Monetized benefits								
Children's health effects	223	600	547	502	453	414	369	358
Adult blood pressure	1724	5897	5675	5447	5187	4966	4682	4691
Conventional pollutants	0	222	222	224	226	230	239	248
Maintenance	102	914	859	818	788	767	754	749
Fuel economy	35	187	170	113	134	139	172	164
Total monetized benefits	2084	7821	7474	7105	6788	6517	6216	6211
Total refining costs	96	608	558	532	504	471	444	441
Net benefits	1988	7213	6916	6573	6284	6045	5772	5770
Net benefits excluding blood pressure	264	1316	1241	1125	1096	1079	1090	1079

Adult blood pressure

Blood lead levels were thought to be associated with blood pressure and hypertension. Medical costs would be saved if these illnesses could be reduced. Moreover, some heart attacks and strokes would be avoided. A value of a 'statistical life' of $1 million was used for the latter. The resulting values show up in the 'adult blood pressure' row of the table. They are seen to be high because of the involvement of mortality-avoidance in this benefit.

Other pollutants

Reducing lead in gasoline also reduces other pollutants. This is because making unleaded fuel the 'norm' reduces the risk of 'misfuelling', i.e. using leaded fuels in vehicles designed for unleaded fuels. The mechanism whereby misfuelling is reduced is through the higher cost of leaded fuels at the new low-lead concentration. This deters drivers from purchasing the leaded fuel. As misfuelling is reduced, so emissions of HC, NO_x and CO are reduced. Damage done by these pollutants was estimated by studies of ozone pollution damage (ozone arises from HC and CO emissions), but estimates were also made of the value of the equipment destroyed by misfuelling. The figures appearing in the row 'conventional pollutants' in the table, are, in fact, an average of the two methods.

Maintenance and fuel economy

Maintenance costs for vehicles were expected to fall due to reduced corrosive effects of lead and its scavengers on engines and exhaust systems. Fewer engine tune-ups and oil changes would be needed, exhaust systems would last longer. Fuel economy was expected to rise as the new technologies to raise octane levels to what they were previously also increase the energy content of fuels. There would also be reduced fouling of oxygen sensors. Maintenance benefits outweighed fuel economy benefits by around 6 to 1.

The net benefits from reducing lead in gasoline are seen to be substantial, even if the blood pressure benefits (which dominate the aggregate benefits) are excluded. Indeed, inspection of the table shows that the regulation would be worthwhile *even if all health benefits were excluded.* In the event, the blood pressure benefits were excluded from the final decision because the research establishing this link was judged too recent to permit adequate review. The lead regulation was also of interest because of the introduction of a 'lead permits system' to reduce the financial burden on the refining industry. Essentially, this allowed 'lead quotas' to be traded between refiners. Refiners who found it easy to get below the limit were allowed to sell their 'surplus' lead rights to refiners who found it expensive to get back to desirable octane levels without lead. The particular feature of the lead-in-gasoline benefit–cost study that made it a powerful aid to decision-making was the clear-cut nature of the net benefits even when uncertainties about benefits were allowed for.

Discounting and the environment

Since discounting attaches a *lower* weight to benefits and costs in the future, it has some unfortunate effects as far as the environment is concerned. Box 7.4 shows what is sometimes known as the 'tyranny' of discounting. Examples of how discounting militates against the interests of future generations are found in the following cases:

(a) Where the *environmental damage* done by, say, a project occurs far into the future, discounting will make the present value of such damage considerably smaller than the actual damage done. Examples of such projects might be the possible damage from stored nuclear waste and long-lived persistent micropollutants such as heavy metals.

(b) Where the *benefits* of a project accrue to people 50 or 100 years hence, discounting will lower the value of such benefits and make it difficult to

Box 7.4 The 'tyranny' of discounting

A simple example shows the way in which discounting can shift heavy costs to future generations. Imagine a nuclear waste repository where safety conditions are of the highest order. Some nuclear waste remains very radioactive for hundreds of years. As with many waste dumps in the past, societies often 'forget' where waste has been dumped, or relax their controls. If this happens with a nuclear waste repository, then it could produce a grave risk for future generations due to leakage. Hypothetically, imagine that the cost of such a leakage is £1 billion (£1000 million) in 100 years' time. If the discount rate is 8 per cent, say, then the present value of the damage from the leaked material 100 years from now would be:

$$\text{£1000 million} \times \frac{1}{(1.08)^{100}} = \text{£1000 million}/2200 = 0.45 \text{ million} = \text{£450 000}$$

The £1 billion damage is recorded in the CBA as only £450 000!

justify the project or policy. An example might be afforestation, particularly in slow-growing hardwood trees in temperate climates.

(c) Where the decision to extract a resource is affected by the discount rate. Chapter 16 will show that exhaustible resources are more likely to be used up quickly the higher is the discount rate, leaving less for future generations.

Because of this apparent discrimination against the future, environmentalists frequently object to discounting *per se*.

There is, in fact, no unique relationship between high discount rates and environmental deterioration. High rates may well shift the cost burden to future generations for the reasons given above, but, as the discount rate rises so the overall level of investment falls, thus slowing the pace of economic development in general. Since natural resources are required for investment, the demand for such resources is lower at higher discount rates. High discount rates may also discourage development projects that compete with existing environmentally benign uses, e.g. watershed development as opposed to existing wilderness use. Exactly how the choice of discount rate impacts on the overall profile of natural resource and environment use is thus ambiguous. This point is important because it indicates the invalidity of the more simplistic generalizations that discount rates should be lowered to accommodate environmental considerations.

One approach to determining a discount rate is through the formula:

$$s = p + u.c$$

where s is the social time preference rate (society's rate of discount); p is the 'pure time preference rate', i.e. the discount rate that arises simply because people prefer the present over the future ('impatience'); c is the growth rate of real consumption per head and u is a measure of the rate at which the extra wellbeing (or 'utility') arising from consumption declines as consumption rises. (In technical language, u is known as the elasticity of the marginal utility of consumption.) Suppose, for simplicity, that $u = 1$. Then:

$$s = p + c$$

Many people feel it is simply wrong to discount the future because today's generation is 'impatient'. If we reject pure time preference on these grounds we are left with:

$$s = c$$

i.e. the social rate of discount simply becomes the growth rate of the economy (measured as growth in per capita consumption).

Environmentalists point to the *presumed* positive value of c in the social time preference rate formula. First, they argue that there are underlying 'limits' to the growth process (see Chapter 3). We cannot expect positive growth rates of, say, 2–3 per cent for long periods into the future because of natural resource constraints or limits on the capacity of natural environments to act as 'sinks' for waste products. A second concern highlights the problems of particular regions. Chapter 3 showed that in some low income countries real per capita consumption *fell* in the 1980s. That is, c was negative. Does this mean the social discount rate should be negative? Arguably, it should, although past negative growth may not be relevant to a discount rate based on expected future growth. More significantly, the pure time preference component of a social discount rate could be argued to be very high. Real borrowing rates in poor economies are often of the order of 10–15 per cent and offer a first guess at personal time preference rates. So, the approach described above for deriving a social discount rate is inconclusive.

An alternative approach is to look at the **opportunity cost of capital**. This is obtained by looking at the rate of return on the best investment of similar risk that is displaced as a result of the particular project being undertaken. It is only reasonable to require the investment undertaken to yield a return at least as high as that on the alternative use of funds. For example, if private business can earn 10 per cent rate of return, governments should earn as least as much, otherwise the money is better allocated to the private sector. This is the basic justification for an opportunity cost discount rate.

The environmental literature has made some attempts to discredit discounting on opportunity cost grounds. As these criticisms are fairly complex, they are not discussed here (see Markandya and Pearce, 1991). But the general feeling is that opportunity cost arguments lead to rates that are 'too high' and these discriminate against the environment.

It is widely accepted that a benefit or cost should be valued less the more *uncertain* is its occurrence. After all, if you are offered £1 now for certain, or £1 next year with some uncertainty as to whether you would actually get the £1, you are virtually certain to prefer the £1 now. The types of uncertainty that are generally regarded as being relevant to discounting are:

(a) uncertainty about whether an individual will be alive at some future date (the 'risk of death' argument);
(b) uncertainty about the preferences of the individual in the future; and
(c) uncertainty about the size of the benefit or cost.

The risk of death argument is often used as a rationale for the impatience principle itself, the argument being that a preference for consumption now rather than in the future is partly based on the fact that one may not be alive in the future to enjoy the benefits of one's restraint. The argument against this is that although an individual may be mortal, 'society' is not and so its decisions should not be guided by the same consideration.

Second, uncertainty about preferences is relevant to certain goods and perhaps even certain aspects of environmental conservation. Economists generally accept that the way to allow for uncertainty about preferences is to include **option value** in an estimate of the benefit or cost; see Chapter 8.

The third kind of uncertainty is relevant but the difficulty is in allowing for it by adjusting the discount rate. Such adjustments assume that the scale of risks is increasing exponentially over time. Since there is no reason to believe that the risk factor takes this particular form, it is inappropriate to correct for such risks by raising the discount rate. This argument is in fact widely accepted by economists but the practice of using risk-adjusted discount rates is still quite common among policy-makers.

The extent to which the interests of future generations are safeguarded when using positive discount rates is a matter of debate. For example, generations 'overlap' – parents, children and grandchildren exist at the same time. Each generation has 'altruism'. Altruism is said to exist when the wellbeing of the current generation is influenced not only by its own consumption, but also by the utility of future generations. This is modelled by assuming that the current generation's wellbeing is also influenced by the wellbeing of the second generation and the third generation. Each generation's discount rate is therefore likely to take account of the next generation's interests. This approach goes some way towards addressing the question of future generations but it does so in a rather specific way. Notice that what is being evaluated here is the current generation's judgement about what the future generations will think is important. It does not therefore yield a discount rate reflecting some broader principle of the rights of future generations. The essential distinction is between the first generation judging what next generations want (**selfish altruism**) and the first generation using resources so as to leave the next ones with the maximum scope for choosing what they want (**disinterested altruism**).

Conclusions on discounting

We have spent some time on the issue of discounting, although we have hardly done justice to the many and frequently complex arguments that are debated on the issue. There are no firm conclusions. We have to remember that the *purpose* of discount rates is to discriminate against the future in order to reflect the underlying value judgement of CBA, namely, that individuals' preferences count. Most of the criticism of discounting rejects the underlying rationale for discounting. It introduces a separate and contradictory objective, namely being fair to the future. It should not, therefore, be too surprising to find that we cannot find a convenient rule for adjusting the discount rate to reflect these contradictory objectives.

A sustainability approach

Chapter 4 introduced the idea that all forms of capital should be maintained intact in some sense, or even enhanced. And it introduced the much stricter idea that the stock of *natural* capital should be kept intact. Is it possible to build these ideas into CBA? Requiring that no project or policy should contribute to environmental deterioration would be absurd. But requiring that the overall *portfolio* of projects should not contribute to environmental deterioration is not absurd. One way to meet the sustainability condition is to require that any environmental damage be *compensated* by projects specifically designed to improve the environment. So, imagine an agency with ten road building projects each of which does some harm to the environment. The idea would be that, subject to assurances that environmental damage was being minimized in each case, the *cumulation* of environmental damage would be offset by a project specifically aimed at enhancing the environment. This may well mean that nine of the projects go ahead, but the tenth is abandoned in favour of the environmental project.

Conclusions

The sustainability approach has some interesting implications for project appraisal. One of these is that the choice of discount rates problem largely disappears. The goal of adjusting discount rates to capture environmental effects is better served by the sustainability condition. If this is correct, the sustainability condition deserves more investigation. Although it may have quite radical implications, it offers the prospect of avoiding belabouring the 'tyranny of discounting' and of asking that all ethical and environmental concerns be accounted for by discount rate adjustment.

Notes

1. Vilfredo Pareto (1848–1923) was an Italian economist who formulated various rules about when society could be said to be better or worse off in terms of welfare (wellbeing). His work laid the foundation for modern **welfare economics**.
2. The variant of the Pareto rule in which people are hypothetically compensated is known as the Kaldor–Hicks rule after Lord Nicholas Kaldor and Sir John Hicks.

Further reading

A. Markandya and D. W. Pearce, 'Development, the environment, and the social rate of discount', *World Bank Research Observer*, **6** (July): 137–52, 1991.

The elements of cost–benefit analysis are explained in

D. W. Pearce, *Cost–Benefit Analysis*, Macmillan, Basingstoke, 1986.

The literature on discounting is quite complex and there are no easy expositions. See:

D. W. Pearce, A. Markandya and E. B. Barbier, *Blueprint for a Green Economy*, Earthscan, London, 1989, Chapter 6.

CHAPTER 8

Valuing concern for nature

Imputing values for non-market goods and services

In the market-place, the individual has fairly clear information (depending on the degree to which advertising is informative rather than persuasive) on which to base their valuation and choices. The product tends to be visible, its characteristics are generally well known, and it has a market price. The individual, on the basis of the available information, weighs up quantity, quality and price on offer. But as we have seen in Chapters 1 and 5, environmental goods and services often have no market price tag and a considerable amount of uncertainty can surround their true value and significance. Many of the environmental assets are also public goods and this is another characteristic that makes it difficult for markets to evolve in such assets.

Given that in the real world, individual consumers and policy-makers have to make trade-offs, it is fundamentally important to know what is being traded-off against what. It is not possible to know this unless we have some idea of the *economic value of environmental assets*. To make comparisons involving an *unpriced good or service*, it is necessary to **impute a value**. The discipline of economics has developed techniques whereby such values can be imputed.

As we saw in Chapters 1 and 7, in the market-place individuals exercise choice by comparing their *willingness to pay* with the price of the product. Imputing values involves finding a willingness to pay measure in circumstances where markets fail to reveal this information. We also noted in Chapter 2 that the values that count belong to those actually exercising the choice: the current generation. But it is a particular feature of environmental costs and benefits that they often accrue to people in generations yet to come (intergenerational incidence of costs and benefits). Counting only the current generation's preferences biases choice against future generations unless there is some built-in mechanism to ensure that current generations choose on behalf of future generations and take their interests into account. We have reviewed the various ethical arguments about intergenerational fairness in Chapter 2, and the further bias against future generations that can be present in economic decision-making because of the practice of *discounting* in Chapter 7. In this chapter we will concentrate on the problems that economists face when they attempt to impute values for non-market environmental assets. Our central message in this chapter is:

> economic (monetary) valuation of non-market environmental assets may be more or less imperfect given the particular asset together with its environmental and valuation contexts; but, invariably, some valuation explicitly laid out for scrutiny by policy-makers and the public, is better than none, because none can mean some implicit valuation shrouded from public scrutiny.

One final caveat is necessary before we analyze the concept of **total economic value** (TEV) and the range of imputation methods that have been developed to estimate the TEV of environmental assets.

The caveat concerns the idea of **intrinsic value in nature** which we looked at in Chapter 2. The TEV which we will be concerned about is related to valuation of preferences held by people (anthropocentric and instrumental value) and does not encompass any value which may intrinsically reside 'in' environmental assets.

In Box 8.1 we take a simplified and hypothetical example of a woodland resource which, among other things, is providing a place for people to enjoy some recreation. The recreation service is initially an unpriced environmental service, but we could observe some consumer behaviour which will give us a clue to demand for recreation, i.e. the number of recreational visits which an average individual makes to this woodland park every year. We can establish a demand curve by varying the 'price' of a visit and seeing how many visits our average consumer makes. How do we impute or simulate the price variable? In practice, a variety of methods can be utilized, some of which we will review later in this chapter, but we start with a simple approach and assume the imposition of an entrance fee.

Suppose that we find that at an entrance fee in excess of £15.00 the individual is unwilling to make any visits. However, at a fee of £15.00 the individual would make just one visit per year, i.e. the maximum WTP for the first visit is £15.00. Now suppose that the maximum entrance fee that the individual is WTP for a second visit is, say £8.50. Maximum WTP for further trips will similarly decline, say £4.00 for a third visit, £2.00 for a fourth and just £0.50 for a fifth visit. Indeed let us suppose that the individual would only make a sixth visit if there was no entrance fee, i.e. his/her maximum WTP for the sixth visit is £0.00. So if, in reality, there is in fact no entrance fee for walking in the woodland then our average individual will indeed make six

Box 8.1 The demand for recreational visits to a wood

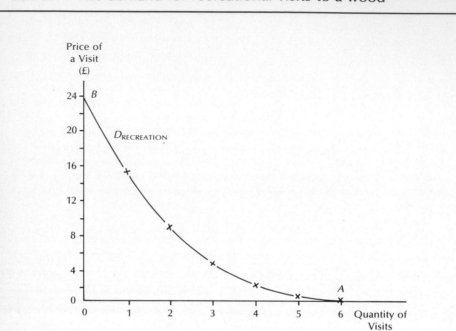

Table 1 WTP, price paid and consumer surplus for a visit

(1) Visit No.	(2) WTP (£)	(3) Price Paid (£)	(4) Consumer Surplus (£)
1	15.00	0.00	15.00
2	8.50	0.00	8.50
3	4.00	0.00	4.00
4	2.00	0.00	2.00
5	0.50	0.00	0.50
6	0.00	0.00	0.00
Totals (£)	30.00	0.00	0.00
	Total Value (total WTP)	= Total Price Paid	+ Total Consumer Surplus

The actual entrance fee paid for a visit is zero. Here the demand curve ($D_{RECREATION}$) shows the maximum amount which a visitor would be WTP for each visit to a wood (column 2 of Table 1). Summing this for each visit gives the visitor's total value for all visits made (area 0*AB*). Here there is, in fact, no (or rather a zero) market price for a visit, i.e. entrance is free (another way of looking at this is to imagine that the supply curve runs along the horizontal axis, i.e. at zero price, any amount of visits are supplied). Therefore the total price paid is zero (i.e. the price line is also a flat line running along the horizontal axis) and the total value area is equal to the total consumer surplus.

visits per annum (i.e. all visits where the WTP is equal to or exceeds the price (here zero) of a visit).

Plotting out these price/quantity of visit combinations, we obtain our demand curve $D_{RECREATION}$ in Panel (b) of Box 8.1. We can now calculate the total value of all visits as the total of the amounts which the individual would have been willing to pay for each of the visits in turn, i.e. £15.00 + £8.50 + £4.00 + £2.00 + £0.50 + £0.00 = £30.00. Now because there is in reality no entrance fee to the wood (i.e. no supply constraint) then the actual price paid by the individual for a visit is zero. We can now calculate total consumer surplus as the difference between the total value and the actual price paid, i.e. £30.00 − £0.00 = £30.00. Here we can see that, for unpriced goods, total consumer surplus equals the total value of the good. This is often the case for many environmental goods. Therefore in Panel (b) the total value is (as always) given by the area under the demand curve (0*BA*) which, for an unpriced good only, is also equal to the total consumer surplus provided by the good.

Total economic value

Environmental economists have gone a considerable way towards a classification of economic values as they relate to natural environments. The terminology is still not fully agreed, but the approach is based on the traditional explanation of how value occurs (i.e. it is based on the interaction between a human subject, the valuer, and objects – things to be valued). Individuals have a number of held values which in turn result in objects being given various assigned values. In order, in principle, to arrive at an aggregate measure of value (total economic value) economists begin by distinguishing **user values** from **non-user values**.

Box 8.2 illustrates the use and non-use values which a multiattribute

Box 8.2   The total economic value of woodland

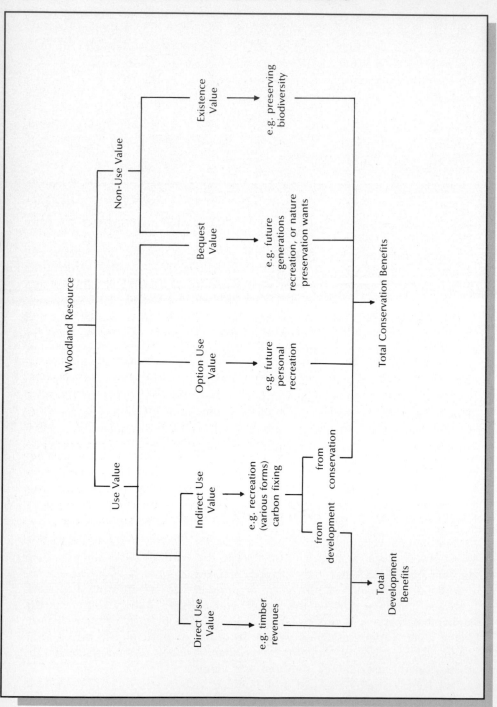

environmental asset such as, for example, a woodland provides. By definition, use values derive from the actual use of the environment. Slightly more complex are values expressed through options to use the environment (*option values*) in the future. They are essentially expressions of preference (willingness to pay) for the conservation of environmental systems or components of systems against some probability that the individual will make use of them at a later date. Provided the uncertainty concerning future use is an uncertainty relating to the 'supply' of the environment, economic theory indicates that this option value is likely to be positive. A related form of value is **bequest value**, a willingness to pay to preserve the environment for the benefit of one's descendants. It is not a use value for the current individual valuer, but a potential future use value or non-use for their descendants.

Non-use values are more problematic. They suggest non-instrumental values which are in the real nature of the thing but unassociated with actual use, or even the option to use the thing. Instead such values are taken to be entities that reflect people's preferences, but include concern for, sympathy with, and respect for the rights or welfare of non-human beings. These values are still anthropocentric but may include a recognition of the value of the very existence of certain species or whole ecosystems. *Total economic value is then made up of actual use value plus option value plus existence value.*

During the 1980s more extensive use of monetary valuation methods was combined with technical improvements in techniques. The result is a large literature consisting of a wide diversity of valuation case studies.

Some scientists have argued that the full contribution of component species and processes to the aggregate life support service provided by ecosystems has not been captured in economic valuation. There does seem to be a sense in which this scientific critique of the *partial* nature of economic valuation has some validity; not in relation to individual species and processes but in terms of the prior value of the aggregate ecosystem structure and its life support capacity. Thus the aggregate ecosystem could be said to possess **primary value**. The prior existence of a 'healthy' ecosystem is necessary before the range of use and non-use values, linked to the ecosystem's structure and functions (see Box 8.2, the woodland ecosystem), can be utilized by humans. We would therefore label all use and non-use values as **secondary values**. It is the various components of total secondary value that are included in total economic value (TEV). But the primary value of the total system is *not* encompassed by TEV.

It is also the case that TEV may fail to fully capture total secondary value (underestimation of 'true' TEV). This is because some ecosystem functions and processes are difficult to analyze scientifically, as well as to value in monetary terms. The **indirect use** values of ecosystems (see Box 8.2) are often surrounded by uncertainty, and the distinction between these values and non-use values is far from clear cut once we realize how complicated and interrelated natural environments actually are in practice. This has recently led some economists to coin a new term, replacing non-use values with **passive use** values. This latter term does seem to better capture the fuzzyness and uncertainty that surrounds the distinction between use and non-use values.

Approaches to valuation

Box 8.3 illustrates *one* (a number of different typologies exist in the literature) way in which the various approaches and methods of monetary valuation can be classified, in the context of environmental resources. Two basic approaches are distinguished, those which value a commodity via a demand curve (Marshallian or Hicksian) and those which do not and therefore fail to provide 'true' valuation information and welfare measures. These latter methods are, however, still useful heuristic tools in any cost–benefit appraisal of projects, policies or courses of action.

The **dose–response approach** requires the existence of data linking human, plant or animal physiological response to pollution stress. If, for example, a given level of pollution is associated with a change in output then it is usually the case that the output can be valued at market or shadow (adjusted/proxy market) prices (loss of crop output from air pollution). But for situations involving human health, complex questions relating to the value of a human life have to be addressed (strictly, analysts seek to value the increased risk of illness or death).

The **replacement cost** technique looks at the cost of replacing or restoring a damaged asset and uses this cost as a measure of the benefit of restoration, (e.g. costs of cleaning building soiled by air pollution). But application of this technique does require careful thought. It is a valid approach in situations where it is possible to argue that the remedial work must take place because of some other constraint. For example, where there is a water quality standard that is mandatory, then the costs of achieving that standard are a proxy for the benefits of reaching the standard.

Another situation where the replacement cost approach is valid would be where there is an overall constraint (a 'sustainability constraint') not to let environmental quality decline. Wetland ecosystems, for example, have been heavily depleted across the globe and are now 'protected' by an international convention (agreement) known as the Ramsar Convention. In these circumstances, wetland replacement costs (these could be wetland restoration elsewhere in a region, wetland relocation, or new wetland creation) might be allowable as a first approximation of the benefits of future wetland conservation, or wetland loss. The so-called **shadow project** approach relies on such constraints. It argues that the cost of any project designed to restore an environment because of a sustainability constraint (see Chapter 7) is then a minimum valuation of the damage done.

Box 8.3 Methods for the monetary evaluation of the environment

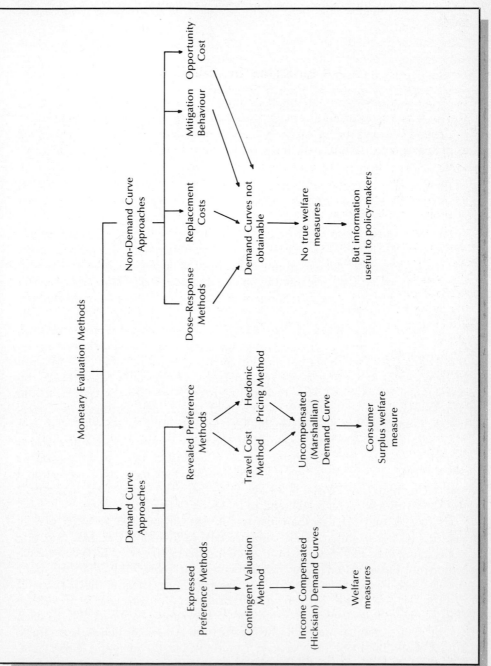

Mitigation behaviour (in terms of **avertive expenditures**) can sometimes be observed in the pollution context. Householders may purchase insulation to 'defend' their homes from noise pollution, as a substitute for a reduction in noise at source.

In the **opportunity cost approach** no direct attempt is made to value environmental benefits. Instead, the benefits of the activity causing environmental degradation – say, drainage of a wetland to allow intensive agriculture – are estimated in order to set a benchmark for what the environmental benefits would have to be for the development (agriculture) *not* to be worthwhile. While this is not a valuation technique, it has proved to be a very useful aid to decision-makers, for example, much of the recent loss of wetlands in Europe due to the operation of the Common Agricultural Policy represents a socially inefficient result because of the heavily subsidized nature of the drainage investments and arable crops that replaced the wetland. Such conversions have now all but ceased as subsidies have been withdrawn or lowered.

Box 8.3 indicates that there are two basic types of demand curve evaluation; firstly, demand can be measured by examining individuals' *stated (expressed) preferences* for environmental goods (elicited via questionnaires); secondly, demand can be *revealed* by examining *individuals' purchases of market priced goods* which are necessary in order to enjoy associated environmental goods.

The **travel cost method** (TCM), which is a revealed preference method, can be used to estimate demand curves for recreation sites and thereby value those sites. The underlying assumption of the TCM is a simple one, that the incurred costs of visiting a site (e.g. petrol costs) in some way reflect the recreational value of that site. Questionnaires are used to ask visitors to the recreational sites where they have travelled from. From visitors' responses, we can estimate their travel costs and relate this to the number of visits per year. Not surprisingly, this relationship generally shows a typical downward sloping demand curve relationship between the cost of a visit and the number of visits taken, i.e. people living a considerable distance from a recreational site (facing high travel costs) make few visits per year, while those living near the site (with low travel costs) tend to make more frequent visits.

Of course, other factors than just travel cost can affect how often people visit a site. For example, if we compare two individuals, one rich and one poor, living the same distance from a site (i.e. facing identical travel costs) we would not be surprised if the rich person made more visits than the poor person. Because of this, analysts usually take into account the income of visitors as one factor explaining the number of visits per year. Other explanatory factors include the number of alternative sites available to each visitor, their personal interest in the type of site, etc. Nevertheless, once these adjustments are made, the analyst can then see the demand curve relationship between the price of visiting a recreational site (i.e. the travel cost) and the number of visits made. Box 8.4 shows a graph illustrating typical results from a TCM survey with each circle recording the travel costs per visit and number of visits made per year for one visitor (a real life study will typically interview several hundred visitors). From this information, statistical techniques can estimate the 'demand curve' for the site, i.e. the representative relationship between the price of a visit to the site (travel costs) and the number of visits made. This demand curve illustrates, for a typical visitor, how many visits would be made at any particular visit price. The demand curve is then used to obtain the total recreational value for the site. We can multiply this figure by the total number of visits made to the site per year to get an estimate of the total annual recreation value of the site.

The TCM seems at first a relatively straightforward technique based upon the defensible assumption that recreational value must be related to travel cost. However, in practice there are numerous problems with this technique a few of which we raise here.

1. *Time costs.* The underlying assumption of the TCM is that travel costs reflect the recreational value of visiting a site. A simple TCM might assume that the only travel cost is related to petrol expenses, however time is also valuable to people in that time spent during a long car journey cannot be spent doing anything else. There is, therefore, a value of time (a 'time cost') which should be added to the travel cost as a reflection of the true recreational value which the visitor gets from visiting a site. So ignoring time costs is generally believed to lead to a significant underestimate of the recreational value which people obtain from visiting a site. However, what is the value of time? Can we put a price on an hour spent in a car? There have been many attempts to estimate a value of time, for example, by comparing the travel time of differing methods of commuting to work with the costs of those differing measures. However, no real consensus has yet been achieved. A further complication is that many people enjoy travelling, for them the journey to a recreational site is not a cost and may even be a benefit. In such cases we should subtract the time benefit of the journey from its travel costs, i.e. simple TCMs (based on travel costs) may now be overestimating the recreational value of sites in such cases.

2. *Multiple visit journeys.* If an individual visits several sites during a single day's journey but is asked to answer a TCM questionnaire at one of them, then how should analysts apportion the visitor's travel costs? During the day the visitor may have incurred high travel costs, however, only a portion of these reflect the recreational site in question. Conventionally analysts have tried to use a percentage of the day's total travel costs, sometimes asking the visitor to set that percentage. However, the margin for error in this context is uncertain.

3. *Substitute sites.* One visitor may travel 20 miles to visit a site which they particularly enjoy whereas another who has comparatively little enthusiasm for the site may travel the same distance from another direction simply

Box 8.4 Evaluating woodland recreation using the TCM

An on-site questionnaire is used at the forest gate or car park to record how often visitors visit the wood, what their travel costs of a visit are, what their income is, etc. Adjusting for factors such as income we can examine the relationship between travel costs and visits per year as illustrated in Panel (a).

Panel (a) The relationship between the number of visits to a site and the price of the visit.

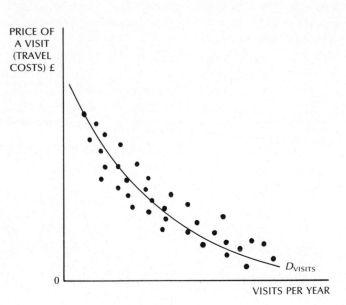

The demand curve D_{VISITS} shows the overall trend relationship between travel costs and visit rates for all the visitors interviewed. Using this information we can estimate the average visitor's total recreational value for the site. Multiplying this by the total number of visitors per annum allows us to estimate the total annual recreational value of the wood itself.

A large scale TCM study of forest recreation in the United Kingdom was undertaken in the late 1980s. Table 1 summarizes results from this study, showing average recreational value per visit at various forests, the annual number of visits to these forests and (multiplying these two together) the estimated total annual recreational value of the forests in question.

Table 1 Estimates of forest recreational values derived from the travel cost method

Location	Average recreation value per visit (£)	Annual number of visits	Total annual recreational value of the forest (£)
Cheshire (Delamere)	1.91	225 000	429 750
Ruthin (Clwyd)	2.52	48 000	120 960
Brecon (Coed Taf)	2.60	41 000	106 600
New Forest (Bolderwood)	1.43	68 000	97 240
Loch Awe (Inverliever)	3.31	3 000	9 930
Lorne (Barcaldine)	1.44	10 000	14 400
Newton Stewart (Glen Trool)	1.61	70 000	112 700
Buchan (Bennachie)	2.26	84 000	189 840
Aberfoyle* (Queen Elizabeth)	2.57	145 000	372 650

Note: All 1988 prices except * 1987.
Source: Adapted from Benson and Willis (1990).

because there is no other available site near their home. Using the simple TCM approach would yield the result that both visitors held the same recreational value for the site, which is clearly incorrect. Some analysts have tried to allow for this by asking visitors to name substitute sites; however, this is both statistically complex and open to error.

4. *House purchase decision.* It may well be that those who most value the recreational attributes of various sites will choose to buy houses near those sites. In such cases, they will incur relatively low travel costs visiting the sites they value so highly, i.e. travel cost will be a gross underestimate of recreational value. Interestingly although this problem has been recognized for many years, it is only very recently that analysts have attempted to include this factor in their questionnaires.

5. *Non-paying visitors.* TCM studies often omit any visitors who have not incurred travel costs to reach the site, e.g. those who have walked from nearby homes. However, this group may well put a very high value on the site.

In summary then, the TCM is grounded upon a simple and fairly well-founded assumption that travel costs reflect recreational value. It allows us to estimate a demand curve and thereby recreational value. However, in practice there are a number of application problems which need to be

119

addressed before we can accept monetary evaluations produced by this technique.

The hedonic pricing method (HPM)

The hedonic price method (HPM) attempts to evaluate environmental services, the presence of which directly affects certain market prices. In practice, by far the most common application of HPM is to the property market. House prices are affected by many factors: number of rooms, size of garden, access to workplace, etc. One such important factor will be local environmental quality. If we can control for the non-environmental factors, e.g. by looking at houses with the same number of rooms, similar garden size, similar accessibility, etc., then any remaining difference in house price can be shown to be the result of environmental differences. For example, in a recent study in Gloucestershire the presence of open water near to a house was shown, on average, to be responsible for a 5 per cent increase in house price (Garrod and Willis, 1991). However, in general the HPM has been applied to the evaluation of environmental costs rather than benefits. For example, just as the water resource raised the value of local housing, so the noise from an airport may lower local house prices. Box 8.5 illustrates a HPM study applied to the valuation of traffic noise.

In order to apply the HPM, the analyst must first collect information regarding all the factors which go to determine house price. This can be a long and arduous task, for example, making measurements of the distance from each house to local facilities such as shops, workplace, etc. Up until recently, these measurements were generally calculated by hand from maps. However, analysts can now massively speed up this operation by the use of a Geographical Information System (or GIS) which holds digitized maps from which such distance calculations can be made by the computer. These GIS computer programs also have a specific application when we are trying to use HPM to place money prices upon landscape values; at the moment most HPM studies just use distance to local landscape features to assess whether they affect house prices. However, GIS maps can include the contours of hills and valleys so that the computer can calculate exactly what is the specific environment affecting each particular house, e.g. whether a house is directly exposed to the noise of a nearby major road or whether it is shielded by other houses. Wider use of this innovative technology may significantly increase the accuracy of HPM studies.

While the HPM approach does appear to be reasonably robust, it nevertheless does have some problems.

1. *User unfriendly*. Estimating the relationship between house price and environmental quality requires a high degree of statistical skill to separate

Box 8.5 Valuing road noise using the hedonic pricing method

The HPM relies upon the assumption that, among other factors (number of rooms, accessibility to shops, workplaces, etc.), the local environmental quality (or lack of it) will determine the price of a house, i.e.:

HOUSE PRICE = *f* (ROOMS, ACCESS, ENVIRONMENT)

The equation states that house price is a function of (*f*) the number of rooms in the house (ROOMS), the distance in miles to local facilities from the house (ACCESS) and some measure of local environmental quality (ENVIRONMENT). Suppose we were interested in valuing the environmental impact of local traffic noise, then we could measure this in terms of decibels of traffic noise inside the houses in question.

We then need to measure each of the items HOUSE PRICE, ROOMS, ACCESS and ENVIRONMENT for a large number of houses so that we can begin to see how, on average, house price changes when each of the influencing factors change. We would expect house price to rise as the number of rooms increase; that house price would fall as the distance to local facilities rises, and finally, for house price to fall as the traffic noise increased, i.e. a typical demand curve relationship. This is indeed the result obtained in an American study of road noise. Table 1 shows the average percentage fall in house price which corresponded to a one unit increase in traffic noise in a number of US areas.

So if a new road scheme was likely to raise traffic noise by one unit in, say, Washington DC, then a monetary value for this increased noise pollution could be found by finding 0.88 per cent of average house prices in the affected area.

Table 1. The impact of traffic noise upon house prices

Area of USA	% fall in house price due to a one unit increase in noise
North Virginia	0.15
Tidewater	0.14
North Springfield	0.18–0.50
Towson	0.54
Washington DC	0.88
Kingsgate	0.48
North King County	0.40
Spokane	0.08
Chicago	0.65

Note: Traffic noise was measured as the equivalent continuous sound level (measured in decibels) which would have the same sound energy over a given period as the actual fluctuation sound level measured at houses in the study.
Source: Nelson (1982)

out the other influences upon house price such as house size, accessibility, etc.

2. *The property market.* The method relies upon the assumption that people have the opportunity to select the combination of house features (size, accessibility, environmental qualitv) which they most prefer given the constraints of their income.

However, the housing market can often be affected by outside influences, for example, the Government may have a large influence over house prices because of changing tax concessions or interest rates, etc. Similarly, if the HPM is carried out over a large area (e.g. highly urban to very rural) then there may be a cut-off distance at which those who are employed in cities are unable to move further into the country. It may even be that there are different perceptions of landscape in such rural areas. In effect then, the demand curve for houses with different environmental characteristics may be significantly constrained by the supply curve so that the market does not operate freely. In such cases both the demand for and supply of houses will have to be taken into consideration considerably complicating the analysis.

Expressed preference methods: The contingent valuation method (CVM)

Both the TCM and HPM methods have, in some way, relied upon individual valuations of environmental goods as revealed in their purchases of market priced goods (petrol, houses, etc.) which are associated with the consumption of those environmental goods (recreation, peace and quiet, etc.). The contingent valuation method (CVM) bypasses the need to refer to market prices by asking individuals explicitly to place values upon environmental assets. Because of this, the CVM is often referred to as an expressed preference method. Although there are variants of the technique, the most commonly applied approach is to interview households either at the site of an environmental asset, or at their homes, and ask them what they are willing to pay (WTP) towards the preservation of that asset. Analysts can then calculate the average WTP of respondents and multiply this by the total number of people who enjoy the environmental site or asset in question to obtain an estimate of the total value which people have for that asset. Box 8.6 discusses a CVM study estimating the value of improving water quality in a river in Pennsylvania.

An interesting advantage of the CVM approach is that it can, in theory, be used to evaluate resources, the continued existence of which people value, but which they never personally visit. An example of such an asset is Antarctica which people are WTP to preserve but would not in general ever want to visit. Closer to home another example of these 'non-use' values was provided when a UK forestry firm announced its intention to drain and plant the Flow Country, an important natural wildlife habitat and wetland area in Northern Scotland. Although few people actually visit the area, a CVM study (this time conducted through a postal survey of households) found that individuals were WTP a far higher sum to preserve the area than could ever be produced from growing timber there.

Compared to the methods previously discussed, the CVM approach may appear comparatively straightforward. However, there are a number of potential problems facing the unwary analyst, a few of which we discuss here.

1. *Understating WTP.* The central assumption of the CVM technique is that the WTP sums stated by respondents correspond to their valuation of the assets in question. Critics have questioned the validity of such an assumption claiming that the hypothetical nature of CVM scenarios make individuals' responses to them poor approximations of true value. However, in a series of experiments where hypothetical WTP questions have been followed up by actual requests for money payments, it was found that the sums which people stated they would be WTP were between 70–90 per cent of the amounts they eventually did pay. This indicates that people 'free-ride', i.e. tend to understate what they would really pay in an attempt to reduce any subsequent actual payments. However, as the magnitude of this understatement is relatively small this may not be too serious a problem.

2. *WTP v. WTA.* In theory the payment question can either be phrased as the conventional 'What are you willing to pay (WTP) to receive this environmental asset?' or in the less usual form 'What are you willing to accept (WTA) in compensation for giving up this environmental asset?' When comparisons of the two formats have been carried out analysts have noticed that WTA very significantly exceeds WTP, a result which critics have claimed invalidates the CVM approach showing responses to be expressions of what individuals would like to have happen rather than true valuations. However, recent work has shown that there are good psychological and economic reasons to indicate that individuals feel the cost of a loss (WTA compensation format) more intensely than the benefit of a gain (WTP format). If true, the observed WTA/WTP divergence then actually supports the validity of the CVM. However, it is also true to say that respondents will be far less familiar with the notion of receiving compensation for losing something than they will be with the notion of paying for something, a concept we all meet every day. This is likely to cause far greater uncertainty and variability in answers to WTA questions than occurs with WTP questions. Therefore, the former are to be avoided in favour of the latter. This, in turn, has consequences for the applicability of CVM to certain situations. We can obviously ask people their WTP for an environmental gain (e.g. to set up a new parkland), but in cases of environmental loss we must ask people their WTP to prevent that loss occurring (e.g. to fund flood defences to preserve marshland areas from

Box 8.6 Valuing river-water quality improvements using the contingent valuation method

The Monongahela River is a major river flowing through Pennsylvania, USA. Analysts asked a representative sample of households from the local area what they would be willing to pay in extra taxes in order to maintain or increase the water quality in the river. The analysts conducted several variants of the CVM survey. In one variant households were presented with three possible water quality scenarios and simply asked how much they were willing to pay for each.

Scenario 1: Maintain current river quality (suitable for boating only) rather than allow it to decline to a level unsuitable for any activity including boating.

Scenario 2: Improve the water quality from boatable to a level where fishing could take place.

Scenario 3: Further improve water quality from fishable to swimmable.

Among the households surveyed some used the Monongahela river for recreation while others did not. The analysts therefore could look at how much the users were willing to pay compared to the responses of non-users. Results for the sample as a whole were also calculated. Table 1 presents the willingness to pay, of users, non-users and the whole sample for each proposed river quality change scenario.

A number of very interesting conclusions can be drawn from these results. Considering the results for the whole sample, we can see that the stated willingness to pay sums draw out a conventional demand curve for water quality, i.e. people are prepared to pay a relatively high amount for an initial basic level of quality. However, they are prepared to pay progressively less for higher levels of water quality. Panel (a) draws out the demand curve

Table 1 Willingness to pay (WTP) for river quality scenarios

Water quality scenario	Averge WTP of whole sample ($)	Average WTP of users group ($)	Average WTP of non-users group ($)
Maintain boatable river quality	24.50	45.30	14.20
Improve from boatable to fishable quality	17.60	31.30	10.80
Improve from fishable to swimmable quality	12.40	20.20	8.50

Panel (a) Demand curve for water quality.

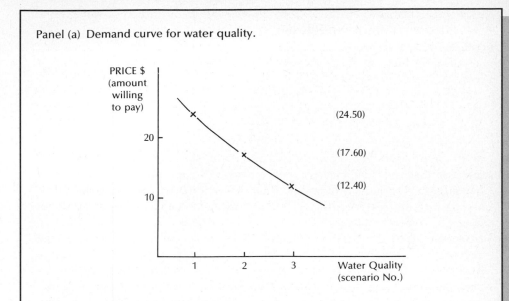

indicated by the results for the whole survey, i.e. for the average household.

From this demand curve we could attempt to calculate the total value of environmental quality at the river. More importantly, we could find the value gain experienced by the average household when a water quality improvement is achieved. The total benefit value of a specific improvement could then be estimated by multiplying this average household value by the number of households which it is thought would be affected by such an improvement. This benefit can then be compared against the cost of achieving such a quality improvement to see if it was worthwhile.

Turning to results for the users and non-users group, we can see that both map out conventional downward sloping demand curves. Furthermore, as we would expect, at every quality level the willingness to pay of the users group exceeds that of the non-users.

Finally, notice that the willingness to pay of non-users is not zero. This is due to the fact that such households, while not personally wishing to visit the river, nevertheless do value its continued existence and even upgrading so that others can enjoy its benefits. This non-use, 'existence' value derives from people's altruistic 'public preferences' showing that the concentration upon people's 'private preferences' as demonstrated by the market prices of marketed goods does not always fully capture the entire range of values which people have for things.

Source: Desvousges *et al.* (1987)

seawater flooding). Nevertheless, it may be that the WTP sum obtained does not reflect what people would consider adequate compensation (their WTA compensation) for losing the environmental asset; indeed the WTP sum may significantly underestimate the true WTA compensation. This problem is a focus of ongoing research.

3. *Part-whole bias.* Critics of the CVM have noted that if people are first asked their WTP for one part of an environmental asset (e.g. one lake in an entire system of lakes) and then asked to value the whole asset (e.g. the whole lake system) the amounts stated may be similar. Why is this? The reason appears to lie in how people commonly allocate their spending; first, dividing their available income up into several broad budget categories (e.g. housing, food, car, recreation) and then subdividing this between the actual items purchased. So for recreation, the first stage is to define the total budget which the individual has available for recreation and then subdivide this into how much they are willing to spend on each site they wish to visit. One approach to this problem is to first ask respondents to work out their overall recreational budget and then ask for their WTP for the environmental asset in question, reminding respondents of their limited recreational budget and that any money they allocate to this asset cannot be spent elsewhere. A second approach is to restrict the use of CVM to the evaluation of broad groups of environmental goods (i.e. wholes rather than parts), again reminding respondents of their limited recreational budget constraints. This restriction, if necessary, would considerably constrain the wide-scale application of the CVM and may itself raise further problems regarding respondents' ability to comprehend such broad amalgams of goods.

4. *Vehicle bias.* When asking a WTP question analysts must specify a realistic route by which such a payment could be made (the 'payment vehicle'). However, respondents may alter their WTP statements according to the specific payment vehicle chosen. For example, in a recent experiment regarding WTP for recreation in the Norfolk Broads, WTP via a charitable trust was noticeably lower than WTP via tax. In this case respondents stated that they doubted the ability of charitable funds to protect the environment and, while they did not like paying taxes, they did feel this was more likely to ensure effective environmental protection. It also compelled a wider group of people to contribute than would have if payment had been via charitable donation. Such results clearly tell us probably as much about the payment vehicles chosen as about the value of the asset in question. An obvious solution to such problems is therefore to use whichever payment vehicle is most likely to be used in reality.

5. *Starting point bias.* Many early studies attempted to prompt respondents by suggesting a starting bid and then increasing or decreasing this bid based upon whether the respondent agreed or refused to pay a such sum. However, it has been shown that the choice of starting bid affects respondents' final WTP sum. As an ancillary part of the water quality study discussed in Box 8.5, a separate group of respondents were offered a starting bid of $25 for the first scenario which produced a final average bid in that group of $27.50. However, when another group were offered a starting bid of $125 for the same scenario they gave a final average bid of $94.70, i.e. starting point significantly affected the final bid. In the light of these findings more recent studies have abandoned the use of starting bids.

This chapter has examined a variety of methods which attempt to extend CBA appraisals by expressing the value of non-market environmental goods and services in money units. While many of these methods represent a considerable improvement upon previous practice, we have attempted to indicate that none of them are panaceas and each method has limitations. There is no simple answer to these problems which remain a focus of considerable ongoing research. However, we remain convinced that such valuation methods have an important role to play and, if carefully applied, provide valid and reliable value estimates. Explicit valuation via these methods is preferable to implicit valuations where the link to individuals and their preferences is unclear or non-existent.

Further reading

For a non-technical survey see:

D. W. Pearce, *Economic Values and the Natural World*, Earthscan, London, 1993.

D. W. Pearce and R. K. Turner, *Benefits Estimates and Environmental Decision-Making*, OECD, Paris, 1992.

R. K. Turner and I. Bateman, 'A Critical Review of Monetary Assessment Methods and Techniques', Environmental Appraisal Group Report, University of East Anglia, Norwich, 1990.

R. K. Turner and T. Jones (eds), *Wetlands: Market and Intervention Failures*, Earthscan, London, 1991.

J. Winpenny, *Values for the Environment*, HMSO, London, 1991.

The more technical journal articles referred to were:

J. F. Benson and K. G. Willis, 'The Aggregate Value of Non-Priced Recreation Benefits of the Forestry Commission Estate', Report to the Forestry Commission, Department of Town and Country Planning, University of Newcastle upon Tyne, 1990.

W. H. Desvousges, V. K. Smith and A. Fisher, 'Option price estimates for water quality improvements: a contingent valuation study of the Monongahela River', *Journal of Environmental Economics and Management* **14**: 248–67, 1987.

G. D. Garrod and K. G. Willis, 'The Environmental Economic Impact of Woodland: A Two Stage Hedonic Price Model of the Amenity Value of Forestry in Britain', Countryside Changing Unit, University of Newcastle upon Tyne, 1991.

N. D. Hanley and S. Craig, 'Wilderness development decisions and the Krutilla–Fisher model: The case of Scotland's Flow Country', *Ecological Economics* **4**, 145–64, 1991.

J. P. Nelson, 'Highway noise and property values: a survey of recent evidence', *Journal of Transport Economics and Policy* **XIC**: 37–52, 1982.

R. K. Turner, I. J. Bateman and D. W. Pearce, 'United Kingdom', in S. Navrud (ed.), *Valuing the Environment: The European Experience*, Scandinavian University Press, Oslo, 1992.

CHAPTER 9

Coping with uncertainty

Introduction

Risk and uncertainty are facts of life, and nowhere is this more true than in the environmental context. The reality is that *we often do not know* what the environmental consequences will be of undertaking a particular policy or project. In large part this uncertainty arises because we do not fully understand how ecological systems function, and because we do not know how man-made substances – or increased quantities of 'natural' substances – will interact with the environment. If we did know, then chlorofluorocarbons (CFCs) would probably not have been introduced. We know now that CFCs damage the ozone layer, and that the ozone layer serves valuable protective functions for life on earth (see Chapter 20). Uncertainties of this kind are pervasive. We cannot be sure what is happening with the increasing release of micropollutants into the environment, for example. Sometimes the result of undertaking action without knowing for certain what will happen is that we create *irreversible consequences* such as the elimination of a species. Once gone, we cannot recreate them. In turn, we cannot be sure what will happen if continued species elimination occurs. It may not matter much (from the human standpoint, that is) if species are lost, but we cannot tell. The *scale* of outcome could be large, or small. So, the context of much environmental policy is characterized by:

- uncertainty about the effect
- irreversibility of some effects
- uncertainty about the scale of the effect.

The issue is, then, how do we handle uncertainty? It turns out that there is no easy answer. In what follows we caution readers that the terminology of risk and uncertainty, and the approaches to them are not widely agreed. We have tried to provide a framework for understanding what is a very large and often very confusing literature.

Risk and uncertainty

The terms 'risk' and 'uncertainty' are often used interchangeably. It is a matter of choice, but it is often helpful to distinguish risk from uncertainty in the following way. Risk relates to a situation where we have at least some idea of the *probabilities* of the effect occurring. For example, we might know that there is a 1/10 000 chance of being in an accident when crossing the road. The 1/10 000 is a probability. Often we do not know the probability at all. This is true uncertainty. Chapter 19 looks at climate change in the context of such uncertainty – we cannot (yet, anyway) assign probabilities to climate change having particular effects. The basic distinction between risk and uncertainty is that with risk we have some idea of the probabilities of outcomes, while with uncertainty we do not.

Managing risks

Of course, much research is devoted to finding out just what the probabilities of adverse effects are. This process of **risk assessment** aims to determine the relationship between, say, the concentration of a pollutant in the environment and its effects on human health. We can, therefore, think of risk assessment as involving an analysis of the 'dose' (the level of pollution) and the 'response' (the human health effect). In this way, risk assessment tries to convert an uncertainty context into a risk context. Once a risk assessment is completed, the next stage is **risk management** which is the whole process of bringing various disciplines to bear on two decisions: (a) how much risk is *acceptable*, and (b) how unacceptable risks should be reduced. The terms 'risk assessment' and 'risk management' tend to embrace uncertainty. That is, even if we cannot convert uncertainty into probabilistic outcomes, the same procedure of assessing doses and responses and determining acceptability and management applies.

Box 9.1 gives an example of risk assessment in terms of the relationship between numbers of people dying in the United States from particular environmental risks. The procedure involves first assessing what the risk of a particular hazard is, measured in terms of fatalities. To standardize the estimates, the fatalities are then expressed 'per million' people, which is the same thing as a probability. So, a risk of 63 000 in 1 million is the same as a probability of 0.063 (63 000/1 000 000), for example. Box 9.1 also shows the costs of the legislation aimed at reducing these risks, divided by the number of lives saved. The result is a 'cost per life saved' or 'cost per death avoided'. At this point some people begin to get uneasy at relating costs to lives saved. It looks as if we are treating human life as if it is just a 'commodity', to be bought and sold in the market-place. But leaving this instant emotional response to one side for a moment, the information in Box 9.1 reveals some

Box 9.1 Risks of death in the United States: selected environmental hazards and their cost of reduction

	Deaths per 1 million people exposed	Cost to avoid 1 death ($ million)
Trihalomethane in drinking water	420	0.2
Radionuclides in uranium mines	6 300	3.4
Benzene fugitive emissions	1 470	3.4
Benzene occupational exposure	39 600	8.9
Asbestos occupational exposure	3 015	8.3
Arsenic/copper exposure	63 000	23.0
Acrylonitrile occupational exposure	42 300	51.5
Coke ovens occupational exposure	7 200	63.5
Hazardous waste land disposal	2	4 190.2
Municipal solid waste landfill standard	1	19 107.0
Hazardous waste: wood preservatives	<1	5700 000

Source: The Council on Environmental Quality (1990)

The risks shown relate to numbers of mortalities for the relevant exposed population. All the hazards shown are the subject of environmental legislation in the United States, so, for example, the risk that is affected by the piece of legislation is the numerical value shown here. Notice that expressing the risks as 'per million' makes some of them look large. The largest risk, for arsenic/copper exposure, is 0.063 when expressed as a fraction, or 63 in 1000 or just over 6 in a 100. The manner in which risk is expressed often influences the extent to which people react to the risk.

The legislation costs money. The right hand column shows what happens when this cost is divided by the numbers of lives that the legislation is expected to save. In this way, cost and 'effectiveness' (lives saved) can be compared – see text.

interesting results. For example, it suggests that the United States can save lives at a cost of $200,000 per life by reducing trihalomethane in drinking water, compared to $19 *billion* for one life saved from improving landfill site quality. If the landfill legislation did not exist its cost would be saved and could have been allocated to the drinking water legislation, saving many more lives in the process. This is an example of **cost-effectiveness analysis**. Far from demeaning the 'value of a human life', cost-effectiveness shows how we can maximize the number of lives saved for a given budget. We know that environmental budgets are not infinite, nor could they ever be. So it makes eminent sense to look at the cost per life saved. Indeed, failure to do so amounts to admitting that it isn't saving life that matters, but some non-specified emotional objective. But there are other complex factors at work to do with the way in which the public *perceives* risk, an issue we address below.

Unfortunately, the kind of information in Box 9.1 is hard to come by for many risks. Governments rarely keep statistics in a form that permits this kind of cost-effectiveness analysis. Often, the cost of a policy is simply not known, while 'dose–response' functions tend to be known only imperfectly and, sometimes, not at all.

Risk and risk perception

The analysis in Box 9.1 looks convincing, but it disguises many problems. The risk data shown are *objective* in the sense that the deaths per million are either based on actual past data, or on *expert* assessment of future risks. But the *public* often perceives risk in very different ways to experts. This disparity between public and expert risk assessment is absolutely fundamental to the problem of coping with risk and uncertainty. Recall that the cost–benefit way of thinking involves us in a process of recording *individuals' preferences* for or against some change. We tended not to ask where the preferences came from, or whether they were 'good or bad' (subject to the law, that is). This is because cost–benefit approaches try to be 'democratic' by using individuals' preferences rather than some expert's view. Otherwise the way is open for the 'tyranny of the expert' whereby expert values are imposed on others. The only qualification is that the cost–benefit approach tries to measure the *intensity* of preference, as well as the mere fact of a preference.

When it comes to assessing risks, however, we have a problem. Suppose the expert assessment of risk is that some dreaded event, say a core meltdown in a nuclear power station, can only happen with a probability of 1 in a million reactor-years. That is, the chance of an accident of this kind would only occur once in 1 million years of producing electricity from one nuclear reactor, or, say, once in 1000 years if we had 100 nuclear reactors. This is an extremely small probability. And it is one that tends to be used when designing modern reactors in the developed world. Most people would agree that such a risk is so small that it is not worth worrying about. Yet the fear of a nuclear accident is so great that in the United States no nuclear power station of any significance has been commissioned for the last twenty years. In the United Kingdom any decision to build a reactor is greeted with a substantial public outcry from environmentalists, with long and expensive planning inquiries as the result. Clearly, there seems to be marked disparity between what the public worry about and what the experts think is important. And this disparity has major implications for the development of certain energy sources and the siting of allegedly hazardous facilities. Indeed, it generates the 'NIMBY' syndrome ('not in my back yard') whereby people oppose the siting of such things as waste disposal sites, incinerators, and power stations in their area. They do this despite the expert evidence that the risks to health from such facilities are very small.

Box 9.2 shows the contrast between expert and public opinion. The expert information is for the United States but the public's opinion can be gleaned from surveys in the United States and the United Kingdom. It can be seen that what concerns the public is fairly similar in the two countries, and most of the exceptions are readily explained. For example, the United States has debated the risks from exposure to radon (naturally occurring radioactivity) in domestic dwellings for quite some time and it has been a regular feature of

Box 9.2   Comparing perceptions of risk: experts *vs.* the public

US Environment Protection Agency Scientific Advisory Board Unranked Priorities	US Public Opinion Poll March 1990 % Saying 'very serious'	UK Public Opinion Poll May 1989 % Saying 'very worried'
Ecological risks		
Climate change	48	44
Ozone layer	60	56
Habitat change	42	45
Biodiversity loss	n.a.	45
Health risks		
Criteria pollutants[a]	56	34–40
Toxic air pollutants[b]	50	33
Radon	17	n.a.
Indoor air pollution	22	n.a.
Drinking water	46	41
Pesticides	52	46
Issues regarded by the public as important but not by the experts		
Oil spills	60	53
Hazardous waste sites	66	n.a.
Industrial water pollution	63	n.a.
Nuclear accidents	60	n.a.
Industrial pollution accidents	58	64
Radioactive waste	58	58
Leaking undergound storage tanks	54	n.a.
Contaminated bathing water	n.a.	59

Sources: UK Department of the Environment (1991); *Science* (1990).

media programmes. This concern is somewhat more recent in the United Kingdom and hence did not figure prominently in the 1989 public opinion polls. There have been similar investigations into indoor air pollution generally in the United States but, to date, very little has been said about this in the United Kingdom. Perhaps of more interest are the items that the US experts implied did not matter very much, but which the public thinks do matter. These are very much in a general category of 'accidents' – nuclear, industrial, oil spills, underground storage tanks in the United States and problems with the nuclear fuel cycle. The only exception is bathing water which has been a specific problem in the United Kingdom because of a Directive from the European Community on the matter. How, then, do the public perceive accidents?

Everyone is familiar with news items about road accidents in which multiple vehicles are involved and the deaths are several or many. This is the phenomenon of the 'group accident'. It partly explains why aeroplane crashes, boat sinkings, gas explosions, nuclear accidents and natural disasters such as hurricanes and tornados are news. Yet the deaths from such events rarely exceed twenty-five people and the events themselves are not very common. Compare that to the more than 5000 people who die every year in road accidents in the United Kingdom. What it suggests is that individuals perceive group accidents differently to accidents in which one person dies. Put another way, if ten people die in one accident this is seen as being somehow far more serious than if one person dies in each of ten accidents. There is what is known as **disaster aversion**. Allowing for disaster aversion in assessing environmental risks is perfectly legitimate if the requirement is that individuals' preferences should count. Moreover, disaster aversion is consistent with the economic theory of risk aversion. To see why, we investigate briefly the nature of this theory. But we shall then discover that other aspects of human behaviour toward risk are not consistent with that theory.

Expected utility

Much of the theory of risk aversion in economics rests on what is known as 'expected utility' theory. The idea is very simple. The context is one of risk so we assume we know the probabilities attached to outcomes. Consider an investment project with benefits that are known subject to certain probabilities. Suppose there is a 20 per cent chance of the benefit being *minus* 5 (for the moment the units do not matter); a 50 per cent chance of it being *plus* 15; and a 30 per cent chance of it being *plus* 20. We can calculate the **expected value** of the benefits as:

$$(0.2 \times -5) + (0.5 \times 15) + (0.3 \times 20) = 12.5$$

We could compare this expected value with the cost of undertaking the action. If it is less than 12.5, then the project looks worth undertaking. Note, however, that the investment might be undertaken and the loss of 5 might occur. In that case we will have invested money for nothing. Somehow, the expected value idea does not seem to capture the relevant concerns about the outcomes of the project. In particular, expected value seems not to capture our likely concerns about the *extremes* of the outcomes. People tend to be *averse* to bad outcomes such as the minus 5 in the example. Expected value approaches do not capture this *risk aversion*[1].

It seems more likely that the individual will attach some weights to the outcomes. The result is the **expected utility** approach rather than the expected value approach. The term 'utility' can be translated as meaning 'wellbeing'. Expected utility then has the same formula as the expected value approach but this time utilities rather than values are substituted. So, if we are very averse to the loss we might weight it more heavily, say by a factor of 5. (Similarly, the 20 might not be 20/15 times as good as the return of 15, but for simplicity let us ignore this.) Now the calculation will be:

$$(0.2 \times [-5 \times 5]) + (0.5 \times 15) + (0.3 \times 20) = 8.5$$

The effect is to make the project much less attractive than it was previously[2].

The expected utility approach seems able to handle the problem of disasters discussed previously, since what would happen is that we would attach a large utility value (or 'disutility' value if it is a loss) to the outcomes we most like or dislike. Some attempts have been made to estimate 'disaster aversion' measures. Box 9.3 shows some suggested rules taken from contexts in which safety investments have to be decided upon.

Why expected utility does not apply

The expected utility model is attractive, but extensive research suggests that it does not describe how people actually behave. Recall that if individual preferences count, then actual behaviour must be studied to see what people actually care about and why they behave as they do. This can be contrasted with the view that ignores how people actually behave and builds up an approach based on how they *ought* to behave if they are to be judged 'rational' or 'consistent'. It is not always easy to keep this distinction in mind. After all, the very purpose of analyzing decisions is to make them better. Better decisions could be ones that always obey the axiom that what people want is best. But we know that societies have always abrogated some individual sovereignty to the state in order to override individual preferences.

In practice, psychologists and economists have uncovered all kinds of behaviour which is inconsistent with expected utility theory. Just a few are listed below:

1. People seem regularly to confuse probability with plausibility. The more they think it could happen ('it seems reasonable'), the higher the probability they attach to it occurring. This **conjunction fallacy** is especially

Box 9.3   Disaster aversion

Table 1 shows some possible rules for deciding on the 'value' of a disaster. Suppose we know that the 'value of a statistical life' (*V*) is £2 million, i.e. society is willing to pay up to £2 million to save a single life in road accidents, health programmes, etc. Assume that the accident in question has a one in a million chance of happening (*f* = frequency of the event) and that it might involve 100, 500 or 1000 people dying (*N* = 100, 500, 1000). Then the 'value of the accident' depends on how people view the group accident event. It has been suggested, and some regulatory agencies use this rule, that an accident involving 100 people is regarded as being the equivalent of 100×100 deaths in individual accidents (the 'square rule'). Others suggest that it is equal to 300 times the number of actual deaths, and so on. Which rule is chosen matters a great deal. In Table 1 it can be seen that one would spend only £4000 to avert a one in a million chance of 1000 people dying in a single accident if no aversion factor is present, but £4 million if the square rule is used.

Table 1   The value of a disaster

$f = 1/1\,000\,000$		
$N = 100$	$N = 500$	$N = 1000$
$fN = 0.0001$	$fN = 0.0005$	$fN = 0.001$
$fn^2 = 0.01$	$fN^2 = 0.25$	$fN^2 = 1.0$
$300\,fN = 0.03$	$300\,fN = 0.15$	$300\,fN = 0.3$
$vfN = £400$	$vfN = £2000$	$vfN = £4000$
$vfN^2 = £40\,000$	$vfN^2 = £1000\,000$	$vfN^2 = £4000\,000$
$v300\,fN = £120\,000$	$v300\,fN = £600\,000$	$v300\,fN = £1200\,000$

important if the event in question is described in some detail, e.g. the effects of a nuclear accident, islands disappearing under rising sea levels, etc. This often happens in association with events that are easy to imagine (explosions, flooding) while events that are hard to imagine tend to attract low subjective probabilities (the issue of **availability**).

2. Everyone is aware of the 'it can't happen to me syndrome'. Because it hasn't yet happened, people think it won't happen. And everyone is a better driver than the average driver! This is the **fallacy of optimism**.
3. Experiments show that people do not correctly perceive low probabilities. Many seem to ignore them altogether, and much depends on how the risk is described (see Box 9.2). In many other cases, people exaggerate the low probabilities, believing some accidents to be more likely than, say, the risk

of fatality in a road accident. This is the **under- or overweighting of low probabilities** issue.

4. People seem 'anchored' to wherever they are at the point in time they are asked to make a decision. This is their 'reference' point, and people value risks with reference to that point rather than in abstract in the way the expected utility approach assumes. They also value losses from the standpoint of the reference point more highly than equivalent gains (the phenomenon of 'loss aversion'), whereas economics has traditionally taught that there will be little difference in these values. This helps explain the difference between *willingness to accept* and *willingness to pay* in economic valuation (see Chapter 8). People also tend to make the risk problem simpler than it really is, as if they cannot cope with a more complex issue. These features of decision-making, together with the distortion of low probability perception, define **prospect theory**. Prospect theory seeks to explain how individuals behave with respect to risk in light of the apparent failure of expected utility theory to explain that behaviour.

5. Prospect theory also suggests that people put the various contexts for valuing risk into separate mental boxes, or 'mental accounts'. They then have little difficulty in weighing up costs and benefits within each account, but find it difficult to make comparisons *across* mental accounts. If this is true, then it goes some way to explaining how people can seemingly entertain contradictory notions at the same time. For example, benefits might be in one 'account' and costs in another! This does not invalidate cost–benefit thinking since, as Chapter 7 indicated, the idea of cost–benefit is to *prescribe* actions. But it raises again the awkward problem of when individuals' actions can be regarded as 'rational' and when they cannot.

6. Much also depends on the context of risk. A risk of being injured or catching a disease is regarded as being very different if it is *involuntarily* borne as opposed to being *voluntary*. So, the risk of dying from lung cancer through smoking (a voluntary process) is often seen as being less than the risk of cancer through exposure to nuclear radiation (involuntary), even though the former risk is substantially greater than the latter. The context issue can be complicated. Risks in the future are usually thought to be less important than risks now (the phenomenon of 'discounting'), but recent research suggests that people often tend to value future risks more highly than present risks, and future benefits more highly than present benefits. This is because they sometimes like to 'leave the best to the last' (in the case of benefits), or dread being vulnerable when they are older and perhaps less capable of looking after themselves (in the case of risks).

Conclusions

All in all, the issue of how people *actually behave* in the presence of uncertainty and risk turns out to be complex. It seems fairly clear that neither expected value nor expected utility are adequate to explain that behaviour, even if expected utility can accommodate many issues, such as disaster aversion. Other theories of risk-taking – such as prospect theory – have been developed to account for the inadequacies of expected utility. They tend to suggest that the context of the risk is important, and that we cannot advocate a single rule to deal with all risk and uncertainty contexts. The phenomenon of loss aversion is important for environmental economics because it is often the case that we are dealing with environmental losses rather than gains. Loss aversion means that those losses may be valued very highly by society. The issue of risk context means that we cannot analyze low probability, high damage events in the same way as we value 'everyday' risk. Somehow we have to account for perceptions of low probability events. Finally, new theories of uncertainty suggest all kinds of ways in which people can be encouraged to deal with risk. As just one example, in some countries it is fairly usual to compensate people if a project perceived as risky is located in their vicinity. This might be a nuclear power station or even a waste landfill site. Compensation may work as a means of getting a more 'rational' appraisal of risk, not just because bearing the risk is itself compensated, but because the compensation creates a new context of sharing in risk compared to the uncompensated case in which the owner of the landfill site, or the nuclear power station is seen to be 'imposing' the facility.

Notes

1. Indeed, the expected value criterion implies **risk neutrality**. Compare the certainty of getting £50 with the gamble of a 0.5 chance of £100 and a 0.5 chance of getting nothing. The expected value of the gamble is also £50. If you are indifferent between the certain £50 and the gamble, then you are risk neutral. If you prefer the certain £50 you are risk averse. And if you prefer the gamble you are a 'risk lover'.
2. The example is extremely simplistic since expected utility involves translating each return into a utility value based on what is called a 'utility function'.

Further reading

Most treatments of the economics of risk in environmental contexts are fairly complicated. An excellent and fairly readable article which summarizes expected utility and the development of other approaches such as prospect theory, regret theory and contingent weighting (the last two are not discussed in this chapter) is:

C. Camerer and H. Kunreuther, 'Decision processes for low probability events: Policy implications', *Journal of Policy Analysis and Management* 8(4): 565–92, 1989.

References

The Council on Environmental Quality, *Environmental Quality: 21st Annual Report 1990*, US Government Printing Office, Washington DC, 1991.

'Counting on science at EPA', *Science* **240** (August 10): 12, 1990.

D. W. Pearce and R. K. Turner, 'The Development of Environmental Indicators', Report to UK Department of the Environment, April 1991.

PART IV

The economic control
of the environment

CHAPTER 10

Using the market to protect the environment

We have shown in Chapters 1 and 5 that the primary virtue of the price mechanism (the market) is that it signals to consumers what the cost of producing a particular product is, and to producers what consumers' relative valuations (based on WTP) are. 'In a nutshell, this is the elegance and virtue of free markets which economists have (generally) found so attractive since the time of Adam Smith' (Pearce *et al.*, 1989).

On the other hand, we have also demonstrated that an *unfettered* price mechanism will use too much of the non-market (zero-priced) environmental goods and services. This problem is then compounded by the 'publicness' characteristics of many environmental goods and services. Because the price for goods and services does not reflect the true value of the totality of the resources being used to produce them, unfettered markets fail to allocate resources efficiently. There is a divergence between private and social cost.

All this is not to argue, however, that freely functioning 'unfettered' markets cannot achieve improvements in environmental quality. If consumers change their tastes in favour of less polluting products (as indicated, at least in principle, by ecolabelling), market forces will lead to a change in the 'pollution content' of final products and services (see Chapter 17). Green consumerism may do little to alter production processes since the consumer is generally not well informed about the precise nature of such processes, and is in any case less able to impact in any direct way on the choice of processes. But process changes will occur if industry also becomes environmentally conscious, and/or the cost signals to industry alter.

There are two ways in which markets can be restructured so as to ensure that environmental services enter into the market system more effectively. First, we could create markets in previously free services. This would require restriction of access to such resource services by charging entrance fees and/or changing property rights, e.g. establishing extended exclusive economic zones in coastal waters. We take a further look at this option at the end of this chapter and in Chapters 15 and 23 but first we concentrate on a second option. This would be to 'modify' markets by centrally deciding the value of environmental services and ensuring that those values are incorporated into the prices of goods and services. This type of regulatory approach is known as the **market-based incentives approach**. It is to be contrasted with a **direct ('command-and-control') regulatory approach** which involves the setting of environmental standards (e.g. for air quality or water quality) enforced via legislation without the aid of market-based incentives.

Economists have for long argued that the market-based incentives approach is more efficient than one based on 'command-and-control' (CAC). The actual pollution control systems operating in industrialized countries, however, have been dominated by direct regulations. Chapters 11, 12 and 13 examine in more detail the policy instruments that can be deployed in a market-based incentives approach to pollution control. Chapter 14 covers the regulatory systems that have so far found favour with the control agencies.

There are two broad sources of inefficiency in the CAC approach:

1. CAC requires the regulator to use up resources to acquire information that polluters already possess. For example, polluters know far better than government what it will cost to abate or clean-up waste emissions. Yet, under the CAC approach, governments must obtain this information.
2. Polluters vary in the ease with which they can abate pollution. Put another way, their costs of control differ. Under the CAC system each polluter has to achieve a given standard, subject usually to some consideration about the type of technology adopted and 'excessive' cost. These technology-based standards are commonly adopted across Europe and in North America. We examine standards such as 'Best Available Control Technology' (BACT) and 'Best Available Control Technology Not Entailing Excessive Cost' (BATNEEC) in Chapter 14. But a key feature of the CAC approach is that control is not concentrated in the sources that find it cheapest to abate pollution. Yet, such a process of concentration would enable overall costs of compliance with the standard to be minimized.

Thus charges/taxes would enable a polluter to choose how to adjust to the environmental quality standard. Polluters with high costs of abating pollution will prefer to pay the charge. Polluters with low costs of abatement will prefer to install abatement equipment. By making abatement more attractive to 'low cost' polluters than to 'high cost' ones, charges tend to cut down the total costs of compliance.

There can be little doubt that as society demands increasingly stringent pollution controls, costs and regulatory intrusiveness are set to escalate significantly. For economists therefore, the balance of argument will fall even more heavily in favour of the exploitation of the market's mechanisms for revealing information, as compared with the excess costs and bureaucracy associated with a strategy based solely on regulatory controls. Governments will be forced to search out cost-minimizing procedures to reduce the projected cost burden of future environmental policy. Economic incentives carry with them the promise of just such cost-effectiveness benefits.

The growing severity and pervasiveness of pollution in the industrialized economies led the OECD (Organisation for Economic Co-operation and Development), a group of twenty-four industrialized countries plus the Commission of the European Community and the former Yugoslavia (which had special status), to elaborate and adopt in 1972 the '**Polluter Pays Principle**' (PPP) as a background economic principle for environmental policy. Recall from Chapter 1 that the laws of thermodynamics ensure that production and consumption activities result in the release of a diverse range of residuals (wastes) into the environment (air, water and land media). Whether the residuals discharged/emitted cause pollution or not depends upon the specific environmental context, but also on one's definition of pollution.

The economic definition of pollution is dependent upon both some physical effect of waste on the environment and a human reaction to that physical effect, i.e. a loss of welfare due to the imposition of an external cost. So the physical presence of pollution does not mean that 'economic' pollution exists. Further, even if 'economic' pollution exists, it is far from always the case that it should be completely eliminated.

The basic tenet of PPP is that the *price* of a good or service should fully reflect its *total cost of production*, including the cost of *all* the resources used. Thus the use of air, water or land for the emission, discharge or storage of wastes is as much a use of resources as are other labour and material inputs. The lack of proper prices for, and the open access characteristic of many environmental resources means that there is a severe risk that overexploitation leading to eventual complete destruction will occur. The PPP seeks to rectify this *market failure* by making polluters 'internalize' the costs of use or degradation of environmental resources. The aim is to integrate use of the environment (including its waste assimilation capacity) into the economic sphere through the use of price signals and the use of economic instruments such as pollution taxes, charges and permits (see Chapters 11, 12 and 13). The use of regulation to internalize externalities is also, however, consistent with the PPP.

Effective international use of the PPP requires a coordinated approach because environmental regulations can become a source of trade distortion if some countries subsidize private investment in pollution control while others do not. To encourage uniform application of the PPP, the OECD Council stipulated that the PPP should constitute a fundamental principle of pollution control in Member Countries in 1972 (implemented in 1974). Internationally, the PPP has become a principle of non-subsidization of polluters. Nevertheless, some Member Country governments argued in favour of accelerated national programmes of pollution reduction measures. This led to the acceptance of certain exceptions to the strict PPP. Financial aid could be given to a polluting sector if that sector was already suffering from significant economic difficulties. But the aid could only be given for a fixed amount of time in a clearly defined programme and international trade distortion should be avoided.

The PPP was also endorsed by the EC in a 1975 Recommendation which attached application conditions similar to those of the OECD and was included in the Singe European Act. In 1989 the OECD adopted a Recommendation on the Application of the PPP to Accidental Pollution. This links the economic principle and the legal principle relating to damage compensation.

Economic efficiency theory suggests that the polluter (firm, individual or government) should pay the full cost of environmental damages caused by its activity. This would create an incentive for the reduction of such damage, at least to the level where the *marginal cost of pollution reduction is equal to the marginal cost of the damage caused by such pollution*. Box 10.1 presents a graphical explanation of the derivation of **optimal pollution levels**, assuming some positive environmental waste assimilative capacity. Box 10.2 uses the example of the paper box producer from Chapter 5 to demonstrate the derivation of the optimal pollution level in a somewhat more formal way.

Empirical estimation of the damage impacts and their monetary equivalents (pollution damage costs) is a far from exact procedure and therefore real world pollution control policy operates on the basis of exogenously determined 'socially acceptable' pollution levels (and related ambient quality states). In principle, making all waste dischargers pay the same price for an extra unit of effluent discharged (via pollution taxes levied per unit of effluent or via tradeable pollution permits/consents signifying a right to discharge a given amount of effluent) will achieve a cost-effective allocation of effluent control costs. That is, it will result in any target for the total effluent load from all firms, being achieved at the lowest possible total of effluent costs (Pezzey, 1988). Economists generally claim that regulations (as opposed to economic instruments like charges and permits) will result in higher total control costs for meeting the same overall effluent target. But note that this analysis implicitly assumes that non-persistent pollutants are being discharged and that polluter behaviour conforms to the rational economic person assumptions of economic theory.

The *standard interpretation of the PPP* therefore requires polluters to pay for controlling effluent down to the acceptable load, but not for the environmental damage caused by the acceptable effluent load. The standard PPP therefore effectively grants polluters a *de facto* right to discharge the acceptable level of effluent free of charge. An *extended interpretation of the PPP* would imply that polluters must pay damage costs as well as control costs. This interpretation would allow incentive charging, making polluters pay in net terms for their acceptable effluent discharges. The incentive charging instrument has the advantage that it may motivate appropriate polluter

Box 10.1   Costs and benefits of pollution

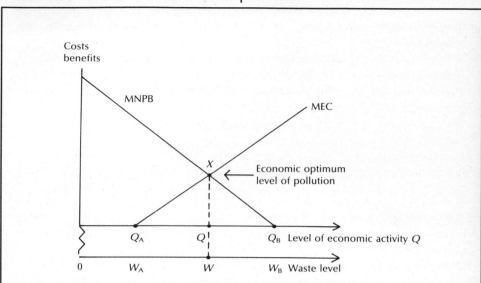

In this simplified pollution (i.e. a substance entering the environment can be neutralized by natural processes, physical and biological, and is therefore non-persistent or benignly held in a sink) model a firm's activity level Q and proportional level of waste W are shown on the horizontal axis. It is also assumed that at any activity level below Q_A the amount of waste generated can be assimilated, given sufficient time, by the environment and therefore any externality is only temporary (i.e. there is contamination but not permanent pollution).

MNPB is the extra benefit a polluting firm receives from changing its level of activity by one unit (i.e. it is the marginal private costs of production minus the marginal revenue received).

MEC is the value of the extra economic damage done by the pollution related to the extra unit of activity.

The main result of this analysis is that the economic optimum level of pollution is determined by the intersection of the MNPB and MEC schedules at X (where MNPB = MEC, with an activity level of Q and amount of waste W). Note that this is a non-zero level of pollution.

A number of important caveats apply to this simple model:

• It is not appropriate for many toxic, non-biodegradeable and persistent pollutants (e.g. persistent residuals like PCBs and other dangerous substances which accumulate over time and cannot be safely assimilated).

- It assumes the release of a single pollutant; in reality a cocktail of pollutants is often found mixing together which greatly increases the damage impact.
- It assumes pollution damage only occurs when individuals recognize a loss of welfare; low doses of pollution over long periods of time may not result in easily identifiable impacts like health effects until it is too late to respond adequately.

Nevertheless, it does serve to highlight an important underlying economic message. Zero pollution is technically not really feasible as a policy objective, and in any case would be prohibitively costly both in terms of investment in equipment and processes to reduce waste outputs and in loss of benefits derived from the goods being produced.

Box 10.2 Output and pollution

In a competitive market situation where firms are not compelled to pay for the external pollution costs they incur, then such firms will produce all units where MR exceeds MVC (internal costs only), i.e. they expand production to the level Q_m in Panel (a). Subtracting MVC from MR gives the firms MNPB (see Panel (b)). The firm produces all units with positive MNPB, i.e. production is expanded to Q_m (as per Panel (a)).

As output rises so the total quantity of pollution emissions increase (see Panel (c)). Emissions exceed assimilative capacity when output exceeds Q_A. When output is below Q_A, all emissions are safely assimilated by the environment, as shown in Panel (d). Initial units of pollution beyond Q_A cause relatively little damage compared to subsequent units (because of the effects of accumulating total pollution levels). This implies that each additional unit of pollution causes more damage than the preceding unit, i.e. we have an upward sloping MEC curve in Panel (e). Note that for output below Q_A we have zero MEC.

Overlaying the MEC onto the MNPB (from Panel (b)) we can see that MEC exceeds MNPB for all units of production from Q_s to Q_m in Panel (f), i.e. output should be reduced to Q_s (by making polluters pay the costs of their pollution emissions). We do not wish to reduce output below Q_s as MNPB would exceed MEC, i.e. below Q_s the value of production exceeds its total (internal and external) costs. Q_s is therefore the socially optimal level of output and the corresponding pollution level is the optimal level of pollution.

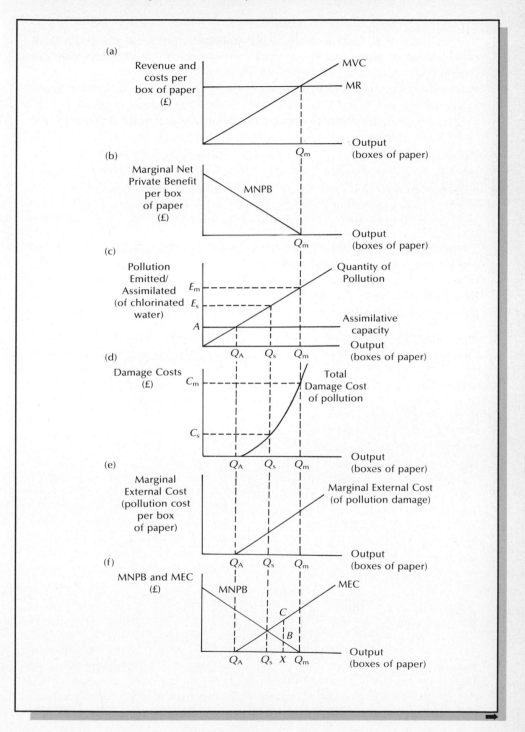

Note that we can trace the effect of reducing output from Q_m to Q_s from Panel (f) up to Panel (c) to see that this implies a cut in total pollution emissions from E_m to E_s. Furthermore, in Panel (d) we can see that reducing output from Q_m to Q_s reduces the costs caused by that pollution from C_m to C_s.

Consider the particular box of paper marked by the letter X in Panel (f). The MNPB earned by the firm for producing box X (the amount XB) is considerably less than the external cost of pollution caused by producing this box (the amount XC). Therefore, while it is in the interests of the paper mill to produce this box, it is not in the interests of society as a whole (the value of the paper consumed is exceeded by the sum of internal plus external costs). Economists state that it is 'socially inefficient' to produce box X.

How can we avoid this social inefficiency? One approach is to make firms pay for the pollution damage they cause, i.e. force them to pay the external costs of their production. If the firm is forced to pay for pollution costs then its MNPB for box X (i.e. XB) is outweighed by the pollution cost bill (i.e. XC). Indeed this will be the case for all boxes between output levels Q_s and Q_m.

behaviour (the search for cost-effective and less polluting technologies) over the long term (see Chapter 12).

Although pollution charges are widely used in Europe, they have been established primarily as revenue sources and have not been calibrated to achieve specific environmental quality targets. The revenues raised have often been 'recycled' back to discharges in the form of grants to cover the capital costs of the installation of new treatment technologies. Practice and economic principles clearly diverge to a considerable extent but this is hardly surprising once one recognizes that pollution control policy inherently exposes contradictory ethical, political and economic efficiency implications, all of which must be managed under a shroud of scientific uncertainty (Lave and Malès, 1989).

The material benefits of modern economic systems cannot be delivered with zero environmental risk founded on zero exposure to pollution. Some sort of cost– and/or risk–benefit balancing process is required in which 'acceptable' trade-offs between risk levels and the costs of reducing exposure are struck. The trade-offs can be made implicitly or explicitly depending on the policy approach adopted. Two broad types of policy approaches toward the internalization of pollution externalities can therefore be distinguished – the *cost–benefit approach* and the *precautionary approach* (Pearce *et al.*, 1992).

A broad definition of the *precautionary principle* says that because of the uncertainties caution should be exercised when setting emission standards, and emphasis should be placed on the prevention of pollution via source reduction measures (i.e. changing/modifying production processes or products) rather than the sole reliance on end-of-pipe treatments (i.e. filters at the end of pipes and gas scrubbing devices in chimney stacks). There is the *risk* that, especially in situations where persistent pollutants are accumulating in the environment, that the assimilative capacity itself may be damaged/destroyed. Given that the economic optimum level of pollution is not zero, and uncertainty surrounds the precise impacts over the long run of the build-up of certain substances in the environment, it is possible (but not certain) that a so-called **dynamic externality** problem could arise (Pearce, 1976). It is this risk of significant long-term pollution damage that the precautionary approach seeks to mitigate. We examine the precautionary principle in more detail in Chapter 14 since it operates through the **mechanisms of regulation**. Box 10.3 examines the Love Canal pollution incident in the United States in order to highlight the risks and damage costs that can be incurred if short-term expediency takes precedence over long-term planning in matters of pollution control.

Box 10.3   When pollution dumping exceeds assimilative capacity: the case of Love Canal, USA

To demonstrate the problems and consequences of adopting a pollution disposal option which only provides a short-term solution, we can consider the infamous case of Love Canal in Upper New York State, USA. Love Canal was begun in the 1890s as a proposed bypass across a curve in the Niagran river running through the city of Niagara Falls. However, due to subsequent economic recession, it was never completed and in the 1940s the partly built canal passed into the hands of the Hooker Electrochemical Company, a large chemical manufacturer who purchased the canal in order to use it as a dump for its highly toxic chemical wastes.

Over the years 1942–52 Hooker deposited some 21 000 tons of waste materials in the trench (Levine, 1982), a short-term solution to the external costs of pollution emission. However, the toxicity of the pollutants dumped into Love Canal was far in excess of the local environment's capacity to safely assimilate it. The build-up of non-assimilated wastes began to poison the ground and overload the environment. Some local residents complained about odours and in 1953 the Love Canal site was closed and capped with clay (a second short-run solution). This stopped the odours and in the

➡

absence of complaints, houses and even a school were built on the site. However, the persistent chemical overload which the area had suffered had completely stripped out any capacity for safe assimilation in the local environment and in the mid-1970s it was noticed that underground waterways (swales) were flushing out high concentrations of highly toxic substances. In 1978 over 200 houses in the area were purchased by the State. A further 700 families were evacuated in 1979. Local residents were found to be suffering a variety of pollution-related illnesses including very high pregnancy/birth problems (affected pregnant women were found to have a 47 per cent chance of an adverse pregnancy outcome). Subsequently, the US Environmental Protection Agency sued Hooker for $125 million while private lawsuits totalled some $14 billion. The Love Canal case was instrumental in setting up the US 'Superfund' programme designed to clean up uncontrolled hazardous waste sites. To date, this has instigated some $1.3 billion of clean-up work (Clay, 1991).

So what should Hooker have done and what targets should environmental pollution policies set themselves to ensure the goal of sustainability? For long-term sustainability the quantity of pollutants released into the environment must not exceed its assimilative capacity. The firm failed to evaluate the safe assimilative capacity of the Love Canal site relative to the highly toxic pollutants being dumped there. A sustainable optimal level of pollution should have been calculated and investments in new processes (e.g. recycling of waste chemicals) carried out to achieve this. This would, of course, have involved higher costs than those of simply dumping in Love Canal, but the long-term consequences for society (and in this case for Hooker) of not facing up to the costs of long-term safe disposal options are clearly greater. If such options are not financially feasible for the firm then the only sustainable solution is to stop production of such waste altogether.

This case highlights the problems of free market operations with respect to external pollution costs. The pressures upon Hooker to maximize profits were, at the time of dumping, the only real factors which affected decisions.

Property right approaches

In this final section we look at a school of economic thought associated with Coase (1960) which emphasizes the importance of **property rights and bargaining** between polluters and sufferers. The **Coasian tradition** rejects intervention by the government (via taxes, subsidies or standard-setting) in favour of market bargaining underpinned by appropriate property rights in order to achieve the social optimum level of pollution. Given the existence of an appropriate property rights system (guaranteed ownership of resources via the force of law) and some other assumptions, Coase argued that polluter and sufferer (from pollution) should be left in an unregulated situation. A bargaining process would then develop (with bribes or compensation changing hands depending on which party – polluter or sufferer – held the property rights) on an automatic basis. We present the Coase theorem analysis in Box 10.4.

The 'Coase theorem' lays down that regardless of who holds the property rights, there is an automatic tendency to approach the social optimum via bargaining. If this analysis is correct, then government regulation of externalities is redundant, the market will take care of itself, with bargaining representing an efficient process.

A number of criticisms of and complications with the Coase theorem have subsequently been explored in the literature. These include the existence of imperfect competition, high transactions costs, difficulties of polluter and sufferer identification and threat-making behaviour. Pearce and Turner (1990) have concluded that the Coase theorem is important in forcing advocates of environmental intervention to define their terms and justify their case more carefully than they might otherwise have done. But there are many reasons why bargains do not, and cannot, occur.

Further, is it really correct to argue that as it makes no difference on efficiency grounds which party has the property right, there is little benefit to altering those rights? In the real world it surely matters a great deal which party has the property right and much public policy (including environmental policy) reduces to struggles over which parties can get the state on their side. Bromley and Hodge (1990) have examined some of the consequences of *reconsidering the property rights structure* that exists in the industrialized countries. Their particular focus was on private property rights in land and the agricultural sector. Contemporary agricultural policy in these countries is anchored to this property rights system.

As we showed in Chapter 6 the Common Agricultural Policy in Europe, and for that matter agricultural intensification throughout the industrialized countries, has led to an extensive range of negative environmental externalities (e.g. pollution, loss of landscape and amenity, impaired recreation, etc.). When governments intervene to correct for policy failure, the agricultural sector (farmers and agri-business) resists efforts to alter the prevailing property rights position. A struggle develops between the presumed 'right' of a landowner and the 'right' of other members of society to be free of the negative externalities generated by agricultural activity. To the extent that the state does intervene to reduce the external costs this has been via regulations, or via financial inducements given to farmers. Bromley and Hodge conclude that 'Any change in the status quo production domain of the farmer must inevitably be purchased by the state with bribes, subsidies, or concessions at other places in the policy arena' (1990, p. 199).

Box 10.4   Coase theorem

Panel (a) illustrates that left unregulated, the polluter will try to operate at $Q\pi$, where profits are maximized. But the social optimum is at Q^*. Thus private and social optima appear to be incompatible. However, the introduction of property rights may change this situation. If the sufferer from pollution has the property rights, then it could pay the polluter to compensate the sufferer (up to the level of activity Q^*). Beyond Q^* it is not feasible for such compensation to take place because the polluter's net gains become less than the sufferer's losses. Thus starting at 0 and giving the sufferer the property rights, there is a 'natural' tendency to move to Q^*, the social optimum.

If the property rights are vested in the polluter then the analysis in the figure starts at $Q\pi$, with the sufferer given the opportunity to compensate the polluter until again the level of activity Q^* is reached.

Panel (a) The bargaining solution to the pollution problem.

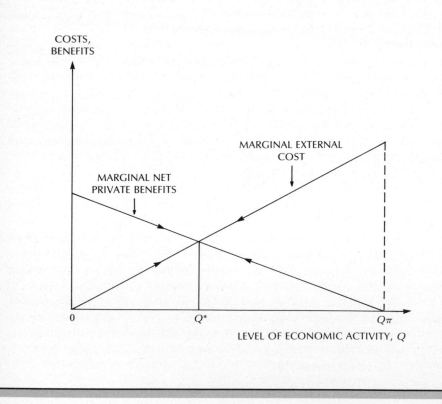

But why not establish an alternative property rights regime, one in which society uses farmers to produce environmental-type goods and services (Bromley and Hodge refer to these as 'countryside and community attributes', (CCA)) and also to produce food and fiber of a certain quality? In the status quo system, food and fiber production comes first and CCA occur as incidental side-effects. In the alternative regime, the desired level of CCA would be set through collective action at the local and/or national level. So the property rights to determine the attributes that shall exist in the rural landscape would now reside not with the farmer, but with society. If a particular farmer should wish to undertake a form of production that would detract from the defined level of CCA, then it is the farmer who must be willing to pay the exchequer for the right to deviate from the plan.

So far the discussion has been conducted in terms of two extreme positions, one in which the complete property rights reside with the landowner and the alternative position in which all the rights reside with the state (acting as our agent and as agent for future generations). In practice, the level of CCA will be determined by actions that are subject to a wide range of alternative property rights, some held by the landowner and some by the state. Currently, for example, landowners do *not* have the right to dump hazardous chemicals into watercourses and receive no compensation for the loss of this right. Landowners *do* have the right to select their own mix of capital and labour. In between come a whole range of situations – allowing soil to erode, loss of wetlands due to drainage, application of chemical fertilizers and pesticides, etc. – which are in dispute. Some move towards the alternative property rights regime would reduce the externalities and 'improve' the provision of CCA, while at the same time reducing the effect of the 'fiscal treadmill' (subsidies, grants, management agreement payments, environmentally sensitive area payments, etc.) that the modern state is currently locked into.

Conclusions

What we have shown in this chapter is that environmental protection policy can be operationalized through an **economic incentives approach** (using economic instruments such as taxes/charges), or through a **regulatory (CAC) approach**, buttressed by the precautionary principle; or through *property (resource) rights* systems. Each approach has its advantages and limitations and a combined approach has much to commend it. Since the environment should not generally be left to unfettered markets (or highly subsidized markets), regulations will be required to underpin most economic incentive and property right systems.

Further reading

D. Bromley and I. Hodge, 'Private property rights and presumptive policy entitlements: Reconsidering the premises of rural policy', *European Review of Agricultural Economics* **17**: 197–214, 1990.

R. Coase, 'The problem of social cost', *Journal of Law and Economics* **3**: 1–44, 1960.

L. B. Lave and E. H. Malès, 'At risk: The framework for regulating toxic substances', *Environmental Science and Technology* **23**: 386–91, 1989.

D. W. Pearce and R. K. Turner, *Economics of Natural Resources and the Environment*, Harvester Wheatsheaf, Hemel Hempstead, 1990.

D. W. Pearce, R. K. Turner and T. O'Riordan, 'Energy and social health: Integrating quantity and quality in energy planning', *World Energy Council Journal* (December): 76–88, 1992.

For a general review of the market incentives approach to pollution control see:

D. Helm (ed.) *Economic Policy Towards the Environment*, Blackwell, Oxford, 1991.

J. B. Opschoor and R. K. Turner (eds), *Environmental Economics and Environmental Policy Instruments: Principles and Practice*, Kluwer, Dordrecht, 1993.

D. W. Pearce, A. Markandya and E. B. Barbier, *Blueprint for a Green Economy*, Earthscan, London, 1989.

On the Polluter Pays principle see:

OECD, *Environment and Economics: A Survey of OECD Work*, OECD, Paris, 1992.

J. Pezzey, 'Market mechanisms of pollution control: Polluter pays, economic and practical aspects', in R. K. Turner (ed.), *Sustainable Environmental Management: Principles and Practice*, Belhaven Press, London, 1988.

The dynamic externality problem was first highlighted in 1976 in an article in the journal *Kyklos*, see:

D. W. Pearce, 'The limits of cost–benefit analysis as a guide to environmental policy', *Kyklos*, **29**(1): 97–112, 1976.

On the Love Canal example see:

D. R. Clay, 'Ten years of progress in the Superfund program', *Journal of the Air Waste Management Association* **41**(2): 144–7, 1991.

A. G. Levine, *Love Canal: Science, Politics and People*, Lexington Books, Massachusetts, 1982.

CHAPTER 11

Charging for the use of the environment

There is a suite of **economic incentive (EI) instruments** that can be deployed in order to encourage environmentally positive behaviour and investments. Box 11.1 illustrates the instruments, the majority of which are charges of one sort or another, currently in place in OECD countries. The incentives that such instruments provide can take the following forms:

(a) direct alteration of price or cost levels;
(b) indirect alteration of prices or costs via financial or fiscal means;
(c) market creation and market support.

Direct alteration of price and cost levels occurs when, for example, charges are levied on products (product charges) or on the processes that generate these products (emissions charges (see Chapter 12) input charges, feedstock charges), or when deposit–refund systems (see Chapter 18) are put into operation. Indirect alteration takes place when, for example, direct subsidies, soft loans or fiscal incentives (e.g. accelerated depreciation) are provided to induce environmentally clean technologies; enforcement incentives (such as non-compliance fees and performance bonds) can also be put in this category. Market creation is often done on the basis of changed legislation or regulation, e.g. emissions trading (see Chapter 13), quota auctioning as a consequence of limiting emissions or catches in a certain area, insurance schemes in response to changed liability legislation, etc. Market support occurs when public or semi-public agencies take responsibility for stabilizing prices or certain markets (e.g. for secondary materials such as recycled paper or steel), see Opschoor and Vos (1989); Opschoor and Turner (1993).

If we define EIs loosely, i.e. if we include financial and fiscal instruments that may not have had the intention of modifying the behaviour of polluters and resource users, then it is possible to produce an impressive list of EIs actually in use. Opschoor and Vos (1989) presented a review of the situation in six countries (Italy, Sweden, the United States, France, the Federal Republic of Germany, the Netherlands). These case studies yielded a total of

Box 11.1 Economic incentive instruments in OECD countries: past or current usage by country

Country	Effluent charge — Air	Effluent charge — Water	Effluent charge — Waste	Effluent charge — Noise	User charge	Product charge	Administrative charge (licensing and control)	Tax differentiation	Subsidies (including grants, soft loans and tax allowances)	Deposit-refund	Emission trading	Market intervention
Australia		×			×		×					
Belgium		×			×		×					
Canada					×							
Denmark					×		×		×		×		
Finland				×	×	×	×	×	×	×		×
France	×				×	×	×		×	×		
Fed. Rep. of Germany		×		×	×	×	×	×	×			
Italy		×			×	×	×					
Japan	×			×	×							
Netherlands		×		×	×		×	×	×	×		×
Norway					×	×	×		×	×		
Sweden				×	×	×	×	×	×	×		
Switzerland				×	×		×	×				
UK				×	×							
USA	×				×	×			×		×	

Source: Adapted from Opschoor and Vos (1989)

eighty-five EIs, or fourteen per country. Roughly 50 per cent of these were charges, only about 30 per cent were subsidies, and the remainder were other types such as deposit–refund systems and trading schemes. Among the more successful EIs are the Dutch water pollution charge, some US experiences in emissions trading, and some deposit–refund schemes in Sweden.

The choice of instrument (or package of instruments) depends upon many pragmatic considerations (not just economic efficiency) that are often overlooked by many policy analysts. It is important that, as well as being efficient, the instruments package is equitable, administratively feasible, dependable and provides dynamic and continuing incentives for improvement (see Box 11.2). Usually a mixed approach is necessary, with each instrument focused on one part of the environmental protection problem.

Clearly the complete list of criteria in Box 11.2 represents the ideal situation and the challenge is to design pollution control and resource management programmes that can meet as many of these criteria as possible. So some degree of trade-off is inevitable since some of the criteria conflict with each other. Box 11.3 illustrates that, on the basis of a simplified criteria list, no one general approach is rated well by all five aggregated criteria. We will now take a closer look at the individual economic instruments with the selection criteria in mind.

Box 11.2   Selection criteria for policy instruments

- Economic efficiency
- Low information requirements – minimal amounts of accurate information are required and the costs of updating it should not be prohibitive
- Administrative cost – complex, highly technical schemes requiring large amounts of information run a high risk of failure or very limited effectiveness
- Equity – heavily regressive schemes are to be avoided
- Dependability – environmental effectiveness of the scheme should be as reliable as possible given the inevitable uncertainties
- Adaptability – the system should have the capability to adapt to changing technology, prices and climatic conditions
- Dynamic incentive – the system continues to encourage environmental improvement, and technical innovation; beyond policy targets if this is feasible
- Political acceptability – does not represent too radical a departure from prevailing and likely future practices and underlying philosophies

Source: Adapted from Young (1992)

Box 11.3 Comparative evaluation of different decision frameworks

Regulatory approach		Economic efficiency	Equity	Administrative simplicity	Acceptability	Risk reduction
No risk (bans) zero emissions	PP	very low	very high	high	very high	very high
Risk-based (regulations)		low	high	high	high	high
Technology-based (standards)		very low	low	very high	high	high
Risk–benefit analysis	CBA	high	low	low	low	low
Cost–benefit analysis (augmented by economic incentives)		very high	low	low	low	low

Note: PP = precautionary principle; CBA = cost–benefit approach.
Source: Adapted from Lave and Malès (1989)

Charges

These instruments represent a straightforward way to price the use of the environment.

Emission charges

These are charges on the discharge of pollutants into air, water or on the soil and on the generation of noise. They are related to the quantity and quality of the pollutant and the damage costs inflicted on the environment (see Box 11.4).

User charges

User charges have a revenue-raising function and are related to treatment cost, collection and disposal cost, or the recovery of administrative costs depending on the situation in which they are applied. They are not directly related to damage costs in the environment.

Box 11.4 Pollution charges: emission charges

Basic aims and advantages	Best practice conditions	Environmental media relevance	Limitations
• Savings in compliance costs • Dynamic incentive effect • Revenue raising potential • Flexible system	• Stationary point-pollution • Variable marginal abatement costs between polluters • Monitoring of emissions is practicable • Potential for polluters to reduce emission and change behaviour • Potential for technical innovation	• Water – good prospects, e.g. surface water charges in France, Germany and Netherlands • Air – medium, monitoring problems, e.g. NO_x charges in Sweden • Waste – low • Noise – high for aircraft, low for other vehicles, e.g. aircraft noise charges in Netherlands and Switzerland	• Limit on number of pollutants that can be covered • Distribution effects • When revenue raised is earmarked, a coherent allocation system is required

Source: Adapted from OECD (1991)

Product charges

These are levied on products that are harmful to the environment when used in production processes, or when consumed or disposed of. The charge rate is related to the relevant environmental damage costs linked to the target product (see Box 11.5).

Marketable permits

These are environmental quotas, allowances or ceilings on pollution levels. Initial allocation of the permits is related to some ambient environmental target, but thereafter permits may be traded subject to a set of prescribed rules (see Box 11.6).

Box 11.5   Product charges

Basic aims and advantages	Best practice conditions	Environmental media relevance	Limitations
• Reduce use of products and/or stimulate product substitution • Incentive effect • Revenue raising • Flexibility • Potentially applicable to diffuse (non-point) and mobile pollution sources	• Products used in large quantities or volumes • Identifiable products • Price elastic demand for selected product • Substitution possibilities • Adapt to existing administrative and fiscal systems	• Water – medium prospects, e.g. charges on fertilizers and pesticides in Norway and Sweden, charges on lubricant oils in Finland and Germany • Air – high, especially for fuels, e.g. charges on sulphur content of fuels in France; charges on motor-vehicle fuels in Finland and Sweden; differential taxes on leaded and unleaded petrol (France, Germany, Norway, UK, etc.) • Waste – high, e.g. charges on non-returnable beverage containers in Finland, on plastic bags in Italy • Noise – medium, e.g. motor vehicle noise – no practical systems as yet	• Not applicable to hazardous waste (ban is preferable) • Low elasticities and substitution possibilities seriously inhibit the effectiveness of the instrument • Trade and competitiveness implications • Potential administration constraints

Source: Adapted from OECD (1991)

Box 11.6 Marketable permits

Basic aims and advantages	Best practice conditions	Environmental media relevance	Limitations
• Savings in compliance cost • Can encompass effect of economic growth • Flexibility • International pollution abatement	• Differences in marginal compliance costs • Maximum ambient pollutant concentrations are fixed • Number of polluters large enough for market to form and operate • Better applied to fixed pollution sources • Potential for technical innovation	• Water – low • Air – high, e.g. US bubbles and offset programmes (see Chapter 13) • Waste – low • Noise – low	• Limited applicability to more than one pollutant simultaneously • Pollution 'hotspots' may be exacerbated • Initial allocation of permits requires careful consideration • Administrative complexity • High transactions costs if there are many polluters • Low levels of banking and trading of permits in US systems

Source: Adapted from OECD (1991)

Deposit–refund systems

They involve a deposit paid on potentially polluting products. If products are returned to some authorized collection point after use, thus avoiding pollution, a refund is paid (see Box 11.7). **Performance and assurance bonds** are similar systems that require the payment of a performance bond or security deposit by a mining, logging or other development firm. If activities conducted by these firms do not comply with environmentally acceptable practice (land reclamation, wetland protection, etc.) then any clean-up costs or restoration costs are paid for out of the deposit/bond funds.

Box 11.7   Deposit–refund systems

Basic aims and advantages	Best practice conditions	Environmental media relevance	Limitations
• Arrange safe disposal, reuse or recycling of products • Flexibility • Rewards appropriate behaviour	• Hazardous or difficult components of the wastestream causing disposal problems • Market for recyclable materials exist • Cooperative arrangements between producers, retailers and users	• Water – low • Air – medium • Waste – high, e.g. car hulks Norway and Sweden; beverage containers in many countries • Noise – not applicable	• Set-up costs, distribution and refilling costs • Possible trade implications

Source: Adapted from OECD (1991)

Conclusions

A review of experience with EIs in OECD countries showed that theory and practice diverged quite significantly (Opschoor and Vos, 1989). Thus, although charges constituted the most commonly used EI, their application was, by and large, suboptimal. They tended to be fixed at too low a rate to achieve the environmental objectives the administrators had in mind. They therefore failed to provide a sufficient incentive effect and served merely to raise revenue. Some countries then recycled these funds back to polluters for investment in pollution control technologies. Other countries allocated the revenue to the financing of environmentally related public goods or services such as collective treatment facilities.

EIs are rarely operated in isolation (deposit–refunds are an example of this practice) and combinations of an EI and direct regulation are quite common. We concluded in Chapter 10 that in future greater thought needs to be given to combined approaches – EIs plus regulations plus resource rights systems. In the next two chapters we take a more detailed look at pollution taxes/charges and marketable permit systems.

Further reading

L. B. Lave and E. H. Malès, 'At risk: The framework for regulating toxic substances', *Environmental Science and Technology* **23**: 386–91, 1989.

OECD, *Environmental Policy: How to Apply Economic Instruments*, OECD, Paris, 1991.

J. B. Opschoor and J. Vos, *Economic Instruments for Environmental Protection*, OECD, Paris, 1989.

J. B. Opschoor and R. K. Turner (eds), *Environmental Economic and Policy Instruments: Principles and Practice*, Kluwer, Dordrecht, 1993.

M. D. Young, *Sustainable Investment and Resource Use*, UNESCO, Parthenon, Carnforth, 1992.

CHAPTER 12

Green taxes

In this chapter we will examine the arguments for and against the imposition of a pollution tax, that is a tax levied on firms discharging/emitting waste and calibrated according to the damage which that firm's pollution causes in the environment.

An optimal pollution tax

The idea of a pollution tax was first put forward by the British economist Pigou, in 1920, who suggested that polluters should face a tax based upon the estimated damage caused by their pollution emissions. Because of this, such charges are known as **'Pigovian' taxes**. To see how a Pigovian tax should be set we again consider the case of a paper mill producing boxes of paper and emitting pollution in the form of chlorinated water, see Box 12.1.

One method of achieving such a reduction in output (and so in pollution emissions) to the social optimum level Q_s is for the government to impose a tax just equal to the damage cost of pollution (MEC) at Q_s. Such a Pigovian tax is shown by the line t^*t^* in Box 12.1. Now, on each unit of pollution which the firm produces it must pay the tax t^* to the government. As the MEC equals the MNPB at Q_s then, if the firm produces any output in excess of Q_s, the amount of money it makes on those extra boxes of paper (given by MNPB) is less than the tax it must pay on those units (t^*). Using this approach, the firm therefore has a strong economic incentive to reduce output to Q_s and so reduce pollution to the optimal pollution level W_s.

The ideal 'Pigovian' tax, on efficiency grounds, must exactly reflect the costs of pollution of the margin. However, it is often impractical to tax the pollution precisely and therefore a number of proxy solutions are often adopted. But because charges or other market-based instruments such as permits equalize the level of marginal pollution abatement costs among firms, they provide the right incentive for the most cost-effective total investment in

Box 12.1 The optimal (Pigovian) pollution tax

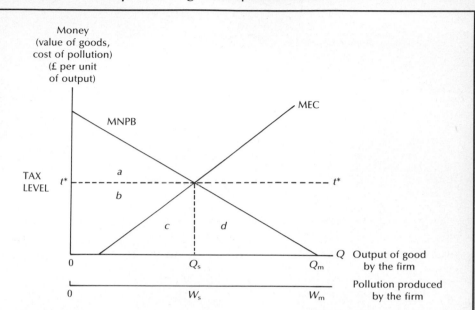

The firm maximizes profit by producing all units of output which have MNPB > 0, i.e. by expanding output to Q_m. However, the social optimum is achieved by stopping production of all units where MEC > MNPB, i.e. by restricting output to Q_s. Imposing tax level t^* upon the firm causes it to stop producing all units where t^* > MNPB, i.e. the firm restricts output to Q_s, the socially optimum level of output. This, in turn, reduces pollution emissions from W_m to W_s.

Source: Pearce and Turner (1990)

pollution clean-up. So compared to standards set without taxes, charges will tend to be a lower cost method of achieving a given standard – see Box 12.2.

Pollution taxes have a number of advantages when compared to the United Kingdom's traditional regulatory approach of setting quantity-based pollution emission standards accompanied by financial penalties (fines) for non-compliance with those standards. These advantages are illustrated in Box 12.3. The setting of a standard is usually made without reference to the value of the goods produced (the MNPB curve). Because of this, the standard will only by coincidence be set at the optimal pollution level W_s. If the fixed pollution standard is set above W_s then the paper mill will still have the chance to produce boxes of paper which have a value (MNPB) less than the

Box 12.2 Taxes versus uniform standards setting

Taxes versus uniform standard setting.

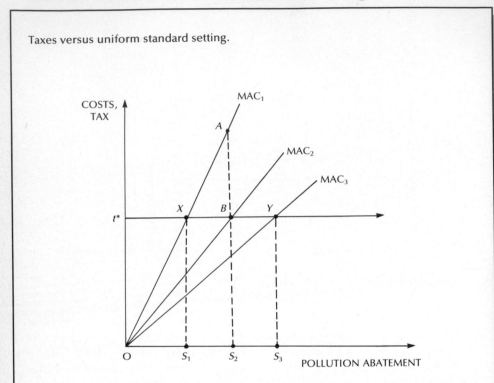

Three polluting firms are being regulated in order to achieve an overall standard equivalent to S_2 of pollution abatement. The government could, for example, either set a standard such that each firm is made to abate pollution by an amount $0S_2$, or it could set a tax t^*, so that firm 1 goes to point X, firm 2 to point B and firm 3 to point Y on their respective marginal abatement cost curves. Total costs of abatement will be higher under the standard-setting solution than the tax solution.

Under standard setting
total abatement costs $= TAC_{st} = 0AS_2 + 0BS_2 + 0CS_2$
Under the tax

$$TAC_{tax} = 0XS_1 + 0BS_2 + 0YS_3$$
$$TAC_{st} - TAC_{tax} = S_1XAS_2 - S_2CYS_3$$
but $S_1XAS_2 > S_2CYS_3$
so $TAC_{st} > TAC_{tax}$

Source: Adapted from Pearce and Turner (1990)

Box 12.3 Comparing pollution taxes with fixed emissions standards and associated fines

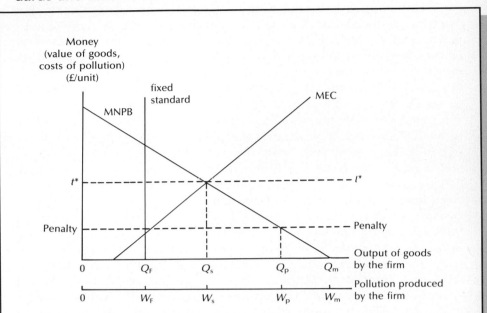

Imposing a fixed pollution emissions standard at Q_F should reduce pollution to W_F. However, if contravention of this standard only incurs a relatively low fine (broken line marked 'penalty') then firms may only cut back on those units of production where penalty > MNPB, i.e. reducing output from Q_m to Q_p (reducing emissions from W_m to W_p). The penalty would have to be raised to the level of the tax t^* in the figure before output and emissions were reduced to their socially optimal levels.

Source: Pearce and Turner (1990)

external costs which they force upon society, i.e. too much output and pollution is allowed.

However, in Box 12.3 we illustrate a case where the fixed standard for emissions (W_F) is set below the optimal pollution level (W_s). If the paper mill consequently reduces output of paper to Q_F, eliminating units of output between Q_F and Q_s with a value greater than their pollution costs, this again is a loss to society. However, now suppose that the government fixes a penalty for exceeding the standard set and that this is at a low level (a common feature in the UK regulatory practice, and shown in Box 12.3 by the dashed horizontal line marked 'penalty'). On all the units up to Q_p the firm would make a marginal profit in excess of this penalty level. So, whereas in Box 12.1 the tax t^* gives the firm a strong economic incentive to reduce output from the agreed market level Q_m to the optimal level Q_s (and reduces pollution to the optimal level W_s) in Box 12.3 the standard (or rather the penalty attached to non-compliance) only gives the comparatively weak incentive to reduce output from Q_m to Q_p (reducing pollution level from W_m to W_p). On all the units from Q_F to Q_p the firm makes more money than the cost of the fine and so it pays the fine rather than reducing its output.

A number of other advantages can be claimed for pollution taxes over the current UK approach of quantitative emissions standards backed by relatively low fines. First, as pollution taxes would be administered via the government's existing tax framework there is a lower risk of evasion compared to that for fixed emissions standards which are policed via irregular on-site inspections. Second, once a pollution standard has been set a firm has no incentive to reduce emissions below this level. This is not true of pollution taxes which always provide an incentive for further reductions in emissions, as reducing the amount of emissions means a reduction in the amount of tax which the firm is liable to pay. This, in turn, leads to a third advantage; that taxes give firms an incentive to commit funds towards research and development on new pollution abatement technology or lower pollution production methods. Fourth, taxes upon existing pollutants may reduce emission of associated pollutants, for example, a tax upon carbon emissions from burning fossil fuels may induce producers to switch to non-fossil fuelling and so reduce emissions of say sulphur dioxide which is also associated with fossil fuels. Recent research estimates that a 20 per cent reduction in carbon emissions would be synonymous with a 21 per cent reduction in SO_2 and a 14 per cent fall in NO_x emissions (Bye *et al.*, 1989).

Problems with setting the tax

While pollution taxes appear in theory to possess several attractive attributes, setting an optimal Pigovian tax in practice is difficult, perhaps most fundamentally because of the uncertainty surrounding the actual damage costs associated with any particular pollutant. Definition of the MEC is a vital precursor to the setting of a Pigovian tax. However, this requires data on and scientific and economic understanding of six separate factors (Pearce and Turner, 1990):

1. The firm's output of goods
2. The pollution 'dose' which this output produces
3. Any long-term accumulation of pollution
4. Human exposure to this pollution

5. The damage 'response' of this exposure
6. The monetary evaluation of the cost of pollution damage

Analysis of this 'dose–response' relationship will clearly be complex and is likely to lead to disputes between interested parties (industrialists, environmental protection groups, etc.). However, a further complication is added by the fact that, in order to evaluate an optimal Pigovian tax we also need to know the benefit value of the good being produced, i.e. ideally we also need to know the MNPB line so that we can find its intersection with the MEC. This again is likely to lead to conflict between interest groups.

In reality then, accurate calculation of an optimal pollution tax level is likely to be an unrealistic goal. The best that we can hope for is to determine an acceptable compromise in the face of imperfect information. What may be more feasible is to calculate the relative magnitudes between a tax on one pollutant and a tax on a second by comparing the levels of damage which each causes. A prime example of this can be found be examining proposals for a carbon tax – that is, a tax upon fuels which, when combusted, release carbon dioxide into the atmosphere thereby exacerbating the 'greenhouse' effect. Burning coal is a major cause of such pollution because it contains a high proportion of carbon. Natural gas on the other hand contains only 60 per cent as much carbon per unit of heat energy as does coal. Therefore, any carbon tax should not be uniform over all fuels but would be lower for low carbon fuels, such as natural gas, and higher for high carbon fuels such as coal. However, this does not solve the fundamental problem of setting the absolute tax level from which these relative taxes can be calculated. Many researchers are examining the fundamental problem of evaluating the damage caused by carbon emissions but, to date, however, no consensus has been reached and a very wide range of numbers have so far been suggested for the appropriate carbon tax rate (Barrett, 1991).

We now turn to consider one of the most controversial questions surrounding the use of pollution taxes: who really pays for them and should they?

Who pays – and should they?

Pigovian taxes are one instrument for achieving the 'Polluter Pays Principle' (PPP), the principle that those who generate pollution (producers and/or consumers) should be the ones liable to pay the damage costs (rather than as now, with society paying most of these damage costs). Returning to Box 12.1 we can see how a pollution tax affects the polluting firm. Before the imposition of the tax the firm received marginal profits (shown by MNPB) on all the units produced up to output Q_m. This profit is equal to areas $a + b + c + d$, i.e. the entire area under the MNPB curve. However, with the imposition of pollution tax t^* the firm reduces its output from Q_m to Q_s, thereby losing marginal profit area d due to lower output and losing areas

$b+c$ in pollution taxes paid to the Government, thus reducing remaining profits to just the area a. Although the shapes of the lines in the upper panel are purely illustrative, this loss of profits may well be considerable and, remembering our discussion in the Box 12.3, likely to exceed that under a fixed emissions standards regime. Some commentators claim that this difference in profits has led industry to put pressure on governments to retain an emission standards regime rather than adopting a pollution tax approach (Buchanan and Tullock, 1975; Theeuwes, 1991).

Forcing a polluting firm to pay for its pollution damages seems to be an equitable idea. However, notice that output Q_s is synonymous with the sustainable optimal pollution level W_s, yet the firm is still being forced to pay tax upon all the units produced up to this level; is this right? Because W_s is sustainable then, at the end of any period, the environment can safely assimilate all of the pollution produced in that period. No net cost is therefore being placed upon society, so why should the firm pay tax even on this pollution? The tax represented by areas $b+c$ therefore appears to be inequitable, we would prefer a different instrument which forced the firm to

Box 12.4   Who pays for a pollution tax?

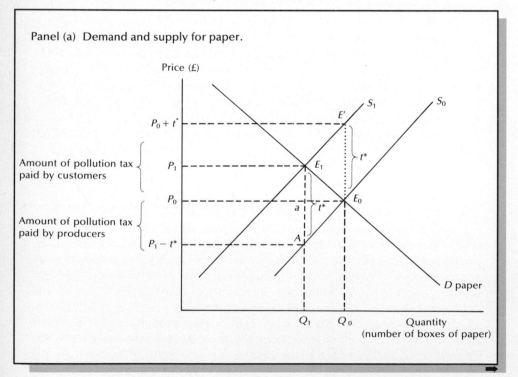

Panel (a) Demand and supply for paper.

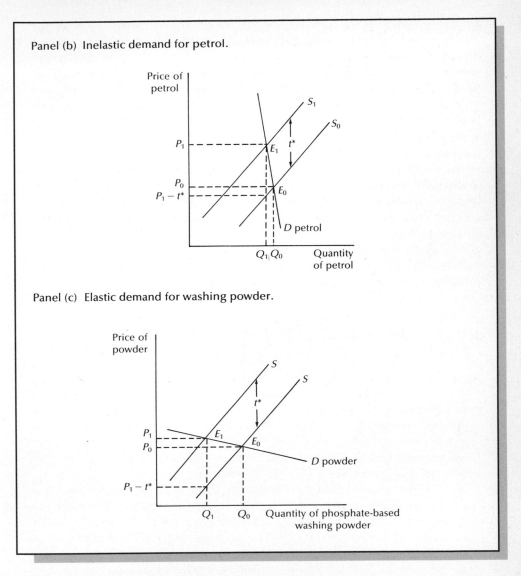

Panel (b) Inelastic demand for petrol.

Panel (c) Elastic demand for washing powder.

restrict pollution to W_s without this extra charge. This uncertainty about the justice of Pigovian taxes has been cited as one reason why policy-makers have generally not implemented them (Pezzey, 1988). However, most of the concern about pollution taxes has, in the main, been focused upon their impact upon consumers, which we now consider.

Panel (a) of Box 12.4 shows the supply and demand curves for the paper produced by our hypothetical paper mill. Before the imposition of a pollution tax, the paper mill has the supply curve S_0. This only intersects with the demand curve D at the equilibrium point E_0, i.e. only at this point is the price level (P_0) such that the amount of paper which people wish to buy is just equal to the amount which the firm wishes to sell (Q_0).

Now suppose that the firm is forced to pay a pollution tax t^* on each box of paper which it produces and sells. This tax raises the firm's costs of producing paper by the amount t^*, i.e. it will only supply the same quantity Q_0 if it receives a new higher price which is equal to the old price P_0 plus the tax t^*. The supply curve shifts to S_1 where the supply quantity Q_0 corresponds to price $P_0 + t^*$, i.e. the new supply curve S_1 is the vertical distance t^* above the old supply curve S_0.

The firm's first reaction is likely to be to try and maintain its existing output and profits by attempting to pass on this tax to consumers in the form of higher prices, i.e. to try to raise the price from P_0 to $P_0 + t^*$ while still supplying the same quantity Q_0 (moving from point E_0 to point E'). However, as the demand curve shows, as the firm raises prices so people buy less paper. If the firm increased prices by the full amount of the tax to $P_0 + t^*$, then this would cause a very dramatic decrease in the amount people would buy. Once the tax has forced the firm to move to supply curve S_1, then the only equilibrium point where supply equals demand is that of E_1 where price is P_1 and consequently quantity produced and sold falls from Q_0 to Q_1.

What implications do these changes have for consumers (those who buy paper) and producers (those who make it)? Consider the producers first; although the price of their product has risen (P_0 to P_1) they now have to pay the tax t^* on each unit sold, therefore they actually only receive the price $P_1 - t^*$. This is below the original price P_0, therefore, in effect they experience a fall in the marginal revenue they receive from each box of paper equal to the difference between P_0 and $P_1 - t^*$. This difference represents the portion of the pollution tax t^* which producers pay on each unit sold. Furthermore, the increase in shop price (P_0 to P_1) has reduced sales from Q_0 to Q_1 so that producers also lose earnings because of lower sales.

Because the imposition of a pollution tax leads to an increase in the price paid by consumers from P_0 to P_1, consumers pay the portion $P_1 - P_0$ of the pollution tax t^*. This price increase also leads to a fall in the amount which consumers buy (from Q_0 to Q_1). The increase in price and decrease in consumption causes a welfare loss to consumers, although this loss is less than the damage cost of pollution which is avoided by introducing the tax, i.e. there is a net welfare gain to consumers from introducing the pollution tax (see Box 12.1).

For any tax, the proportion paid by the consumer compared to that paid by the producer will depend upon the shape of the demand and supply curves for the good in question. In Panel (a) of Box 12.4, these consumer/producer proportions are roughly equal. However, consider Panel (b) which illustrates an example of a pollution tax imposed upon petrol purchases. Here the supply curves are drawn as before but the demand curve is much steeper, so that even if prices rise sharply consumers are only prepared to slightly reduce their consumption of petrol (this is known as an inelastic demand curve and arises here because consumers generally do not have any substitute transport fuel other than petrol into which they can switch their purchases when petrol prices rise). Suppose that a carbon tax (t^*) was put on petrol, shifting supply from S_0 to S_1. Here the price the consumer pays rises sharply from P_0 to P_1 while the amount received by petrol producers only falls slightly from P_0 down to $P_1 - t^*$. So, in a case of inelastic demand, consumers are likely to pay the majority of any pollution tax.

Now consider Panel (c) which illustrates the case of phosphate-based washing powder. Suppose that a pollution tax was placed upon those washing powders which contained phosphates. Because there are many different washing powders consumers can switch to buying non-phosphate brands which still perform the same function of cleaning clothes (this 'substitution' option was not so available in the case of petrol as consumers had no alternative fuel and are unwilling to radically change their driving patterns). The availability of alternatives produces a relatively flat demand curve showing that if price increases consumers drastically cut back on their purchases of phosphate-based washing powder (and increase purchases of untaxed phosphate-free brands). In such a case then, with the imposition of a phosphate pollution tax (t^*), manufacturers of those affected brands have little ability to push this tax off onto consumers as higher shop prices (P_1 is only slightly above P_0) and have to pay the majority of the tax themselves. Therefore, the price received by producers falls from P_0 to $P_1 - t^*$.

Panels (a), (b) and (c) use identical supply curves throughout, showing the effect of varied demand curves. However, similar changes in the *incidence* of a pollution tax (who pays for it) can be derived by varying the slope of the supply curves (the interested reader can verify this by holding the demand curve constant and varying the slope of the supply curves).

We have already considered the fairness of forcing producers to pay a pollution tax, but is it fair that consumers should often be forced to pay higher prices as a result of imposing such a tax? In principle the answer must be 'yes'. To oversimplify somewhat, producers only produce those goods which are demanded by consumers. Therefore consumers can be seen to be at least partly responsible for any pollution which such production creates. One of the major advantages of a pollution tax is that it sends correct signals to both consumer and producer. By lowering producer profits and raising consumer prices, the tax shows both groups the cost of the pollution damage caused by these products and encourages them to switch towards production and consumption of products with lower pollution profiles.

However, critics have argued that the effect of higher consumer prices will be to punish the poor proportionately more than the rich. Such taxes are called **distributionally regressive** as the rich will be able to pay for the price rises they induce with comparative ease compared to the poor. Box 12.5 shows how the introduction of hypothetical 15 per cent value added tax

Box 12.5 The regressive effects of a carbon tax[a]

(1) Decile (10% group) of gross income	(2) Change in fuel consumption (%)	(3) Change in tax paid per week (£)[b]	(4) Change in tax paid as a % of total spending
Poorest	−9.6	1.08	1.8
2	−9.5	1.36	1.5
3	−8.3	1.41	1.2
4	−6.8	1.49	0.9
5	−4.8	1.49	0.7
6	−4.1	1.44	0.7
7	−3.4	1.57	0.6
8	−1.9	1.59	0.5
9	−0.1	1.69	0.5
Richest	+1.1	2.05	0.4
Average	−4.1	1.52	0.7

[a]The tax assumed is a 15% value added tax (VAT) on domestic fuel, the effects shown are for income groups ranging from the lowest 10% to the highest 10% of the population.
[b]This assumes that all consequent adjustments to the imposition of the tax have been fully made by consumers, e.g. reordering of spending priorities.
Source: Johnson *et al.* (1990); reprinted in Pearce (1991).

(VAT) on domestic fuel (imposed to cut down on emissions of 'greenhouse gases' such as carbon dioxide) would impact most severely on the poorest members of society. Column (1) divides the UK population up into ten equal groups ranked from the lowest 10 per cent to the highest 10 per cent income group. Column (2) shows the percentage by which each income group changes its consumption of fuel when the pollution tax is imposed. As expected, the poorer the income group the more it reduces consumption of fuel; this in itself is regressive as poorer homes are already those most likely to be underheated. Column (3) shows by how much an average family in each income group will increase its spending per week on fuel as a result of the pollution tax. Because poor homes already consume less fuel than rich homes, then it is the poorer income groups who pay less extra tax. However, when we take account of the lower incomes of these groups, we see from column (4) that poorer households will be paying a higher proportion of their total spending on the tax (1.8 per cent) than do rich households (0.4 per cent).

This provides significant evidence that pollution taxes are **potentially regressive**, hurting the financially weakest members of society.

While pollution taxes have the potential to be distributionally unfair, there is good reason to believe that this problem can be overcome. This is because the money raised through imposing the tax is not lost but flows instead to the government. Returning to Panel (a) of Box 12.4 we can see that the government receives a total tax income equal to the tax per unit (t^*) multiplied by the number of units produced and sold after imposition of the tax (Q_1). The government can in turn compensate for the unwanted regressive aspects of taxes by giving money back to those worst affected. Such a redistribution to consumers could either be in the form of increased tax-free income allowances or through lowering taxes on other basic commodities (both of which will be of proportionally greater help to the poor than the rich).

A recent UK study (Barker and Lewney, 1990) showed that the revenue gained by imposing a tax on fuel emissions could help pay for a substantial cut in the current rate of VAT. This sort of tax redistribution could also be applied to firms hit by the impacts of pollution taxes, for example, the government could use the funds raised to pay for grants towards the installation of low pollution technology or alternatively it could afford to lower the current rate of corporation tax, a popular move which would give a general boost to UK firms.

Through redistribution of tax funds, a pollution tax can therefore be made **fiscally neutral**, that is, have no net impact upon tax revenues, while still encouraging both consumers and producers to move towards low pollution profile goods. A pollution tax also has the added bonus that, whereas most taxes (e.g. income taxes, investment taxes, etc.) distort the economy by discouraging acts which are essentially 'good' (i.e. earning, investing, etc.), a pollution tax attempts to correct a market failure by stopping something which is essentially 'bad', i.e. pollution.

The power of a pollution tax

How effective is a pollution tax likely to be in reducing emission levels or rather, how high will the tax have to be set before it becomes effective? The answer to this question depends, as we have already shown from Box 12.4, upon the relative shapes ('elasticities') of the relevant demand and supply curves. If demand for the product is highly elastic (responsive) to price and consumers can easily move towards purchasing adequate substitutes then imposition of a pollution tax is likely to be effective. Examples of such cases might include domestic cleaning fluids which contain zinc and thereby cause contamination of waste water. Because there are many non-zinc cleaning products available if a pollution tax increased prices of polluting brands, consumers are likely to move to buying non-polluting alternatives.

The effectiveness of a pollution tax is likely to be much lower where the demand is inelastic (unresponsive) to price changes and/or there are few suitable substitutes available. Up to ten years ago the previously quoted example of petrol would have been appropriate here. However, new technology and the introduction of new products, such as unleaded petrol, gives the opportunity for pollution taxes to work in this case (Opschoor, 1991). But in the absence of available substitutes, the power of a tax to reduce pollution can be limited by consumers' willingness to carry on purchasing high quantities of the relevant goods even in the face of higher prices. Carbon taxes upon fuel are likely to face such problems and Barrett (1991) concludes his summary by stating that 'to lower CO_2 emissions very substantially would require a large carbon tax – larger, certainly, than the taxes already implemented, or for which there exist firm proposals'.

International problems

Before concluding we need to highlight what is perceived by critics to be one of the major weaknesses in the implementation of pollution taxes, their implications for any single nation, unilaterally imposing such taxes upon its own economy. If one country imposes a pollution tax on its own industries then they will be put at a disadvantage compared to foreign competitors so that domestically produced goods may become less attractive to consumers relative to imports. This means, for example, that a carbon tax 'is likely to be introduced on a significant scale only if it is introduced by a number of countries acting together' (Pearce, 1991).

Such concerted action will require some form of international agreement or treaty. However, here again there are problems. First, it will always be in the interest of any one country to see all other countries, except itself, sign such an agreement. In this way, it benefits from their reductions in global emissions without itself having to suffer increased production costs, thereby gaining a competitive advantage over all foreign countries whose firms now have to pay the pollution tax. This 'free-rider' effect is a very strong incentive against such agreements. A second problem is that, even if such an agreement could in principle be reached, in practice this treaty would be unusual in that, to ensure equity, instead of all countries abiding by a common rule, the rule for each country should be different. This is because each country creates a different amount of damage based upon the size and technology of its economy. Furthermore, because of the differences in the levels of technology between countries, each country would also face a different pollution abatement cost in the process of achieving its specific pollution reduction goals. There would therefore be extreme difficulty in getting all countries to agree on one common level of pollution tax per unit of emissions.

A further international complication arises due to those countries which inevitably do not sign any such international pollution tax treaty. Suppose that we consider again a carbon tax placed upon fuel prices. If a carbon tax treaty were signed then this would have the effect of reducing fuel demand in signatory nations. This depressed world fuel demand would lead the oil exporting nations to lower their prices in an effort to protect their falling profits. However, this falling fuel price would have two effects; first, it would offset some of the effects of the tax in signatory nations so that the slump in demand would be somewhat countered; second, it would be taken advantage of by non-signatory nations who would expand their demand for this cheaper fuel. The net impacts of such a carbon tax treaty, in terms of emissions reductions, could therefore be significantly smaller than we might initially expect (Barrett, 1991).

Conclusions

In theory, pollution taxes provide an important route for internalizing the external pollution damage costs caused by companies and restricting their pollution emissions to a sustainable optimal level. They also have several desirable side-effects in that they can also send signals to consumers regarding the pollution consequences of their purchases. Furthermore, the regressive impacts of these taxes upon the poorer sections of society can be adequately compensated for by a system of tax redistribution. Because of these factors, taxes deserve consideration as an economic incentive tool for the reduction of pollution. However, in practice there are some formidable problems to be addressed. The accurate determination of an appropriate pollution tax level is dependent upon accurate information regarding the damage costs of that pollution and the benefits of its associated production of goods. Furthermore, in order that pollution taxes can be adopted on any significant scale, a previously unknown level of international agreement is likely to be necessary. The feasibility of such agreement remains uncertain.

Further reading

T. Barker and R. Lewney, 'Macroeconomic modelling of environmental policies: The carbon tax and regulation of water quality', Department of Applied Economics, University of Cambridge, 1990; mimeo referenced in Barrett (1991).

S. Barrett, 'Global warming: Economics of a carbon tax', in D. W. Pearce (ed.), *Blueprint 2: Greening the World Economy*, Earthscan, London, 1991.

J. M. Buchanan and G. Tullock, 'Polluters profits and political response: Direct control versus taxes', *American Economic Review* **65**: 130–47, 1975.

B. Bye, T. Bye and L. Lorentsen, 'SIMEN: Studies of industry, environment and energy towards 2000', Discussion Paper No. 44, Central Bureau of Statistics, Oslo, 1989.

P. Johnson, S. McKay and S. Smith, *The Distributional Consequences of Environmental Taxes*, Institute of Fiscal Studies, London, 1990.

J. B. Opschoor, 'Economic instruments for controlling PMPs', in J. B. Opschoor and D. W. Pearce (eds), *Persistent Pollutants: Economics and Policy*, Kluwer Academic Publishers, Dordrecht, 1991.

D. W. Pearce (ed.), *Blueprint 2: Greening the World Economy*, Earthscan, London, 1991, Introduction.

D. W. Pearce and R. K. Turner, *Economics of Natural Resources and the Environment*, Harvester Wheatsheaf, Hemel Hempstead, 1990.

J. Pezzey, 'Market mechanisms of pollution control: Polluter pays, economic and practical aspects', in R. K. Turner (ed.), *Sustainable Environmental Management: Principles and Practices*, Belhaven Press, London, 1988.

A. C. Pigou, *The Economics of Welfare*, Macmillan, London, 1920.

J. Theeuwes, 'Regulation or taxation', in D. J. Kraan and R. J. in't Veld (eds), *Environmental Protection: Public or Private Choice*, Kluwer Academic Publishers, Dordrecht, 1991.

CHAPTER 13

Trading environmental permits

Introduction

Tradeable, or 'marketable', permits are instances of **market-based instruments** for the control of environmental pollution and the conservation of natural resources. As Chapter 10 showed, a market-based instrument (MBI) approach to environmental policy makes *use* of the market-place, by modifying market signals in order to induce environmentally more friendly behaviour. The MBI approach regards traditional forms of regulation, based on 'command-and-control', as unnecessarily bureaucratic and inefficient.

The basic idea underlying tradeable permits is simple. First, an acceptable level of pollution is determined. This may be expressed as some allowable concentration of, say, lead in gasoline, a production or consumption target for chemicals (e.g. CFCs), or an allowable national emission level as is likely with carbon dioxide some time in the future. Permits are then issued for the level of emissions, etc., up to the allowable level. If, say, 100 units of pollution is allowable, 100 permits each with a value of 1 unit of emission might be issued. There are various ways of determining the initial issue of the permits. Because of the disruption that might ensue by alternative allocations, a popular initial allocation is one based on historical emission levels. This is known as **grandfathering**: rights to pollute are based on past emission levels. While this is not the only way to determine the initial allocation, the experience so far with tradeable permits shows that it is important to find an acceptable formula for this initial allocation, and that grandfathering tends to be acceptable to all parties. Clearly, grandfathering does nothing to *reduce* pollution or excessive resource use unless either (a) the initial allocation is for less pollution than already takes place (i.e. quotas are allocated pro rata to existing emissions but the overall level is less than the current total), or (b) the initial allocation is reduced over time. Any polluter achieving lower pollution than the number of permits they possess receives a *credit*. For example, polluter A has permits to emit 10 units of pollution but actually

181

emits 8. The credit of two is then tradeable. This works to the advantage of polluter A if reducing the pollution by 2 units is cheaper than the price of selling permits equal to 2 units. In technical terms, there is an incentive to *sell* permits if the (marginal) abatement costs are below the ruling price for permits, and to buy if abatement costs are above the price of permits.

Once the initial allocation is made, polluters are then free to trade the pollution rights. It is this *tradeability* that is the hallmark of the permit system since it is tradeability that accounts for the main attraction of such a system – its role in keeping down the costs of complying with regulations. Basically a firm that finds it comparatively easy to abate pollution will find it profitable to sell its permits to a polluter who finds it expensive to abate pollution. Essentially, it will sell the permit if it receives a price higher than the costs it will have to bear of abating pollution now that it has no permit. The high cost polluter, on the other hand, will find it profitable to buy permits if the price is below what it will otherwise cost to abate pollution. Both low and high cost polluter therefore stand to gain and this provides the incentive for them to trade. Moreover, by trading, the control of pollution will tend to be concentrated among those polluters who find it cheap to control pollution. Permit holding will tend to be concentrated among those who find it expensive to control pollution. Yet the overall environmental standard is safeguarded because nothing has happened to alter the overall number of permits and it is this that determines the level of pollution.

Clearly, such a description is simplistic, but it captures the essence of the tradeable permit system. One important point to note is that trade need not be between *different* polluters (external trading). It can be between different sources within a single firm (internal trading). The result is the same, however, because the firm will gain by concentrating abatement in its low cost sources and concentrating permits in the high cost sources. Box 13.1 gives a numerical example of how tradeable permits might work.

Permit trading in practice: the US experience

We would expect the actual experience of permit trading to result in no decline in environmental standards and a reduction in the costs of compliance compared to what would have been incurred in a CAC system. By and large, this is the experience of the United States where a tradeable permits system exists as part of the US Clean Air Acts of the 1970s, and which have been expanded under the new Clean Air Act of 1991.

Some terminology is needed to understand the US system. **Netting**, introduced in 1974, is a procedure whereby a firm can create a new emissions source provided it offsets the resulting emissions by reductions elsewhere in the same plant. Netting always involves *internal trading*, i.e. the firm is not allowed to acquire permits from outside. **Offsets** were introduced in 1976 in

Box 13.1   How tradeable permits work

Imagine two factories, A and B, which emit sulphur oxides into the atmosphere. Each has different costs of controlling emissions: the costs of controlling one tonne of sulphur oxides in factory A is £20 per tonne, and in factory B it is £30 per tonne. These marginal costs are shown by the height of the two blocks in the diagram. Assume that overall emissions are five tonnes from each of A and B. Now suppose the regulator uses a command and control solution and requires that A and B *each* reduce emissions by one tonne, a total reduction of two tonnes. The cost to A is £20 and the cost to B is £30, so that overall compliance costs are £50. Emissions are now ten tonnes minus the reduction – i.e. eight tonnes.

Instead of using the CAC approach, the regulator could issue permits for eight tonnes of sulphur oxides emissions. A and B are both 'equal' polluters because each emits five tonnes of pollution. The regulator therefore decides to allocate the eight tonnes allowance equally between A and B: each gets permits for four tonnes of sulphur oxides (the 'grandfathering' solution – see text). But the regulator allows trading to take place. This means that the permits will acquire a market value because they can be bought and sold. Let the resulting market price be £24 per tonne sulphur, as shown in Panel (a). A can reduce a tonne of sulphur at a cost of only £20. *It will therefore pay A to reduce emissions below the number of permits he has.* That is, although A need only reduce by 1 tonne (from 5 to 4) he gains by reducing more than this, say to 3 tonnes. This gives a *credit* of 1 tonne which can be traded with B. B will happily buy the permit because it will allow him to avoid cutting emissions at all. The end result is that A cuts by

Panel (a) Establishing the price of permits.

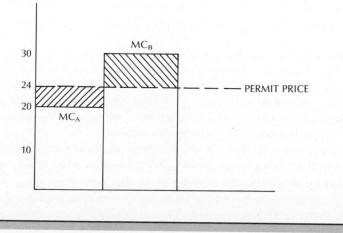

183

two tonnes and B does not cut at all. But this is what the regulator wants – an overall cut of two tonnes. So, the level of environmental quality is as good as it would be under the CAC approach.

But, interestingly, both A and B have gained through the permit trade. The relevant sums are shown in Table 1.

Table 1 The benefit of trading permits

	Factory A	Factory B
Total cost of reducing emissions by 1 tonne: no trade	20	30
Actual control costs with trade	40	0
less sale of permits	24	0
plus purchase of permits	0	24
Net costs with trade	16	24
Gain from trade	$20 - 16 = 4$	$30 - 24 = 6$

Note: Notice the gain from trade, $4 + 6 = 10$, is the difference between the marginal costs.

areas where the Clean Air Act standards had not been met ('non-attainment areas'). Stringent rules applied to new sources would have meant that such areas could attract little or no new industry. However, by offsetting the new source by even greater reductions in existing sources, these areas are allowed to acquire new industry. Such offsets can be obtained by internal *and* external trading, i.e. from buying up permits from within the same source or from other firms. **Bubbles** are perhaps the most famous part of the US tradeable permits system. They were introduced in 1979. A 'bubble' is an hypothetical aggregate limit for existing sources of pollution (whereas netting and offsets relate to new sources). Within the overall bubble limit firms are free to vary sources of pollution so long as the overall limit is not breached. Bubbles are allowed to extend beyond a single firm, but in practice bubbles have tended to be placed round single firms. **Banking** was introduced in 1979 and operates just like a bubble but through time, i.e. the firm is allowed to bank credits and use them at some stage in the future.

Box 13.2 summarizes the US experience and shows the effects on cost savings and on environmental quality. Box 13.2 reveals the following points:

1. Nearly all trading has been internal. Only the offset system has resulted in moderate external trading. While the bubble system does permit external trading, hardly any has occurred. This appears to be due to the high costs

Box 13.2 US experience with tradeable permits

	Bubbles		Offsets	Netting	Banking
	Federal	State			
Number of trades	42	89	2000	5000–12 000	<120
Cost savings	300	135	large	525–12 300	small
$US million					
Air quality				probably	probably
impact	zero	zero	zero	insignificant	insignificant
Nature of trade:					
internal	40	89	1800	5000–12 000	<100
external	2	0	200	0	<20

Source: R. Hahn and G. Hester (1989). See also R. Hahn (1987).

of acquiring information about other firms' willingness to trade, and the costs of obtaining the regulator's permission to trade.

2. The cost savings are considerable, with a minimum of $1 billion and perhaps as much as $13 billion having been saved.
3. Banking has hardly been used at all.
4. The extensive use of netting compared to bubbles, even allowing for the predominance of internal trades, is surprising since bubbles apply to existing sources whereas netting applies only to new or modified sources.

Explaining the less than hoped-for level of trading activity in the US permits system so far is not easy. Companies such as Armco, Du Pont, USX and 3M have traded permit credits, but the take-up has otherwise been quite low. Commentators have suggested five main reasons:

1. New sources are subject to far stricter regulations about emissions quality. This means that firms are keen to adopt any offsetting procedure when a new source starts up. Netting is the appropriate procedure in these cases and this does much to explain the dominance of netting in the US system. Moreover, existing sources have inherited abatement equipment, bought before the bubble policy was introduced in 1979, so that the costs of adjustment under a bubble policy are high.
2. Uncertainty about pollution credits. There has been considerable uncertainty about just what emission credits ensue under the banking legislation. Firms are not always sure how the regulator will determine baseline emissions and hence how emission credits will be determined. This uncertainty is heightened when other firms' credits are the subject of the

trade (i.e. when external trading is involved). Firm A has to be sure that firm B really will reduce emissions to create credits that can be traded. In contrast, internal trading involves far greater certainty because the firm is dealing only with itself.

3. It is more expensive to acquire information about external trading since firm A needs to find out what other firms have banked credits, and the price at which trade is likely to take place. Similar problems have arisen in other countries where attempts have been made to establish waste exchange information services.

4. Firms will not trade with other firms because of the prospect of permit prices rising. Permits will be hoarded as long as the expected price rise is greater than the cost of hoarding, i.e. greater than interest rate.

5. Hoarded permits can be used as a deterrent to new entrants.

Permit trading is the central feature of a more recent US Clean Air Act in the context of acid rain control. Regulators claim they have learned from the experience of the previous tradeable permit systems and that most of the problems should be avoidable in the new system.

Objections to tradeable permits

Objections have been raised by various 'interest groups': environmentalists, industry and government.

In the United States, environmentalists' objections have been focused on two main issues: whether environmental quality is sacrificed under a tradeable permits system, and whether it is morally right to 'permit' pollution even for a price. Box 13.2 shows that the environmental quality argument has little or no foundation. The second objection has to be countered by an educative process. All regulatory systems 'permit' pollution if by pollution is meant waste. No economic process is waste-free. The issue has therefore to be one of whether a tradeable permits system somehow permits more waste than a CAC system. As we have seen, there is no reason at all for this to be the case. It is significant that many environmental organizations in the United States now welcome tradeable permits.

The US experience suggests that certainty about the regulatory system is highly valued. With CAC systems the firm is, by and large, clear about the nature of the regulation and what is and what is not permitted. This is also true for CAC systems that are less rigid, such as the UK system in which there is considerable scope for flexible adjustments in light of dialogue with the Inspectorate of Pollution. As European Community Directives play an increasingly important role, however, we might expect more and more 'standard-setting' to replace the system of negotiation over achieving standards.

Regulators will naturally be sensitive to the concerns of both environmentalists and industry. None the less they will also have their own concerns, primarily arising from the costs of considering, formulating and implementing any departure from the established CAC approach. It is worth remembering that the CAC mode of thinking is ingrained in environmental regulation in most countries, reflecting as it does the experience of over 100 years of public health, workplace and environmental legislation. Anxiety also tends to increase the less that is known about the new system.

Regulators and industry are also likely to be concerned about the administrative costs of any regulatory system. Under a tradeable permits system, the administrative costs could be very high if there are a great many polluters. Where there are comparatively few, the costs of administration are low, but a new problem arises in that one or two polluters may corner the market in permits and refuse to trade them. This would act like a barrier to entry for new firms and the permits could therefore contribute to non-competitive behaviour.

New Zealand fishery quotas

Tradeable permits can also be used to regulate excessive resource use, as with overfishing. The New Zealand Individual Transferable Quotas Scheme (ITQ) was introduced in 1986. Australia also has an ITQ system for Southern Bluefin Tuna and proposes another for the south-east trawl fishery, and the United States has recently introduced one for the Atlantic surf clam industry. In the New Zealand system, initial quotas were grandfathered (fishermen were allowed to dispute historical catch records). Government then bought back some quotas at ruling market prices, thus reducing the total allowable catch (TAC). After that, a fixed price of 80 per cent of the first-stage price was offered to remaining fishermen. Finally, any remaining reductions needed to get to TAC were pro-rated across the remaining fishermen. Fishermen can resell quotas to other New Zealand fishermen. New entrants face minimum quota allocations. Quotas and actual catches are matched at the end of each month. Fishermen also pay a royalty to the government for the quotas, and the royalty is doubled if foreign vessels are leased for the catch. Since the catch was already monitored, the ITQ system has imposed few additional administrative burdens.

The ITQ system has worked well, despite having to face substantial changes in some TACs as better information came to light. Large outlays of government money to buy back quotas have been avoided by making some quotas a proportion of the TAC. Trade in quotas has been facilitated by a Quota Trading Exchange which has brokers who act as intermediaries. But, in fact, most trades have taken place privately, with all trades being reported to the quota managers. Some oddities have emerged. Observed prices for quotas sometimes seem well above their value in terms of permitted catch, and there has been a wide variation in the price of quotas for the same catch. Analysis suggests that these events may be expected during the transition from an 'open access' fishery to a managed regime, but that lack of information and some inherent stability in quota markets is also present. Some 'deterrent pricing' may also be occurring, whereby larger firms bid up the price of quotas to deter entry by new fishermen (a standard potential problem with tradeable permits). The other main problem has been disputes about the government's changes in the royalties charged – and this has been resolved by agreeing fixed charges for five-year periods.

The New Zealand experience suggests that:

(a) grandfathering is a politically acceptable allocation system, followed by buy-back or proportional reductions. This would be highly appropriate for any European resource-use control system;

(b) the 'royalty' charges need to be specified at the outset and maintained so as to induce certainty in expectations about the system;

(c) control is comparatively easy when an in-place monitoring system – the catch records – exist. In the pollution context there is an obvious need to monitor the pollutant itself, so that one would expect such a system to work least well when monitoring is subject to significant error.

Conclusions

Tradeable resource and pollution permits offer an innovative and challenging way of tackling many environmental problems. Because they leave the polluter with the flexibility as to how to adjust to the environmental standard, they make compliance with regulations less expensive than would be the case with CAC. They do not sacrifice environmental quality because the overall level of quality is determined by the overall number of permits, and that is set by the regulatory authority. They appear to be more acceptable to resource users and polluters, at least once they have been in operation for a while and bureaucratic control is minimized. Their potential is not limited to traditional pollutants. As we have seen, they are being experimented with fairly successfully in the control of resource overuse. They have significant potential for controlling carbon dioxide emissions as well. Indeed, it is quite widely suggested that there could be *internationally traded* carbon dioxide permits. The attraction would be that countries which find it costly to reduce CO_2 emissions would buy permits while those finding it easy to cut back emissions could sell permits. There may also be some attraction to 'over-issuing' permits to poor countries who could then sell them to richer countries. Chapter 19 looks at this issue in more detail.

Further reading

R. Hahn and G. Hester, 'Where did all the markets go? An analysis of EPA's emissions trading program', *Yale Journal of Regulation* **6** (1, Winter): 109–53, 1989.

Most of the literature on tradeable permits is fairly difficult. A useful exposition of the elementary theory and the US experience is:

T. Tietenberg, *Environmental and Natural Resource Economics*, 2nd edition, Scott Foresman & Co, Glenview, Illinois, 1988, Chapter 15.

Tradeable permits feature distinctly in:

R. Stavins (ed.), *Project 88: Harnessing Market Forces to Protect Our Environment*, a Public Policy Study sponsored by Senators Wirth and Heinz, Washington DC, December 1988

and its sequel

R. Stavins (ed.), *Project 88: Round II*, Washington DC, May, 1991.

These documents cover the US experience mainly but also touch on European initiatives in market-based instruments.

Excellent detailed analysis of US experience is provided in:

R. Hahn and G. Hester, 'Marketable permits: Lessons for theory and practice', *Ecology Law Quarterly* **16**: 361–406, 1989.

CHAPTER 14

Setting environmental standards

Efficiency, rent-seeking and regulatory capture

National governments now have wide-ranging responsibilities to protect society's health, welfare and environment from the risks posed by pollution. Despite much advice from economists (based on the analysis we have reviewed in Chapters 10 to 13) most administrators tend to prefer CAC regulatory instruments (in particular, environmental standards and/or targets) and limit the extent to which market-incentive instruments are deployed, though, as we saw in Chapter 11, such economic instruments are far from totally absent in all industrialized countries.

The economist's case is that the CAC approach is inferior in efficiency terms to an approach based on charges/taxes, etc. But there is a related question that needs to be asked – are environmental standards 'internally' efficient in their own right? To the extent that the standards-based CAC approach is successful, society benefits from the reduction or elimination of environmental damages. But society pays for these benefits as costs for goods and services escalate. So a national CAC programme may be considered efficient as long as the benefits of a better/cleaner environment have a greater value than the costs society pays to achieve them (Luken and Clark, 1991). We will take a look at the only detailed study to pose that question, in the context of US air and water pollution control policy, later in this chapter. As we shall see the results are less than encouraging for advocates of the CAC approach.

For the moment we will concentrate on why it is that administrators have favoured CAC, and what the main elements of that approach have been. According to Young (1992), the main reasons why CAC has found favour are that less information is required to introduce regulations; they can be depended upon to achieve a prespecified policy target; and they have a high degree of acceptance because of the political and administrative support they generate (refer back to Box 11.1 and check the instruments selection criteria list).

It is also possible to show why industry might favour the CAC approach. For established firms within a regulated industry, the potential benefits of what is called 'regulatory capture' are very strong. This 'capture' concept refers to the tendency for the regulator and the polluter to seek common ground and cooperation. Once captured, administrators begin to see that they need to protect existing members of an industry and, therefore, regulate it accordingly. New entrants are excluded, subsidies are offered and difficult decisions are put off until prospects 'improve'.

The tendency of existing firms to pursue protection through regulation is known as 'rent capture'. Rent-seeking behaviour (persuading governments that subsidies, etc., are essential) tends to bias investment decisions and spawns inefficiency and further extensions in regulatory capture (Young, 1992). CAC therefore provides no dynamic incentive for innovation or improvement beyond the targets set, and generally translates into inefficient resource use. Regulations whenever feasible should be augmented by economic incentive instruments.

The precautionary principle

In cases where persistent substances are being released into the environment, or cases where human health damage effects are likely, or in situations where uncertainty is great, precaution is at a premium. If the aim is to totally prevent some discharge/emission or other action, then regulation may well be more efficient, more dependable and more politically acceptable than economic instruments, though deposit–refunds can play a specialized role in this context (see Chapter 11).

But sometimes the regulations take the form of a *safe minimum standard* (SMS) (see Chapter 4) and risk–benefit analysis and trade-offs will be required. SMSs can be augmented by pollution charges/taxes and in particular by tradeable permits (offsets). Recall that the latter instrument is based on some aggregate emission quota which should be related to the SMS.

Accepting that there may be much uncertainty, it is still reasonable to argue that when it is suspected that the intensity of resource use (e.g. polluting behaviour) is close to breaching an ecological threshold (in this case, the waste assimilative capacity of the receptor media, air, land or water), a regulation is probably more dependable than a tax. Further, in the long run, regulations are much more likely to ensure that resource use remains within constraints necessary to ensure sustainability.

In Box 14.1 we illustrate a possible range of definitions of the *precautionary principle*. It is based on three fundamental principles:

1. When scientific evidence is incomplete, it is prudent to act in advance of certainty on the grounds that it is better to be roughly right in due time, bearing in mind the consequences of being wrong, than to be precisely right too late.

Box 14.1 Elements of the regulatory approach to pollution control

Panel (a) The precautionary principle.

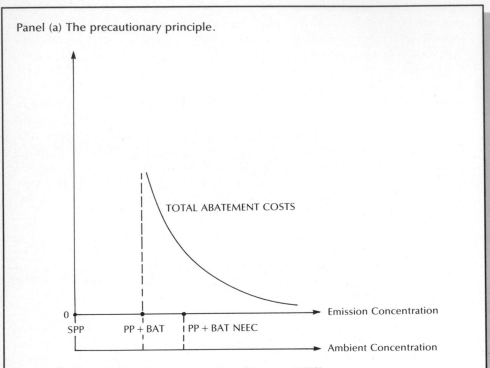

Source: Adapted from Ramchandani and Pearce (1992).

Panel (a) illustrates a range of definitions of the precautionary principle. At the extreme is what can be called the 'strict' Precautionary Principle (SPP). The assumption behind the enforcement of such a standard would be that the future effects of current discharges/emissions are unknown, but may in the future impose significant damage cost burdens. The implication of this approach is that all potentially hazardous releases are considered an unacceptable risk to the future safety of the environment. SPP is therefore a zero-release goal. In reality, however, zero emission is practically impossible due to technological limitations, or impracticable because of excessive costs. The Precautionary Principle emission standard is based on the emission/discharge quality, and receiving environmental status and quality has little or no effect on the determination of such standards.

The **critical load** (CL) concept which has recently been adopted as the basis for international negotiations on reducing air emissions of sulphur and nitrogen (to combat acidification and eutrophication), on the other hand,

Panel (b) The critical load approach to pollution control.

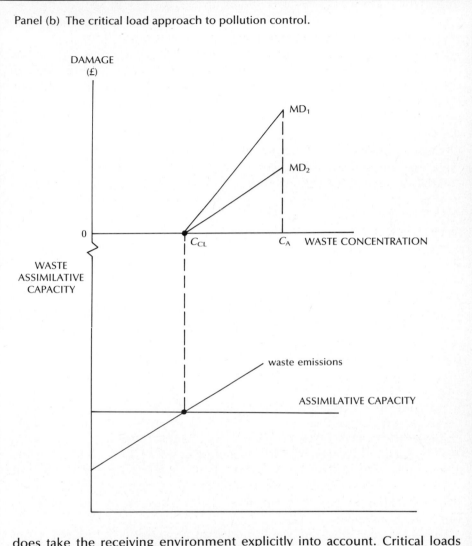

does take the receiving environment explicitly into account. Critical loads are thresholds of damage which indicate the degree to which deposition will have to be reduced if emissions are to be 'environmentally acceptable' (i.e. lack of harmful biological effects). CLs undoubtedly represent a cost-effectiveness improvement over the simple approach of uniform percentage emission reduction, since the effects and costs of abatement do vary across regions. However, they should still be used with some caution if inefficient environmental policy is to be avoided. In Panel (b) CL occurs at an ambient concentration level $0C_{CL}$ 'damage' occurs due to a breaching of the assimilative capacity of the environment, or because of the breaching of a threshold related to the accumulated stock of persistent pollutants.

But a biologically determined CL_b is not necessarily equivalent to an 'economic' CL_e. The latter is defined in terms of human welfare and the perception and valuation of environmental changes. In Panel (b) we assume for convenience that the two critical loads are the same (C_{CL}). If we consider just two locations 1 and 2, economic damage in 1 is measured by MD_1 (marginal damage) and in location 2 by MD_2. Even if the two locations are identical in biophysical, etc., terms they may still vary in economic damage (measured in terms of willingness to pay to prevent damage). Thus area 1 could be an area of high recreational demand or cultural importance relative to area 2. Using the CL approach both sites would be treated equally since they both face the same 'exceed load' situation. But damage (in economic terms) will be different at the two sites. At site 1, it is $C_{CL}.d_1.C_A$ and at site 2 it is $C_{CL}.d_2.C_A$, and $C_{CL}.d_1.C_A > C_{CL}.d_2.C_A$. Hence, the CL approach runs the risk of economic inefficiency.

For this reason, target loads, which are set nationally, need to take into account not only environment sensitivity but also, among others, technical and economic considerations. Thus the CL approach and the SPP approach may be modified by referring to technological capability. Releases of pollution can then be controlled in line with Best Available Technology (PP + BAT in Panel (a)). The problem then becomes that at any given time a best technology does not exist. Another layer of control can always be added, or there is a bench-scale technology under test that promises more effective pollution control (Lave and Malès, 1989). In the United States and Germany the authorities choose the most advanced technology that is commercially available, reliable, has an 'acceptable' level of control and is available at a 'reasonable' cost. In the United Kingdom, BAT is interpreted as a technique which is deemed to be 'available' only if it is 'procurable' and also if it has been developed (or proven) at a scale which allows its implementation in the relevant industrial context with the necessary business confidence.

Given only the prevailing state of relevant technology and innovation, a PP + BAT solution may impose a more or less strict standard on emissions than a CL approach. The actual relative level of PP + BAT standard will depend on the type and availability of existing technologies, the interpretation of the BAT concept by pollution control authorities, the degree of acceptance of the PP in certain contexts and countries and the assimilative capacity of the environment.

The PP and BAT approach is given an even more practicable orientation when the costs of achieving a specified emission target level are explicitly considered. This results in the establishment of a PP + BATNEEC approach (see Panel (a)). The NEEC portion of BATNEEC means that the presumption in favour of BAT can be modified by two sorts of 'economic cost' considerations, i.e. whether the costs of applying BAT would be excessive in relation to the environmental protection achieved; and where the costs of applying BAT would be excessive in relation to the nature of the industry and its competitive position. There is, however, no great consistency in the way authorities have interpreted the term excessive cost. Sometimes what is referred to is a financial cost to the polluting firms (i.e. pollution abatement equipment, etc., and/or loss of market competitiveness); and at other times the wider external costs of pollution are included.

Critics of the technology-based standards approach tend to focus on its vagueness in terms of guidance on questions such as how clean should the environment be made, what are acceptable risks and what precisely are excessive costs (e.g. what do we do with threatened plant closures in areas of high unemployment?). Difficult ethical, political and economic efficiency questions are shrouded rather than illuminated by this approach, value judgements are made implicitly rather than explicitly.

It can also be argued that this approach to pollution control is biased against technological innovation (i.e. it provides no incentive for regulated polluters to exceed their prescribed target level of abatement). Nevertheless, it has still proved attractive to control agencies. What it does provide is a measure of environmental quality 'certainty' (as long as there is adequate monitoring and enforcement). This 'certainty' argument is especially relevant when persistent, toxic and bioaccumulating substances are present. But it remains the case that while the underlying ideas of persistence, bioaccumulation and toxicity are important indicators of the probable hazard posed by a substance are sound, they are not easy to operationalize in environmental management practice (Grey *et al.*, 1991).

2. Where damage to ecosystems risks the loss of high-value environmental functions and services (i.e. life support systems) the overall capacity of such systems to act as a buffer for environmental wellbeing must be adequately protected. This means leaving a natural cushion (SMS) in the functional equilibria of natural systems.
3. The burden of proof to protect natural 'cushions' is beginning to fall upon the would-be polluter rather than the would-be victim, or the pressure groups who champion the cause of ecosystem integrity. This means that costs of reparation or compensation are increasingly becoming the cost of doing business (O'Riordan, 1992).

Environmental policy and the environmental agenda in the 1990s

Most environmental decision-making has proceeded piecemeal, i.e. by way of compartmentalized and only loosely coordinated effort directed at specific issues and problems. Nevertheless, the general objective in all countries is an 'improved' environmental planning and management process, with greater emphasis on long-term considerations. 'Improvements' is taken to encapsulate goals such as better ambient environmental quality states; reduced risks to human health; and a more efficient (cost-effective) pollution control system.

For many environmentalists the 'improvement' route should eventually lead to an ideal integrated comprehensive decision-making process. But such a fully comprehensive process, even if it were possible (which is doubtful), may well be both impracticable and undesirable. Thus, for example, in the United States, the 'cradle-to-grave' philosophy of waste management has imposed massive reporting requirements and expensive controls, but achievements have been limited. On the other hand, the problems of the overly restrictive past UK approach to pollution control are becoming obvious, and in many cases likely to become more severe in the future. Thus policies which seek to mitigate pollution damage in a single environmental medium and foster only end-of-pipe abatement measures (e.g. air emission filters, etc.), as opposed to more fundamental source-reduction measures (e.g. process changes and in-plant recycling systems, etc.), can only be of limited effectiveness.

It is likely therefore that 'green' pressure in the United Kingdom will give rise to continued efforts to improve the quality of the ambient environment via a more integrated approach to pollution control policy. The Environmental Protection Act of 1990 has to work its way through the regulatory system, it will emphasize *two* new systems of control. 'Integrated pollution control' (IPC) obliges Her Majesty's Inspectorate of Pollution (HMIP) to adopt a multimedia control approach, such that in cases where substances are released to more than one environmental medium, the 'Best Practicable Environmental Option' (BPEO) should be selected by the polluter.

Traditionally, UK pollution control policy has been based on a regulatory standards-based (ambient quality standards and waste emission standards) approach. The new policy retains the conventional technology-based standards approach, with the core concept of 'Best Available Technology Not Entailing Excessive Cost' (BATNEEC). The BATNEEC philosophy will oblige HMIP to draw polluters' attention to technologies which are cleaner than those in place, provided their adoption is not 'excessively' costly. Both IPC and BATNEEC will add significantly to industrial costs.

At the European level, the focus of much environmental legislation has, of course, shifted towards Brussels through the medium of environmental

Box 14.2   EC directives

According to Article 189 of the EEC Treaty of Rome, a directive shall be binding, as to the result achieved upon each Member State, but shall leave to the national authorities the choice of form and methods. Piecemeal moves to protect the environment up until the Single European Act of 1987 were consolidated under that Act and environmental protection was given an explicit place in the Treaty via Articles 130R, 130S and 130T. The establishment of the internal market as from 1 January 1993 will require the harmonization of different national laws and environmental measures will also need attention in this context. The goal of **uniform minimum environmental standards** has the advantage of preventing 'pollution havens'; and allowing the establishment of a safety margin approach in the areas of human health and ecosystem damage where scientific data is deficient and uncertainty is high. **Variable minimum standards**, on the other hand, seem more realistic given the existing differences among EC regions in terms of industrial and population concentrations. It can also be argued that regions that produce strong transboundary pollution should be made to maintain higher standards. A European Environmental Agency would have to negotiate such standards.

Directives (see Box 14.2). The Drinking Water Directive has already shown the power of Brussels to implement tough standards with considerable cost implications for industry and the consumer. The Environmental Impact Assessment Directive (applying to certain classes of development projects) was implemented in 1988 and yet to come are proposals on waste management and civil liability; on freedom of public access to information about industrial emissions; and on ecolabelling and environmental audits (based on so-called product life-cycle or cradle-to-grave analysis) for companies. The cost implications in each case are significant.

At the global level, negotiations continue to get framework agreements on the protection of tropical forests and biological diversity. GATT discussions now include debates about the environmental implications of trade agreements. Even more significantly, the foundations of a global agreement on controlling greenhouse gases to reduce the threat of global warming are being laid, following on from the Montreal Protocol agreement of 1987 (strengthened in 1990) which seeks to control ozone layer depleting chlorofluorocarbon emissions (see Chapters 19 and 20).

The overall message seems clear, environmental legislation and pressures continue to mount. Their aggregate effect will mean significantly greater costs for industry in the coming decade, and higher consumer prices for polluting products as a result.

While the Polluter Pays principle itself will continue to evolve it has now been buttressed, to a greater or lesser extent, by four other basic principles, all of which will play a part in guiding environmental policy formulation in the future. The full principles list is as follows:

(a) the *PPP* to force those creating the pollution to pay the costs of meeting socially acceptable environmental quality standards;
(b) the 'prevention or precaution principle', which explicitly recognizes the existence of uncertainty (environmental and social) and seeks to avoid irreversible damages via the imposition of a safety margin (safe minimum standards) into policy; it also seeks to prevent waste generation at source, as well as retaining some end-of-pipe measures;
(c) the 'economic efficiency/cost effectiveness principle', applying both to the setting of standards and the design of the means (policy instruments) for attaining them;
(d) the 'subsidiarity principle', to assign environmental decisions and enforcement to the lowest level of government capable of handling them without significant residual externalities;
(e) the 'legal efficiency principle' to preclude the passage of regulations that cannot be realistically enforced.

Are national environmental standards efficient?

Finally, we return to the question we posed at the beginning of this chapter: are standards 'internally' efficient? Some relevant evidence has recently been presented in a study undertaken in the United States (Luken and Clark, 1991). The US Environmental Protection Agency (EPA) is responsible for administering the national environmental programme in the US. EPA carries out its mandate principally by establishing and enforcing national environmental standards. It has three dominant regulatory approaches:

1. *Technology-based standards* (mandated by the Clean Water Act of 1972), that reflect the capabilities of the best available pollution control technologies (BACT). These standards require polluters to meet uniform discharge limits.
2. *Ambient-based standards* (mandated by the Clean Air Act of 1970) set to protect human health and welfare. Industrial polluters are required to install pollution control equipment only to the extent necessary to meet ambient standards.
3. *Benefits-based standards* (also mandated by the Clean Air Act of 1970) that require risks to society from pollution to be traded off against the costs of risk reduction. Thus existing industrial polluters are required to install pollution control equipment only to the extent that there would be a

reasonable balance between the benefits of pollution reduction and the costs of pollution control technology.

The Luken and Clark (1991) study was the first systematic, geographically specific, efficiency assessment of US (or any other country's) environmental regulation on policy. It was an ex-post evaluation that sought to measure the net benefits (if any) that resulted from EPA's regulation of conventional air and water pollution from the pulp and paper industry between 1973 and 1984. The results of the study are summarized in Box 14.3. But two major conclusions emerged:

1. Ambient and benefits-based standards are more efficient than technology-based standards, because the latter do not require any measure of actual environmental results.
2. Efficient pollution control policies must be flexible enough to take into account 'local' conditions, including the numbers of gainers and losers from the policy. This suggests that national environmental standards *per se* may be inefficient.

Box 14.3 Benefits and costs of regulatory standards in the United States (1973–1984)

The results in Table 1 indicate that the technology-based standard for water pollution management failed on efficiency grounds, both in aggregate terms and in 57 of the 68 pulp and paper mills that were studied. The ambient-based standard for air pollution was more successful, yielding an aggregate net benefit and local net benefits in 22 of the 60 plants investigated. But the benefits-based standard was the most successful approach with an aggregate net benefit and local net benefits in 29 out of the 60 plants studied.

Table 1

Type of standard	Mills with $B > C$/mills analyzed	Total benefits [$ 1984 10^6]	Total costs	Net benefits
Technology	11/68	$36.6	$96.6	$-60.0
Ambient	22/60	$25.2	$23.8	$1.4
Benefits	29/60	$86.9	$55.8	$31.1

Source: Luken and Clark (1991)

One further set of *ethical arguments* has recently been put forward to explain the administrator's preference for regulations. Frey (1992) argues that the use of economic incentive instruments (which he calls 'pricing') may **crowd out** (i.e. cause a substitution of) any existing environmental ethic in the sector in which pricing is applied. There may also be a spillover effect into sectors not being targeted by economic incentive policy, leading to a reduction in the strength of the environmental ethical commitment in those sectors. The end result of the loss of ethical commitment in industry due to the application of pricing policies could (though this is not inevitably the case) lead to an increase in pollution in the targeted sectors and also more generally. This possible result is what environmental pressure groups in many countries have voiced concern about.

Now it is also the case that regulation (CAC) may also provoke a crowding out of environmental ethics because polluters feel 'overjustified' (i.e. already doing more than they have to as laid down in the environmental standard). However, Frey (1992) argues that this is less likely because regulations are accompanied by an explicit 'signal' of disapproval of polluting acts. Pricing does not carry the same 'societal signal'. Carrying this line of argument to the limit, perhaps *subsidies* (generally not approved of by economists) would be supportive of existing environmental ethics in industry and the public sector. Subsidies allow individual self-determination to be maintained and also allow for the argument that nature be conserved on intrinsic value grounds (see Chapter 2).

Conclusions

It seems fair to conclude that environmental regulations (standards) are often both inefficient in themselves and in relation to economic incentive instruments. However, in the contexts of uncertainty over possible pollution-related environmental damage, or known hazardous waste risks, regulatory standards offer the 'best' approach. Such a regulatory approach is consistent with the precautionary principle and may also offer ethical gains for some individuals.

Further reading

F. Cairncross, *Costing the Earth: What Governments Must Do, What Consumers Need to Know, How Business can Profit*, Business Books, London, 1991.

T. O'Riordan, 'The precaution principle in environmental management', GEC 92–03, CSERGE Working Paper, University of East Anglia and University College London, 1992.

D. W. Pearce, R. K. Turner and T. O'Riordan, 'Energy and society health: Integrating quantity and quality in energy planning', *Journal of the World Energy Council* (Dec.): 76–88, 1992.

R. Ramchandani and D. W. Pearce, 'Alternative approaches to setting effluent quality standards: Precautionary, critical load and cost benefit approaches', WM 92-04, CSERGE Working Paper, University of East Anglia and University College London, 1992.

M. D. Young, *Sustainable Investment and Resource Use*, UNESCO, Parthenon, Carnforth, 1992, Chapter 6.

Other references

B. S. Frey, 'Pricing and regulation affect environmental ethics', *Environmental and Resource Economics* **2**: 399–414, 1992.

J. S. Grey *et al.*, 'Scientifically based strategies for marine environmental protection and management', *Marine Pollution Bulletin* **22**: 432–40, 1991.

L. B. Lave and E. H. Malès, 'At risk: The framework for regulating toxic substances', *Environmental Science and Technology* **23**: 386–91, 1989.

R. A. Luken and L. Clark, 'How efficient are national environmental standards? A benefit–cost analysis of the United States experience', *Environmental and Resource Economics* **1**: 385–414, 1991.

PART V

Natural resources

CHAPTER 15

Renewable resources

Introduction

Natural resources are often categorized as 'renewable' and 'exhaustible'. A renewable resource regenerates itself: so, fish and trees are renewable resources. An exhaustible resource is fixed in overall quantity, so that any use of it in a given time period means that there is less of it available for other time periods. Strictly, however, the renewable/exhaustible distinction is misleading. First, a great many renewable resources – fish and trees, for example – are exhaustible if they are not managed in a **sustainable fashion**. A better distinction might therefore be between renewable and *non-renewable* resources. The former will, under a suitable management regime, regenerate themselves. The latter do not have this capability. Second, many resources are mixtures of renewable and non-renewable elements: soil for example.

This chapter looks at renewable resources and asks how they *are* managed and how they *should be* managed. The answers to these questions give us some insights into why renewable resources often come under threat of overuse and even extinction.

The fishery

One of the most written about renewable resources is the fishery. Each year we can catch a number of fish and leave the rest to grow, mature and reproduce. Next year we can take the addition to this year's stock and leave the stock as it was to grow again, and so on. For example, imagine there are 1000 fish and each year they increase by 10 per cent, i.e. by 100. We can catch 100 fish and the stock will fall to 1000 again. Then it will grow naturally by 100 again; we catch 100, and so on. The 100 fish caught every year are the **sustainable yield**. Notice that by catching the sustainable yield, and no more than the sustainable yield, the stock is left constant (at 1000).

Typically, however, the yield will depend on the size of the stock. If, instead of 1000 fish we started with 500, we cannot assume that the yield would be 10 per cent, i.e. 50 fish. Quite often the yield varies with the stock in complex ways. One important variation arises if the stock gets very small. If we have 20 fish we cannot assume that they will increase by 2 each year (10 per cent). Once stocks fall to very low levels they often become *non-viable*, i.e. reproduction does not take place. There might therefore be a **critical minimum size** for the stock. If we go below that minimum, the stock is likely to die out without reproduction. Critical minimum sizes are important for many species of animal such as elephants. They are also important for *habitat* i.e. once a habitat for a given species falls below a certain size it is unlikely to support wild species.

Box 15.1 shows how yield might vary with stock. When the stock is very small, the critical minimum size argument may apply and the stock does not grow at all, but, for convenience, we abstract from this possibility here (we come back to it). So, when stocks are small they grow fast. One reason for this might be that there is plenty of food available 'per capita' when the stock of fish is small. But this growth of the stock (i.e. the yield) will tend to slow down as the fish compete for food supplies. The yield therefore reaches a maximum – the so-called **maximum sustainable yield** (MSY) – after which it declines. It carries on falling until it reaches zero yield. This will occur when the stock of fish has reached the *carrying capacity* of their environment. Any further increase in stock would begin to lead to some fish dying from lack of food resources. The stock of fish that relates to the carrying capacity is known as the **natural equilibrium** stock: it is the number of fish that will exist if they are left completely alone. At the natural equilibrium any deaths are exactly offset by new births. If, for some reason, deaths decreased, then the fishery would go below its carrying capacity and the growth process would accelerate so as to go back to the carrying capacity level. If the fish went beyond their carrying capacity, deaths would accelerate and outweigh births and the fishery would return to its carrying capacity.

Box 15.1 shows this stock–yield relationship in two ways. It shows how the yield varies with stock, and it shows how yield varies with **fishing effort**. Fishing effort is the time and resources devoted to catching fish, so it might be measured in workhours or numbers of trawlers, or numbers and size of nets, and so on. It will be seen that fishing effort varies inversely with stock size. The exact relationship is complex. All we need is the intuition behind the relationship which is that the bigger the effort, the lower the stock; the lower the effort, the bigger the stock. Box 15.1 shows how to go from the stock–yield relationship to the effort–yield relationship, and how to go from the purely biological diagram to one that is expressed in terms of revenues and costs. The revenue–cost diagram shows very clearly that setting the catch at MSY is not economically efficient. It is better to restrict the catch through lower fishing effort and make larger profits than at the effort level associated with catching the MSY.

Box 15.1 Simple analytics of the fishery

Panel (a) shows how yield and stock relate to each other. When the stock is small the growth (yield) of the fishery is high. As competition for food resources occurs, the rate of growth of the yield (the slope of the curve) begins to tail off and yields reach a maximum at MSY. The rate of growth of yield then becomes negative (i.e. the curve starts to slope down) until point S_{CC}, where yields are zero, i.e. birth and death rates are exactly equal. In interpreting Panel (a) note that the *yield* is the vertical distance between the horizontal axis and the growth curve. The *rate of growth* of the yield is the slope of the growth curve.

If we assume that fishing effort and population size are inversely related – as effort increases population size falls, and vice versa – then Panel (a) can be turned round and read in terms of yield and fishing effort, as shown in Panel (b).

Now suppose that each tonne of landed fish sells for the same price, and that the catch is always equal to the yield. Then the yield curve can be reinterpreted as a *revenue* curve (see Panel (c)) since (catch) × (price) = revenue. We now begin to interpret the fishery diagram as an economics diagram. To get a measure of *cost* is simple. Suppose effort is measured by workdays and each workday costs the same amount however many workdays are employed. Then, the bigger the effort the bigger the cost. The *total cost* curve will appear as in Panel (c).

We now have *total revenue* and *total cost* and the transition from the purely 'biological' diagram to an economic one is complete. In the jargon of economics, this diagram is **static** because it does not allow for the inclusion of time. Unfortunately, as soon as time is introduced it becomes quite difficult to present the issue in reasonably simple terms. See the text for the general implications of allowing for time. But even the static diagram is helpful. It shows us, first, that what might appear to be a sensible point to aim for – the maximum sustainable yield – is not a point of maximum profits from the fishery. MSY makes no mention of cost, so it should not be surprising that it turns out not to be an 'efficient' point. None the less, many people still think, erroneously, that catching the MSY is the best way to manage the fishery. The static diagram has a number of other uses (see text for further discussion):

(a) The most profitable use of the fishery is at E_{PROF}. Note that this is a lower level of effort than would be called for by taking the MSY.

(b) If profits attract new fishermen into the industry, the industry will expand as long as profits can be made. This will take the fishery to point E_{OA} where profits (other than those just sufficient to keep a trawler in business) are zero. E_{OA} is the 'open access' equilibrium.

Panel (a) Fishing mortality (F. y^{-1}).
Panel (b) Mean annual total fleet horsepower (HP.10^2).

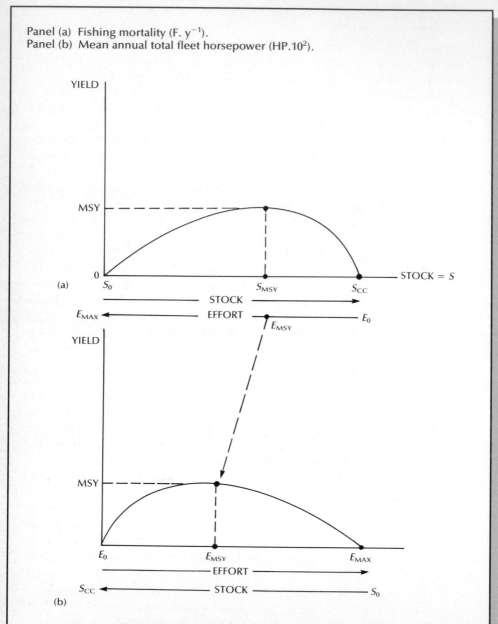

(c) Maximum effort (E_{MAX}) would run the risk of overfishing. On this diagram neither profit maximization nor open access runs that risk. But if the total cost curve was less steep the open access equilibrium would get closer and closer to the risk zone.

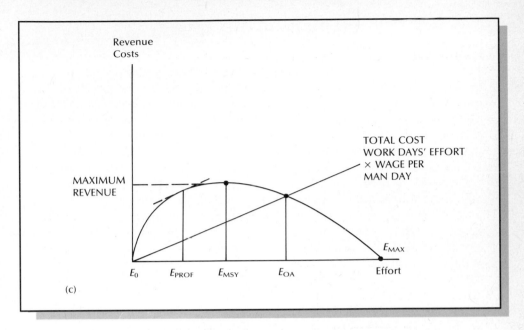

The diagram also reveals some other important findings. If the fishery is open to all comers, as many of the world's fisheries are, then any level of profit will attract new entrants so long as it is above the level just necessary to keep fishermen in business. In Panel (c) of Box 15.1 this profit incentive is shown by the distance between the total revenue and total cost curves. As long as this is positive, new trawlers will come into the industry – especially foreign trawlers fishing in waters that a country may regard as its own. The harder it is to 'police' the fishery, the easier it will be for foreign trawlers to come in. But even within fisheries that are well policed, there can still be too many domestic fishermen. It terms of Panel (c), this process of new entrants will not stop until the point E_{OA} where profits fall to zero. All trawlers are then earning just enough to keep them in business and no more. Any new fishermen will, however, give rise to losses. Some will therefore go out of business. E_{OA} is then an equilibrium since any number of trawlers less than E_{OA} will give rise to profits which will attract new entrants, and level of effort higher than E_{OA} will give rise to losses and reduced effort. E_{OA} is the *open access* solution to the fishery management question. It is the use that will be made of the fishery if there is open competition. Open competition will tend to arise when there are *no property rights* or when property rights are ill-defined, i.e. when no-one owns the fishery or, if they do, their claim to ownership can easily be challenged or ignored. The open access solution is inefficient. Better use could be made of the fishery by restricting entry and placing the fishery under the sole ownership of one company or one consortium. Then E_{PROF} becomes relevant.

209

The tragedy of the commons

It is this kind of analysis that has led many commentators to argue that 'free entry' to renewable resources such as fisheries should not be permitted. Not only is it inefficient, as Box 15.1 suggests, but it risks the extinction of the resource. To see this observe that E_{OA} is the equilibrium closest to the point of maximum effort. From the previous diagrams we see that maximum effort coincides with minimum stocks. If we have some critical minimum size, then, there is a real risk that maximum effort will cause the resource to be made extinct. Since the open access solution is closest to E_{MAX}, open access gives the greatest risk of extinction. Moreover, the lower is the total cost curve, the more risky it becomes. Low total costs mean that it is relatively easy to make a catch. That is why fishery resources that are close to shore, or in easily accessible waters are more at risk than others. It is also partly why the African elephant has come close to extinction risk: high velocity rifles, even vehicles, make it relatively easy to shoot an elephant for its tusks. We can say that the cost per elephant is very low. We can think of severe deterrents, such as shoot-on-sight policies adopted by some countries, as raising the cost curve again. But the other factor providing a high incentive to shoot elephants is the high price of the tusks relative to the costs of poaching. That suggests another way of controlling poaching, namely, to reduce the demand for ivory so that its price falls. This is the logic behind the idea of 'banning' the trade in elephant ivory.

The risks associated with the open access solution are often summarized by talking of the **tragedy of the commons**. This is a somewhat unfortunate phrase because 'the commons' refers to *common property*, i.e. resources owned by a community, whereas open access refers to a situation in which no-one owns the resource. Really, then, it should be the 'tragedy of open access' and even then it is not necessarily the case that open access will cause a resource to be made extinct. As the diagrams in Box 15.1 show, the open access solution poses a greater risk of extinction, but much depends on the nature of costs and revenues.

Time and discounting

The diagram in Box 15.1 is essentially 'static' – it says nothing about the way in which *time* might affect the picture. Chapter 7 introduced the concept of *discounting* to reflect the fact that we tend to regard costs and benefits in the future as being of less importance than costs and benefits now. A unit of money in one year's time will be valued less highly that the same unit now (leaving aside inflation). We tend to be impatient, preferring benefits now to benefits in the future. Also, future people are likely to be richer than people now, so £1 now is likely to yield more 'wellbeing' (utility) than £1 to a later generation. Finally, there is also the fact of the 'productivity of capital': if we invest in a machine it will tend to yield a flow of services over time with values higher than the cost of the investment. Whether we look at it from the point of view of individual valuations over time ('time preference'), or from the standpoint of the capital market ('capital productivity') we discount the future at a positive rate.

The discount rate is of critical importance in determining the rate at which *renewable* (and exhaustible) resources are used. Without going into the derivation, we may state a basic rule as follows:

Biological Rate of Growth + Growth in Capital Value = Discount Rate

The biological rate of growth is the rate at which the fishery grows, i.e. the growth in the total weight of the stock of fish. The growth in capital value refers to the possibility of collecting capital gains by leaving the fish unharvested. Such gains will occur if the price of fish is rising through time so that, by leaving the fish in the sea, their value appreciates.

What this rule says is that the fishery should be harvested in such a way that this rule is obeyed. Consider some hypothetical numbers in order to illustrate the rule. Imagine that the discount rate is 10 per cent, the biological growth rate is 3 per cent and prices are growing at 5 per cent. The choice is between harvesting 100 tonnes of fish now at $100 per tonne, or waiting. The relevant calculations are:

	Fish now	Wait
Revenue	$10 000	$10 800[a]
Discounted value	$10 000	$9 818[b]

[a]Actually $10 815 because the stock grows at 3% to become 103 tonnes, which are then sold at $105 per tonne.
[b]$9818 = $10 800/1.1

Waiting is not worthwhile and the harvest takes place now. If the discount rate exceeds the combined 'own growth' and capital gain, the resource will be harvested sooner rather than later. If the discount rate now is 6 per cent, the calculations can be repeated to obtain:

	Fish now	Wait
Revenue	$10 000	$10 800
Discounted value	$10 000	$10 189

It now pays to wait because the discount rate is below the combined growth and capital gain effects.

211

Finally, if the discount rate is just equal to the sum of the growth and capital gain effects, the discounted values from fishing now or waiting will be equal. Thus, if the discount rate in the above example is 8 per cent, the discounted value of the catch obtained by waiting will be $10 000, the same as making the catch now.

Why is the discount rate important and how does it relate to the problem of conservation? The examples show that if the discount rate of the resource user is very high, or simply high relative to the biological growth rate of the fishery, then there will be an incentive to fish now rather than wait. Moreover, the high discount rate will lead to overexploitation of the fishery and will risk its extinction. If we think of species that have been hunted to extinction or near extinction, it is easy to see that many of them are slow growing, i.e. they do not reproduce 'naturally' at very fast rates. Elephants and whales are good examples. But that means that their biological growth rates are likely to be less than the discount rate, and hence they are at risk of overharvesting.

Some examples of overharvesting

The SouthEast Asia fisheries

Overfishing in the SouthEast Asia region (mainly that of the countries of Thailand, Singapore, Indonesia, Philippines, Malaysia and Brunei) is well documented. Catch rates per unit of fishing effort have declined considerably since 1961, by at least a factor of 10 for most species. Studies show that 60–70 per cent of the decline in catches is due to fishing effort. Most fishing is done by very large numbers of small trawlers which also use nets with small mesh sizes which means they catch many of the young of available species. Box 15.2 shows clearly the way in which effort in the Philippines demersal and pelagic fisheries has moved round the growth curves introduced earlier, well beyond the point of maximum economic profit (rent) and towards effective open access equilibria. The result is the total dissipation of the profits in the fishery with consequent low average incomes for fishermen. Major increases in profits could be achieved by restricting fishery effort as has happened in many of the world's fisheries. Some bans have been enacted in the region. In 1976 a ban was put into effect in the Southern Samar Sea, and Indonesia banned trawling in 1980.

The North Pacific seal fur industry

In the nineteenth century substantial harvesting of the North Pacific fur seal took place during the seals' migrations along the west coast of America to the

Box 15.2 Overfishing in the Philippines

Panels (a) and (b) show actual catch rates, revenues and costs in the Philippines pelagic fishery. Catch is measured on the vertical axis in tonnes. The 'effort' measure is the horsepower of the trawling fleet. The points

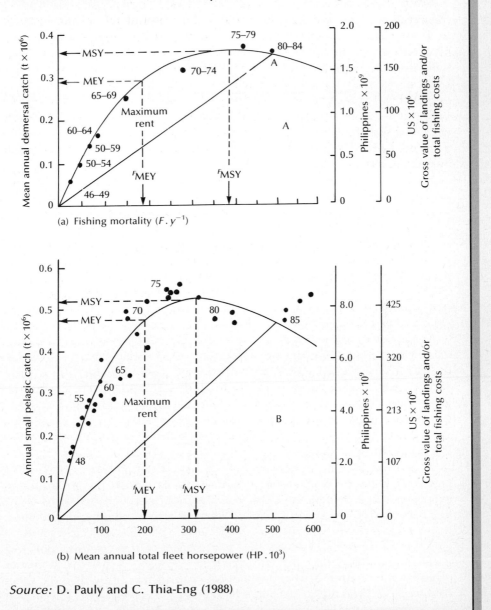

(a) Fishing mortality $(F . y^{-1})$

(b) Mean annual total fleet horsepower $(HP . 10^{3})$

Source: D. Pauly and C. Thia-Eng (1988)

shown relate to specific years, e.g. 1965, 1970, etc. Thus, in 1960 the industry was catching around 300 000 tonnes of fish per year with about 100 000 horsepower. Towards the end of the 1970s the industry was catching in the region of the MSY – around 500 000 tonnes with over 300 000 HP. By 1985 the industry had reached the open access solution: catch had fallen below 500 000 tonnes with 500 000 HP, five times the 1960 level of 'effort'. Costs and revenues were about equal, i.e. zero profit was being earned. After 1985, effort expanded even beyond the open access solution, revenues were less than costs.

Bering Strait. The resource was effectively an open access one with vessels from the United States, Canada, the Soviet Union, Japan and the United Kingdom taking part. In the 1890s massive exploitation occurred, followed by falling catches and many firms leaving the industry. Various attempts to curtail catches were made, culminating in a treaty in 1911 which regulated the catch (and which exists today). The industry thus typifies what one might expect from an open access situation. As we saw, open access could threaten extinction. On the other hand, there are incentives under open access to secure a common property approach by collectively regulating the catch. The question is, would the industry have driven the resource to extinction, or was it moving towards self-regulation of a common property form?

A 'bioeconomic' model of the industry was constructed by researchers (Patterson and Wilen, 1977) to show the conditions under which firms would enter and exit the industry. Basically, if profits were to be made, entry would occur. If losses accrued, firms would leave. By building in price data, and using vessel numbers to measure effort, the 'steady state' stock of seals (i.e. the stock that could be sustained indefinitely) was estimated to be some 580 000 seals, with a sustained maximum yield of around 75 000 seals. In fact, the stock of seals was over 1 500 000 in 1867, fell to under 400 000 in 1897 and then recovered somewhat to 1900. The model suggests that the *actual* catch rates were oscillating about the commercially optimal stocks and catch rates. Put another way, although there was an effective open access situation, the *survival* of the North Pacific Seal *may* not have been at issue. As Box 15.1 predicts, there are some open access situations which do not result in extinction. None the less, the risks were real, not least because the fate of the industry was causing serious political divisions between the hunting nations. In the end, the North Pacific Fur Seal Treaty of 1911 limited catches and, in effect, made the United States the 'sole owner' of the resource. Box 15.1 predicts that sole ownership will conserve the resource because it creates profits, whereas open access runs the risk of extinction. Why then did other nations agree to let the United States become the effective owner? The answer is that because the sole ownership made profits possible, the United States

214

was able to (and still does) compensate the other nations for forgoing their catch.

The blue whale

The blue whale is the world's largest creature. This fact alone justifies the efforts made to preserve it after wholesale slaughter, especially between 1928 and 1938 when catches peaked at 26 000 whales per year. The figures for catches are as follows:

1910–1919	26 819 per decade
1920–1929	69 217
1930–1939	170 427
1940–1949	46 199
1950–1959	35 948
1960–1969	7 434
1970–1979	23
1980–1991	0

Prior to human exploitation there may have been some 220 000 blue whales in the southern hemisphere and 8000 in the north. Current estimates put the remaining populations at 11 000 and 3000 respectively. Other authorities suggest there are even less. One study of blue whales suggests that the maximum sustainable catch was around 9900 whales per annum, a figure clearly exceeded in 1930–39 when annual catches averaged around 17 000 whales per annum. An optimal *commercial* catch, taking into account costs of whaling and the commercial value of blubber, oils, etc., would have been some 9000 whales per annum provided the population was allowed to achieve its optimal level of 67 000. This could only be done by abandoning all whaling until that level was achieved. The 67 000 figure might be compared to the existing population of 14 000 or less whales.

Such an exercise is interesting since it shows that *on purely commercial grounds* the catch rates for blue whales were non-optimal. The catches were tending to reveal the open access solution rather than the maximum profit solution. But given the scientific value of blue whales, and their 'existence value', it is clear that the commercial analysis dictates too low a stock in any event.

Property rights and the management of renewable resources

It is widely suggested that the communal management of natural resources will break down because of the incentive to **free ride**, i.e. to try to make individual gains without contributing to the collective control of the resource. But communal management might work if 'assurances' can be obtained, i.e. that others will obey the rules of collective management and conservation if we do. Since open access gives rise to risks of extinction, and communal ownership may also break down, it is suggested that **privatization** is one solution to inefficient resource use; and that **state control** may be the only other viable regime. Box 15.3 shows four types of resource management regime in terms of their characteristics of *rights, duties* and *privileges*. Property is a right to a flow of benefits, and that right is secure only as long as others observe a duty to honour the right. Rights are protected against others' claims by their duties to honour the right. A privilege on the other hand, is a use unaccompanied by any right and can be exercised because others have no rights either: this is the open access case.

Box 15.3   Resource management regimes

- **State property**   Individuals have duty to observe the rules of resource use determined by the controlling agency. Agency has right to determine use rules.
- **Private property**   Individuals have right to undertake socially acceptable uses, and duty to refrain from unacceptable uses. Others have duty to respect individual rights.
- **Common property**   A management group has right to exclude non-members. Non-members have duty to abide by the exclusion. Co-owners comprise the management group and have rights and duties with respect to the use of resources.
- **Open access**   No defined users or owners. Individuals have privilege, but no right to use the resource.

The categories show the various forms of resource management regime. Both open access (no owners) and communal ownership may risk conservation of the resource. But open access does not *necessarily* lead to overuse, and communal property regimes can be very successful at managing renewable resources sustainably. Private ownership is likely to conserve the resource unless the owner's discount rate is high (see text). State ownership may conserve the resource – much depends on the motives of government and their capability to control the resource.

Source: Modified from D. Bromley (1989).

We briefly review the different property rights prescriptions for managing renewable natural resources (and other resources).

Privatization

One often repeated policy prescription for the problems of overuse of resources under open access and common property is privatization. This may take several forms, one of which is the conferment of **land title** to individuals through documentation, together with enforcement of land titles by the authorities. Title without enforcement will be largely meaningless. Documented land title is often needed in contexts where owners may be threatened by outsiders with rival claims to the land, or where land improvement raises land values which act as a magnet to land speculators. Lack of ownership security is likely to result in various forms of uncertainty which contribute to resource degradation. First, the land owner will be unable to realize the value of any improvements, so that there will be little incentive to invest in longer term measures such as soil conservation which protect the environment. Second, if land values rise the occupier will not be able to resist takeover by land speculators or wealthier, more powerful people. Such groups may be even less interested in conservation, perhaps because land acquisition is a hedge against inflation or as a means of securing tax concessions. Third, secure tenure enables owners to apply for and secure credit from banks and other credit agencies. Insecure tenure means that the landholder has no collateral acceptable to the lender.

For these reasons, and others, one school of thought argues that 'privatization' is the only real solution to the environmental risks that open access and common property regimes pose. Some go further and argue that privatization will emerge 'naturally' as resources get scarce. Thus, in societies where population pressure is low there is no need to establish exclusive rights to tracts of land that are not under immediate pressure. There is no need for a right to sell or buy land because land is in excess supply. As population grows, so pressure on hitherto open access resources may result in the development of rules and conventions about resource use, effectively turning open access resources into common property resources. Nor is land the only resource where this may happen. As the world recognized the threat of ozone layer depletion, it acted by seeking to slow down and then ban the chlorofluorocarbons (CFCs) that were causing it. We can think of this as turning an open access resource (stratospheric ozone) into a common property resource.

Privatization, however, is extremely unlikely for many resources. The ozone layer is a good example again, as is the atmosphere. Moreover, privatization may carry with it further problems in that the single owner may then disregard any external effects imposed on other people. The

217

privatization example is therefore unlikely to be 'optimal' from society's point of view. Regulation is still required.

State ownership

Prima facie, state ownership of land and natural resources should 'solve' the 'tragedy of the commons' since the externalities ingrained in the overuse of common resources become internalized to the single owner, the state. But for state ownership to work efficiently the state must be able to monitor the use of resources, establish acceptable rules of use by individuals and communities, and enforce those rules. Typically, this has not been the experience with state ownership. Chapter 6 has already explained why governments are often motivated by factors other than the public interest – we do not dwell on this further in this chapter.

Communal management

Many people argue that local communities best understand their own environments and hence are best capable of managing natural resources in a sustainable way. The empirical experience tends to support both the supporters and critics of communal management regimes. The reasons for the break down of communal schemes have been varied and have not necessarily risen from the 'tragedy of the commons', i.e. from the conflict between individual and collective objectives. Some of the factors at work have included:

(a) *Population growth* – this places obvious pressures on communal systems as existing land has to be parcelled upon between increasing numbers. The same goes for other resources: as population grows so the demand for, say, energy resources results in increasing emi sions of pollutants, such as carbon dioxide. This 'uses up' the capacity of the atmosphere to absorb those pollutants. While a communal management regime may exist, e.g. through some international convention, rapid population growth makes it more and more difficult for countries to abide by any agreement they may have signed.

(b) *Technology* – this can induce overuse, as with the introduction of chainsaw technology in the Amazon forest and the high velocity rifle in poaching the African elephant. But the record is not a consistent one.

Yet communal management can be successful. A study of forty-one villages in South India suggests that villages do provide public goods and services without the external sanction of government (Wade, 1986). Villagers organize their own standing fund as distinct from local government monies, maintain village guards to protect crops, and pay 'common irrigators' whose task it is to distribute water to the rice fields. The villages also supply schooling, repair wells, rid the village of monkeys, and so on. Oxen and buffalo are needed for traction but the villages have no common land as such. The animals therefore graze close to the crops in the growing season, and livestock feeding is strictly controlled by field guards. An animal found to be grazing on crops is 'arrested' and its owner has to pay a fine to secure its release. At the end of the crop gathering, the stubble becomes common property for livestock use. But the use of this common property is regulated by agreements between the village council and the herders, even down to allocating livestock to land at night to secure manure. What the herders pay the village for the common grazing is recouped in the charges they make for the manure. Other detailed and extensive regulations are applied to livestock.

Much the same form of regulation applies to irrigation water, a notable source of conflict. The common irrigators decide how the water is to be allocated. Each field is entitled to be 'adequately wetted' so that no downstream user is disadvantaged by farmers closer to the irrigation source. What is the incentive for these examples of strict communal management? The main one appears to be the size of the collective benefit. That is, while incentives to defect, to 'free ride', remain in existence, the village authorities devote considerable time and effort to demonstrating that the returns to collective management are very much higher. Moreover, the system of sanctions for defecting is enforced from within the system rather than from outside. The study concluded that the villagers organized resource management because their resources were under considerable demand. If they did not collectively protect them, they would lose substantially.

Conclusions

Renewable resources are most under threat of overuse and even extinction under conditions of open access and the lack of property rights. These conditions have often been referred to as 'tragedy of the commons' situations. This terminology is unfortunate because 'the commons' refers to common property, i.e. resources owned by a community and not freely accessible to everyone. Efficient management of renewable resources requires some management regime based on rights, duties and privileges. The two polar case regimes would be private ownership of the resources and state ownership. Both are problematic for a range of environmental resources. This has led many people to argue that communal management of the resources is the best way to achieve sustainable usage. The empirical evidence of such local community resource management systems is mixed but by no means uniformly negative. When and if the size of collective benefit to be derived from strict communal management is large, the community makes sure that sustainable usage rules are enforced.

Further reading

D. Bromley, 'Property relations and economic development: The other land reform', *World Development* **17**(6): 872, 1989.

D. Patterson and J. Wilen, 'Depletion and diplomacy: The North Pacific seal hunt 1880–1910', in P. Usleding (ed.), *Research in Economic History*, Vol. 2, JAI Press, Greenwich, Conn., 1977.

D. Pauly and C. Thia-Eng, 'The overfishing of marine resources: Socioeconomic background in Southeast Asia', *Ambio* **17**(3): 200–6, 1988.

A. M. Spence, 'Blue Whales and Applied Control Theory', Technical Report 108, Institute for Mathematical Studies in the Social Sciences, Stanford University, 1973; reprinted in Y. Ahmad *et al.*, *Environmental Decision-Making*, Vol. 2, Hodder and Stoughton, London, 1984, pp. 43–71.

Be warned, however, that this is a mathematical article.

R. Wade, 'The management of common property resources: Finding a cooperative solution', *World Bank Research Observer* **2**(2, July): 219–34, 1986.

The economics of renewable resources quickly becomes complicated. We have concentrated on getting across some of the basic ideas. More elaborate treatments can be found in

D. W. Pearce and R. K. Turner, *Economics of Natural Resources and the Environment*, Harvester Wheatsheaf, Hemel Hempstead, 1990.

Even though the article confuses open access and common property resources, it is still worth reading:

G. Hardin, 'Tragedy of the Commons'; reprinted in H. E. Daly, *Valuing the Earth: Economics, Ecology, Ethics*, MIT Press, Cambridge, Mass, 1992.

Much of the common property literature is concerned with communal management regimes in the developing world (as the examples in this chapter show). But the 'global commons' – the atmosphere, international waters, the stratosphere – are the modern focus of some of the literature. We look at these in more detail in later chapters.

CHAPTER 16

Non-renewable resources

Introduction

In this chapter we turn our attention to non-renewable resources. The distinguishing feature of such resources is that they are fixed in overall quantity and therefore the more we extract and use today the less there will be for future periods. The *sustainable yield* concept is not relevant in the context of these resources and instead the main questions to be answered concern the *rate* at which these resources should be *depleted* and the total *amount* that should be extracted. But before we examine the economic principles of non-renewable resource use, we take a closer look at the notion of **natural resource scarcity** and its measurement.

Resource availability and scarcity

In simple economic terms, scarcity will be reflected in costs and prices. In practice, the measurement and prediction of current and future resource availability and scarcity is complicated. It requires a combination of physical science, materials science/engineering and economic data, methods and techniques. Matching the potential stock of non-renewable resources against future resource usage rates (linked to population growth, technical progress, social and economic expectations, etc.) is clearly going to remain an uncertain business. Therefore the 'scarcity debate' will continue to be partly a matter of **environmental ideology** (we outlined the various technocentric and ecocentric positions in Chapter 2).

The 'limits to growth' (LTG) position which we examined in Chapter 3 is linked to what we can call a **Malthusian** perspective (after Malthus whose famous essay on scarcity was published in 1798). From this perspective, **absolute physical scarcity** (i.e. running out of resources) is predicted to be the most likely outcome in the near/medium-term future. A related neo-

Malthusian position emphasizes the importance of environmental limits to resource extraction activities. Essentially the argument is that to continue to exploit lower and lower quality (grade) resources will require massive amounts of energy and will result in unacceptable levels of pollution and landscape and amenity losses.

Taking an opposite **Ricardian** perspective (after Ricardo's work published in 1817) a much more optimistic picture of resource scarcity emerges. Resource depletion effects will show themselves in rising costs and material prices over time as extraction companies are forced to exploit lower grade resource deposits. However, these effects will be offset by other factors. Extraction companies will put more effort into exploring for and discovering new deposits and technological advances will allow such deposits to be utilized (e.g. more efficient mining/drilling methods and new 'processing' methods to raise the 'quality' of the resources). In addition, the *market* will react to the rising price/cost signals by encouraging substitution (new materials and/or new ways of using materials), more efficient resource usage and increased scrap recycling activities.

Given these different viewpoints what evidence is there relating to resource scarcity?

Some evidence on resource scarcity: physical scarcity indicators

Physical measures of scarcity can be calculated by combining geological data on minerals or energy *reserves* with some forecast of the demand for these resources. But estimates of the size of non-renewable reserves are under constant revision. The Geological Survey of the United States, for example, produces national and worldwide estimates of reserves and potential reserves of minerals. Its 1972 classification system (known as McKelvey's Box) is the most widely accepted and clearly distinguishes between *reserves* and *resources*. The reserves category includes all geologically identified deposits that can be economically recovered and is subdivided into proved, probable and possible reserves on the basis of geological certainty. All other deposits are labelled resources, either because they have not yet been discovered or because their exploitation is not currently feasible (technical and economic problems are inhibiting their extraction). The resources category is again divided into paramarginal and submarginal groups. The former are those resources that are recoverable at prices as much as 1½ times the current price levels, and the latter are resources that are not recoverable even at these higher prices. In 1976, an extended version of the McKelvey classification was published and we examine this system in Box 16.1.

The basic purpose of the McKelvey system is to assist long-term planning by bringing together information on the probability of discovering new

Box 16.1 McKelvey Box-type diagram: resources and reserves

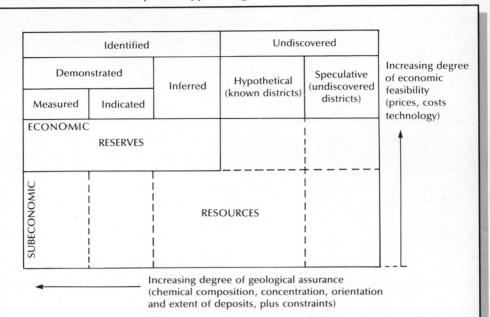

Source: US Geological Survey Bulletin 1450–A (1976)

- Original Resource – the amount of a resource before production.
- Identified Resources – those whose location, grade, quality and quantity are known or estimated from specific geologic evidence. The category includes economic and subeconomic components and can also be subdivided on geologic certainty grounds into measured (proved), indicated (probable) and inferred (possible).
- Demonstrated Resources – measured plus indicated.
- Measured – size, shape, depth and mineral content of the resource are well established.
- Indicated – geologic data not as comprehensive as for measured but still probably good enough to estimate size, shape, etc., characteristics of deposits.
- Inferred – assumed continuity of data, estimates not supported by samples or measurements.
- Reserve Base – that part of an identified resource that meets specified minimum physical and chemical criteria related to current mining and production practices, including those for grade, quality, thickness and depth. The reserve base is the in-place demonstrated resource from which reserves are estimated. The reserve base includes those resources

that are currently economic (reserves), marginally economic, and some of those that are currently subeconomic.

- Reserves – that part of the reserve base which could be economically extracted or produced at the time of determination.
- Undiscovered resources – the existence of which are only postulated, comprising deposits that are separate from identified resources.
- Hypothetical Resources – undiscovered resources that are similar to known mineral bodies and that may reasonably be expected to exist in the same producing district or region under analogous geologic conditions.
- Speculative resources – undiscovered resources that may occur either in known types of deposits in favourable geologic settings where mineral discoveries have not been made, or in types of deposits as yet unrecognized for their economic potential.

It is possible to further extend the Box by including supplies of secondary (recyclable) materials. The reserve category will include recycled scrap flows (see Chapters 1 and 18) and the resource category will include the bulk municipal solid waste stream which is as yet not recycled.

deposits, on the development of economic extraction processes for currently unworkable deposits and on known immediately available deposits. Thus resources are being continuously reassessed in the light of new geologic knowledge, scientific and technical progress and changing economic and political conditions. Known resources are therefore classified on the basis of two types of information: geologic or physical/chemical characteristics (grade, quality, tonnage, thickness and depth of material in place); and financial profitability based on costs of extraction and marketing at a given point in time.

The resource scarcity pessimists tend to use so-called **static stock index** calculations to support their arguments. This type of calculation uses only data on proved reserves (which underestimate 'true' supply or ultimately recoverable resources) and combines it with resource demand estimates forecasted to increase exponentially over time (i.e. rapidly increasing demand). The result is the rapid depletion of many important resource stocks (minerals and fuels), a number before the end of the twentieth century.

If this is the case, why has this not been headline news in the 1980s or 1990s? The answer is that even if we alter only one side of the pessimist's calculation (the supply side) we get quite different results. Basing the calculation on estimated reserves, not just those already proved, or on recoverable resources indicates that we are safe from absolute depletion of our important mineral resource stocks for at least the next 100 years. However, these calculations do assume that we will not meet any insurmountable, technological, energy-supply or environmental damage problems over the same period. In Box 16.2 we present some examples of the pessimistic and the more optimistic physical scarcity forecasts.

Box 16.2 Resource scarcity forecasts

Taking the 'limits to growth' (LTG) approach, Table 1 suggests that a number of non-renewable resources face imminent exhaustion, e.g. in the absence of new discoveries gold, silver and mercury 'in the ground' should already be exhausted. But because the reserves concept is constantly changing by 1980 some of the metals reserve estimates had increased significantly, or remained roughly constant (Table 2).

Taking a Ricardian and technocentric position, it is possible to show that physical scarcity is unlikely to be a significant problem for most of the materials currently in use. This optimistic forecast has been calculated both on estimates of identified reserves and recoverable resources (see Table 3). It also assumes that no severe technological, energy or environmental problems linked to resource extraction will have to be tackled in the next one hundred years or so.

Table 1 The 1972 exponential exhaustion indices in years ($S =$ known global reserves)

	S	$5 \times S$		S	$5 \times S$
Aluminium	31	55	Molybdenum	34	45
Chromium	95	154	Natural Gas	22	49
Coal	111	150	Nickel	53	96
Cobalt	60	148	Petroleum	20	50
Copper	21	48	Platinums	47	85
Gold	9	29	Silver	13	42
Iron	93	173	Tin	15	61
Lead	21	64	Tungsten	28	72
Manganese	46	94	Zinc	18	50

Source: Meadows *et al.* (1972), pp. 56–60.

Table 2 Revised estimates of global reserves: selected metals and minerals

	LTG 1972 (10^6 tonnes)[a]	US BOM 1980 (10^6 tonnes)[b]
Copper	308	505
Nickel	66	64
Lead	91	127
Zinc	123	162

[a]*Limits to Growth.*   [b]US Bureau of Mines.

Table 3 Depletion prospects based on recoverable resource estimates: selected metals and minerals

Material	Demand growth per annum (%)	Estimated identified reserves (tonnes)	Depletion of estimated reserves by year 2100 (%)	Depletion of estimated recoverable resources by year 2100 (%)
Chromium	3.3	1.0×10^{10}	12	—
Cobalt	2.8	5.4×10^6	150	36
Manganese	2.7–3.3	2.8×10^9	120	18
Molybdenum	4.5	2.1×10^7	249	5
Nickel	4.0	2.1×10^8	152	35
Titanium	3.8	7.1×10^8	102	38
Tungsten	3.4	6.8×10^6	236	11
Zinc	2.0	3.3×10^8	581	37

Source: Goeller and Zucker (1984)

Price or cost-based scarcity indicators

Three more 'economic' measures of scarcity have been used in the published literature:

(a) real costs of production (i.e. cost of inputs required to extract and process a unit of resource output);
(b) real prices (i.e. relative prices);
(c) shadow prices (i.e. proxies such as the cost of producing an additional unit of proven reserves) for the unobservable **user cost** of the resource (the forgone value of using a resource now rather than in the future). We say more about user cost in a succeeding section of this chapter.

The results of the studies that have applied these 'economic' scarcity measures to minerals and fuels data have not been particularly consistent. The results are summarized in Box 16.3. Overall, the evidence, such as it is, does not support the dire predictions of the LTG camp. The world is not going to suddenly run short of the important minerals and fuels it needs for economic development.

Non-renewable resource extraction: some economic principles

Extraction companies have to go through a complicated and interrelated three-stage process (exploration, development and extraction – see Box 16.4) in order to supply the market. A primary feature of the mineral-extracting industry is that, unlike most other producing sectors, production in any given period is *not* independent of production in any other period. The current rate of extraction of a mineral affects the amount of that mineral that may be extracted in future periods. Therefore the cost of extracting a unit of the mineral today depends not only on the current level of usage of the necessary production inputs (labour, energy, etc.) and their prices, but also on the levels of input usage in the past and on the impact of current extraction on the future profitability of the mineral deposit.

Current extraction activity can affect the level of reserves available in the future in two opposite ways. An increase in the rate of extraction in the present can *reduce* the level of reserves for a specific deposit. Equally, the same increase in extraction can *increase* exploration and development activities which will lead to an increase in the level of future reserves.

Minerals extracting industries have also been subject to considerable government intervention. This intervention has been driven by policy objectives such as the stimulation of economic growth, the need to ensure national self-sufficiency in strategic materials, increased stringency in environmental protection measures and resource conservation.

In Chapter 15 we showed that the discount rate is of critical importance in

Box 16.3 'Economic' resource scarcity indicators

Two very well known US studies (Barnett and Morse, 1964; Barnett, 1979) examined the trend in unit costs of production for a range of fuels and minerals, and found no evidence of increasing scarcity over time. The apparent increases in the 1970s were not considered to be 'true' reflections of scarcity but rather the influence (thought likely to be only temporary) of the OPEC oil cartel and its price escalation policy.

More recent work by Slade (1982) suggested that exploration, substitutability and technical progress gains have now been overwhelmed by scarcity. Slade's model seems to indicate that the trend in resource relative prices is quadratic (i.e. U-shaped) for some eleven commodities and is therefore increasing quite rapidly during recent times (see Panel (a)). But Anderson (1985) examined the same price data and came to an opposite conclusion. His results revealed very little difference between linear and quadratic relative price trends (Panel (b)). We illustrate both Slade's and Anderson's results for nickel in Panels (a) and (b).

Panel (a) History of deflated prices and fitted linear and quadratic trends for nickel.

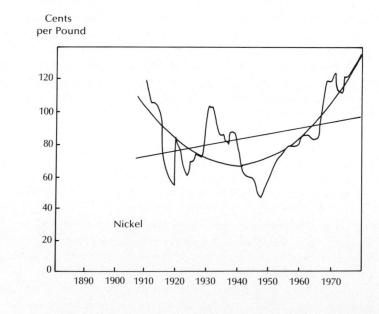

Source: Slade (1982) p. 122, Fig. 6.

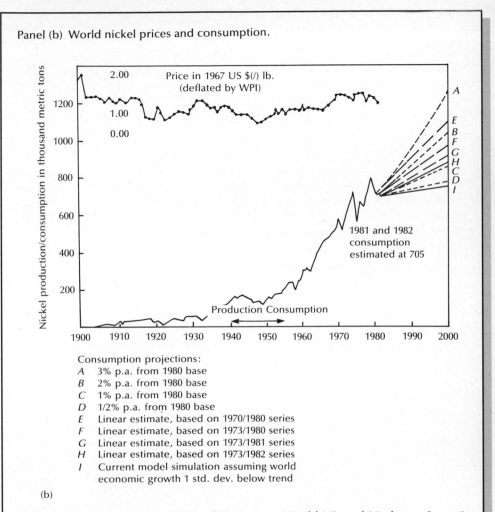

Panel (b) World nickel prices and consumption.

Consumption projections:
A   3% p.a. from 1980 base
B   2% p.a. from 1980 base
C   1% p.a. from 1980 base
D   1/2% p.a. from 1980 base
E   Linear estimate, based on 1970/1980 series
F   Linear estimate, based on 1973/1980 series
G   Linear estimate, based on 1973/1981 series
H   Linear estimate, based on 1973/1982 series
I   Current model simulation assuming world
    economic growth 1 std. dev. below trend

(b)

Source: Ontario Ministry of Natural Resources, *World Mineral Markets – Stage 2* (October 1981); quoted in Anderson (1985).

Note that Anderson has used a longer time series, at both ends, and has also presented the data on a compressed *y*-axis scale. We are grateful to our colleague Norm Henderson for pointing out this example to us.

The most comprehensive study to date (Hall and Hall, 1984) tested the hypothesis that scarcity (measured by unit costs and by relative prices) decreased in the 1960s but increased in the 1970s in the United States. Their results shown in Table 1 indicate that oil, gas and electricity did become more scarce in the 1970s (and the same was true for timber).

Table 1 The scarcity of resources

Resource	Unit cost test	Relative price test
Coal	60s down, 70s up	Not significant
Oil	60s down, 70s up	60s down, 70s up
Gas		60s?, 70s up
Electric power	60s down, 70s up(?)	60s down, 70s up
Non-ferrous metals	60s up, 70s down	60s, 70s?

Notes: 'Down' means scarcity decreases; 'up' means scarcity increases. ? means the result is statistically not significant or the direction of change is indeterminate.
Source: Hall and Hall (1984), pp. 369–70.

Box 16.4 Simple economic model of resource extraction

The supply of non-renewable resources is a three-stage interrelated process, Panel (a).

Panel (a) Non-renewable resource supply process.

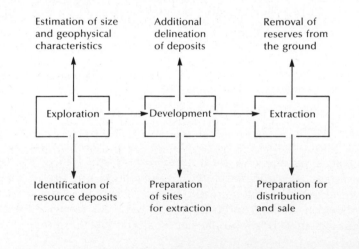

Current decisions are related to past decisions, as well as to expectations of the future prices and costs. The current rate of extraction affects the amount that may be extracted in future periods. Consequently, the cost of extracting a unit of some mineral today depends not only on the current level of mineral usage and necessary inputs and their prices, but also on the level of input usage in the past, as well as on the impact of current extraction on the profitability of the deposit. For a given inventory of already discovered sites, a decision to develop relatively low-cost sites today leaves only higher cost sites for the future. Reductions in the total stock of resource-bearing sites and the tendency for earlier discovery of large and more accessible sites lead to increased exploration costs over time.

Activity at each stage of the supply process satisfies a *derived demand* for inputs to subsequent stages, e.g. new discoveries are an input to development and new reserves are an input to extraction. Changes in the price of final output and in supply costs influence decisions at all three supply stages. Thus final output price changes influence exploration and development decisions, as well as extraction decisions. Development cost changes clearly affect development activities, but also the derived demands for new discoveries and extraction decisions through changes in the cost of replacing reserves.

The decision process is subject to a significant degree of uncertainty. Because extraction companies lack full knowledge of future prices and costs, they must predict both future prices and the uncertain consequences of current decisions on future prices.

The supply process is also affected by the impact of numerous governmental regulatory changes (especially taxation and environmental protection measures). It is also affected by different market structures, e.g. monopoly or near-monopoly markets.

Resource owners seek to maximize the sum of **discounted net revenues** over time, rather than current profits. Depending on their expectations about future prices and costs, resource owners try to balance the gains from increased extraction dependent on price (revenues), with the costs of increased extraction. The extraction costs are made up of increased operating costs plus the user cost of extraction. At the margin, marginal (i.e. per unit of output) extraction operating costs plus user cost is compared with resource price in order to determine the optimal (economically efficient) output over time, i.e. output, Y_1, in Panel (b). To determine the 'full' user cost, all the external costs of resource extraction including pollution damage and landscapes and amenity losses should be included.

The analysis begins in time period t, the current period. The extraction company faces operating costs per unit of output (extraction) given by the curve MC_t (marginal costs in time, t). MC increases with output over the relevant range. The highest cost curve $MC_t + UC$ includes the user cost element.

231

Panel (b) The dependence of quantity extracted upon costs and price.

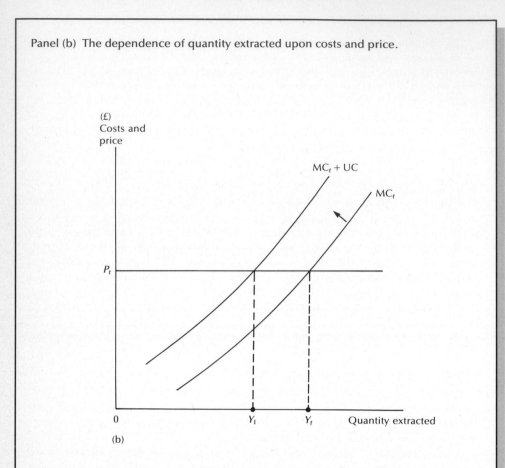

(b)

If we assume the firm has no effect on price (i.e. competitive market conditions) then price in period t, P_t, is shown as a horizontal line. Now the firm will increase its rate of extraction as long as the price it receives, P_t, is greater than the marginal cost (MC) of extraction. It would not increase its rate of extraction if MC > price. In equilibrium $P = MC$. If only current marginal operating costs of extraction are considered, the firm will extract an amount Y_t. The effect of current extraction on future costs and profits decreases current output below the level it would have been at in the absence of these future effects.

Source: Adapted from Anders *et al.* (1980).

determining the rate at which renewable and non-renewable resources are used. The basic rule for a renewable resource was:

Biological Rate of Growth + Growth in Capital Value = Discount Rate

Non-renewable resources have no growth function and have a fixed size, so the rule becomes:

Growth in Capital Value = Discount Rate

In other words, the non-renewable resource should be depleted in such a way that the rate of growth of the price of the extracted resources should equal the discount rate. This rule is known as the **simple Hotelling rule** (after Hotelling's analysis published in 1931), because it applies only to the simplest of cases, for example, situations in which the firm faces zero costs of extraction.

Natural resource economics treats resources 'in the ground' as capital assets. By leaving resources in the ground (preserving them), the resource owner can expect capital gains as the resource price rises through time. The owner will be indifferent between holding the resource in the ground and extracting it if the rate of capital gain equals the rate of interest(s) on alternative assets, since the owner could extract now and sell and invest the revenue elsewhere in the economy (at a positive rate of interest).

So long as we maintain the unrealistic assumption of costless extraction, the price of the resource in the ground is the same as the price of the extracted resource (known as the wellhead price). However, once we drop this assumption (and we now have positive extraction costs) the two prices differ. The price in the ground (known variously as the royalty or rent) is now less than the wellhead price (the difference being the extraction cost). Given that there is a fixed amount of the mineral available for extraction, the full costs of extraction would include an additional element (now called the user cost). The user cost reflects the opportunity cost of current extraction on future profit, because a unit of output extracted now cannot be extracted (and sold for a profit at prices prevailing in the future) in the future. This 'lost' future profit caused by the reduction in the quantity of the mineral available is as real a cost to the mineral extractor as current input costs. So,

extraction costs = user cost + current operating costs; and
optimal price = extraction cost + user cost (see Box 16.4)

The resource owner will try to maximize total profits (revenue – costs) over some time horizon and will select that *rate* of extraction and, since the entire mineral deposit is not generally exploited, that total *level* of extraction that maximizes the present value of the discounted profits stream. An owner might achieve profit maximization by postponing extraction if, for example, it was expected that the price of the mineral would increase substantially in the future (i.e. increase in user cost of current extraction); or if extraction costs were thought likely to fall in the future because of a technological breakthrough in mining/processing methods.

233

On the other hand, if current interest rates paid out on financial investments were to increase then this would serve to increase current rates of mineral extraction in known deposits. A resource owner has the option of extracting to the maximum extent now and investing his profits in order to gain the higher rates of interest. Current profits have, in effect, been made more valuable relative to future profits (in economic terms, the owner has discounted future profits more heavily).

Changes in the rate of interest may also influence the level of effort that extraction companies put into exploring for and developing new sites for future extraction. They also influence investment in new capital equipment, both in deposits already being worked and at new deposits. Increases in the rate of interest would reduce exploration effort and reduce capital equipment investment, thereby offsetting the trend to increased rates of extraction in known deposits.

Conclusions

Summarizing the results of our simple economic model, we can see that the extraction firm is faced with two related and fundamental decisions:

(i) the rate at which to extract resources, and
(ii) the length of the period over which to extract (or the total amount of the reserve to extract).

The economic extraction rate is determined by equating discounted expected price with discounted marginal extraction cost, remembering that extraction costs encompass not just the effect of current extraction on current costs but also the effect of current extraction on future extraction costs and profits (user costs).

The total amount of a reserve that it is economical to extract depends on expected future prices for the resource in question and the effect of current extraction on the future costs of extraction.

Overall, although the measurement of resource scarcity is a far from straightforward task and the published results of the various 'economic' scarcity studies are not consistent, it is not likely that the world is suddenly going to run short of the minerals and fuels it needs for future economic developments.

Further reading

F. J. Anderson, *Natural Resources in Canada*, Methuen, Toronto, 1985.
H. Barnett, 'Scarcity and growth revisited', in V. K. Smith (ed.), *Scarcity and Growth Reconsidered*, Johns Hopkins University Press, Baltimore, 1979.

H. Barnett and C. Morse, *Scarcity and Growth: The Economics of Natural Resource Availability*, Johns Hopkins University Press, Baltimore, 1963.

H. E. Goeller and A. Zucker, 'Infinite resources: The ultimate strategy', *Science* 223 (February): 456–62, 1984.

D. C. Hall and J. V. Hall, 'Concepts and measures of natural resource scarcity', *Journal of Environmental Economics and Management* **11** (September): 369–70, 1984.

D. H. Meadows, D. L. Meadows, J. Randers and W. H. Behrens III, *The Limits to Growth*, Universe Books, New York, 1972.

Ontario Ministry of Natural Resources, *World Mineral Markets – Stage 2*, October 1981, quoted in Anderson (1985).

M. E. Slade, 'Trends in natural resources commodity prices: An analysis of the time domain', *Journal of Environmental Economics and Management* **9**: 122, 1982, Fig. 6.

US Geological Survey Bulletin 1450-A, 1976.

A good basic text on minerals economics is:

G. Anders, W. P. Gramm, S. C. Maurice and C. W. Smithson, *The Economics of Mineral Extraction*, Praeger, New York, 1980.

See also,

D. Bohi and M. A. Toman, 'Understanding non-renewable resource supply behaviour', *Science* (February): 927–32, 1983.

Environmental economics
in action

CHAPTER 17

Business and the environment

Introduction

Part I made it clear that the responsibility for environmental degradation lies with all sections of national and global communities: industry, farmers, *and* governments and citizens. Much environmental literature tends to imply that only industry and agriculture 'pollute'. But it is ordinary citizens who drop litter, and who generate most municipal solid waste. Citizens as consumers send market signals to producers to say that they want their supermarket products packaged for the sake of hygiene and convenience. Consumers can change production and distribution systems to make them environmentally more 'friendly', as the 'green consumer' phenomenon has demonstrated. Ordinary citizens drive cars, often when they could choose alternative modes of transport that are less polluting (rail, public road transport). As we saw in Chapter 6, governments often act against the interests of the environment, sometimes out of indifference, often because they are not aware of how their actions affect the environment.

None the less, industry and agriculture are significant polluters. How then does the business sector fit into the broad structure of environmental economics outlined in the previous parts of this book? While there is a formidable literature on the topic of business and the environment, much of it is devoted to 'green' claims by businesses themselves. Underlying the reticence of many firms to the espousal of environment is a concern about the costs that environmental policy at both government and business level will impose on the business sector.

The costs of environmental policy

Halting or mitigating environmental damage is not costless. Improving the environment means spending resources. OECD countries typically spend around 1.5–2.0 per cent of their national income on pollution abatement (private and public sector expenditures). Few comparisons exist of the national benefits and costs from pollution control. In the United States, in 1981 the benefits that accrued from legislation to control air and water pollution were probably some $37 billion. The costs of the legislation in that year were some $14 billion, indicating that there are major *net* benefits to be obtained by controlling pollution (Portney, 1990). Pollution prevention at the national level pays. But many of the benefits do not accrue directly to business. To get some idea of the impact of environmental policy on the business sector we need to look at how *employment* and *GNP growth* are affected. This is done in Box 17.1 where some of the evidence relating to the GNP and employment impacts of environmental policy is assembled.

While the evidence is still being gathered, the economic approach suggests (a) that environmental damage can make significant inroads into a nation's economic performance, and (b) that policies to control the damage pay off in economic terms.

There are many caveats to such a conclusion, but it looks to be correct, at least for past environmental policy. This does not mean it will be true in the future, nor does it mean that past policy was *efficient*. Regulatory costs could almost certainly have been lower. Benefits could probably have been higher had policies been better targeted. Past policy could probably therefore have yielded even higher benefits, but future policy might be more expensive.

How is this conclusion relevant to corporations? First, it provides a slightly different focus to the way in which the business sector has *traditionally* viewed the environment, which is as a 'drag' on enterprise and economic performance. It suggests that, overall, economic performance is not worsened by improved environmental quality, and may even improve.

Second, it points to the need for a *collective* corporate response. Any *single* enterprise can clearly do little to improve a nation's health and economy by unilaterally investing in environmental improvement. Only if business collectively invests in environmental health will improvements come. It is, after all, industry that converts raw materials and energy into products. It is the consumption of raw materials and energy that creates pollution.

Some environmental issues and the implications for business

Many of the current environmental concerns are international or global in nature: acid rain, ocean pollution, tropical deforestation, global warming, ozone layer depletion. We can illustrate the relevance of these problems to business.

Box 17.1 The effect of environmental policy on economic growth and employment

While industry is rightly concerned about the costs that environmental policies might impose on them, there is little evidence that, in the aggregate, environmental policy constrains economic growth. Part of the reason for this is that the expenditures are not that large, but the other reason is that the expenditures are income to other sectors of industry, e.g. the pollution abatement sector. If that sector is very strong it may even be the case that environmental regulation introduced in a number of countries at once will actually stimulate growth and employment through the creation of export markets. The studies summarized below show that impacts of policy on growth and employment have, so far, been modest or negligible.

Policy	Effect on economic growth	Effect on employment
Dutch National Environmental Protection Plan: approximate doubling of environmental expenditures	Negligible	None or positive
Hypothetical carbon tax in the UK; increased pollution abatement expenditures and water clean-up	Negligible	Positive
Hypothetical carbon tax in Norway	Reduction of 0.4% p.a.	Negligible
Past environmental policy in the USA: Study 1	Reduction of 0.2% p.a.	Not known
Past environmental policy in the USA: Study 2	Negligible	Not known
Past environmental policy in France, Germany, Italy, UK	Negligible	Negligible

Source: D. W. Pearce (1991)

Acid rain

Chapter 22 looks in more detail at the phenomenon of acid rain: a general term to cover both wet and dry depositions of pollutants formed mainly by sulphur dioxide and nitrogen oxides. It seems clear that acid rain is implicated in damage to fish and other species in lakes, especially in southern

Norway and parts of Sweden. Some authorities also think that leaf loss and inhibited growth of forests is due to acid rain. The corrosion of building surfaces may also be due to these pollutants. The evidence for continuing health damage is perhaps rather limited. Cleaning up acid rain means using lower sulphur fossil fuels, and fitting pollution abatement equipment to coal burning power stations and other major plants. While the balance of costs and benefits may be uncertain, there are international agreements to reduce emissions in OECD countries. Signatories (including the United Kingdom) to the Long Range Transboundary Air Pollution Protocol, which came into force in 1987, are bound to reduce sulphur dioxide by 30 per cent below its 1980 level. A nitrogen dioxide agreement of 1988 means that these emissions must not rise above their 1987 level, after which they must fall.

Why does acid rain occur? In economic systems that give considerable emphasis to the free working of the market-place, there is no incentive for any polluter to take account of the environmental damage caused by their actions unless, of course, regulation forces them to do so. Chapters 5 and 6 dealt with this phenomenon of *externalities*. Externalities tend to be endemic to economic systems based on free or nearly free markets. But the victims of pollution can at least lobby government to 'make the polluter pay', which is exactly what does happen when environmental legislation is introduced. All regulations involve the polluter in bearing some cost for preventing, reducing or cleaning up pollution. Some of the cost can be passed on to consumers, but the polluter still suffers because the resulting higher prices for their products in the market-place will tend to discourage demand for them. Box 17.2 shows how business will not bear *all* the cost of any regulation: some of it is passed on to the consumer.

Acid rain, however, involves an additional dimension. While the sufferers of acid rain damage may well be within the same country emitting the pollution, much of the damage is, in fact, borne in other countries. Mainland Europe, for example, pollutes Scandinavia – see Chapter 22. The usual lobbying forces of those who suffer damage now have to be replaced by *international* lobbying aimed at making the polluting country pay. This is more difficult simply because there is no supranational authority to determine who is to blame, by how much and what should be done. These two facts – the 'failure' of markets to account for external damage, and the fact that some air pollutants cross national boundaries – do much to explain the acid rain phenomenon.

What are the implications for business? The first is that the market need not be the enemy of the environment, something that is more likely to surprise environmentalists than businessmen. By keeping materials and energy costs down, business minimizes the flow of energy and materials – and therefore pollution – per unit of economic output. Cost minimization becomes waste minimization, *provided* corporations pay as much attention to materials and energy costs as they do to labour and capital costs.

Box 17.2 The incidence of an environmental regulation on industry and consumer

When a regulation is imposed on industry it raises the firm's costs. For example, acid rain control would mean introducing flue gas desulphurization equipment, or switching to more expensive, lower sulphur fuels. This is shown below as a leftward shift of the MC (marginal cost) curve. For convenience, suppose that firms price their products so that price (P) equals marginal cost (MC). Then, prices in the market-place will rise from P_1 to P_2. But costs have in fact risen by more than P_1P_2 – the actual cost increase is P_1C. Consumers therefore meet some of the cost of regulation through higher prices (P_1P_2) but the firm also bears some of the burden (P_2C). Unless the demand curve is totally inelastic (i.e. is vertical) consumers and producers must always share the financial burden of a regulation.

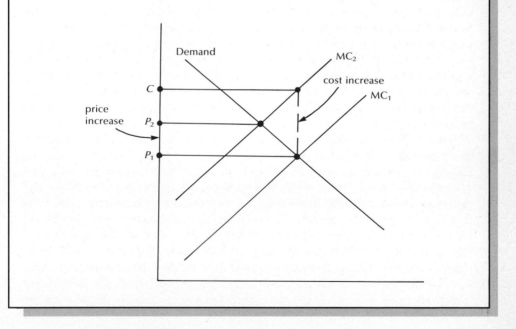

The second implication is that markets do not go far enough. They fail to take full account of environmental costs within a nation, and they fail on a grander scale when the environmental costs are transmitted across national boundaries. It is not tenable to argue that the environment is safe with unfettered free markets. Few businessmen might advance such a proposition, but others do. There has to be environmental regulation.

Tropical deforestation

The world's tropical forests are disappearing at a rate of perhaps 2 per cent per annum – Chapter 23 looks at the issue in more detail. As yet there are no international agreements which set targets to reduce this rate – discussions began in the late 1980s in an effort to get an international convention on the sustainable use of all the world's forests, including the tropical forests. The loss of tropical forest involves many kinds of economic cost. Logging or clearance for agriculture and livestock is often not the most *financially* rewarding use of tropical forest land. Neither is it sustainable since forest soils have limited capability for supporting crop production or ranching over the decades. Forest destruction dislocates indigenous peoples; it causes pollution of rivers as the forest soils are washed away; it removes the protective function of forests with respect to the watersheds of which they are part; it lowers the stock and range of biological diversity, and causes anguish to the many people who want to see these ecosystems preserved or used sustainably. All of these are economic costs. We have little idea at the moment of what those costs amount to, but the evidence is beginning to suggest that tropical deforestation simply doesn't pay economically – see Chapter 23.

Why does tropical deforestation occur? The causes are complex and not always as easily put down to population growth and poverty, the conventional explanations. Both play their part – as population expands the pressure for more agricultural land grows and the 'frontier' is invaded by agricultural settlers. But invading tropical forests is not always that easy – road-building programmes assist by opening up the forest area. Roads are often built by logging companies, the farmers follow. What is less often appreciated is that governments themselves encourage forest exploitation – it is the phenomenon of government failure again. The prevailing philosophy has often been one which views the forest as a resource for exploitation, not sustainable use. Tax concessions and subsidies are sometimes given to ranchers to clear the land (a policy which largely ended in the Brazilian Amazon in 1987 as the costs of deforestation became clearer). Land rights can often be obtained only by clearing the land as the means of recognizing title. The rights of indigenous people have all too often been ignored, especially where they are not registered or formalized.

Like most environmental degradation, deforestation occurs because of a combination of important fundamental factors:

(a) markets and governments tend to recognize only the *cash* value of the forest, not its economic importance in terms of 'unmarketed' benefits like watershed protection;

(b) *rights* to the land tend to be biased in favour of colonizers and developers, not indigenous people;

(c) *incentives* in the form of tax breaks and concessions encourage conversion of forested land to agriculture and timber production;
(d) there are *underlying presssures* from population growth, giving rise to demands for agricultural land and fuelwood; and *underlying enabling factors* such as road-building which opens up the forest.

Does business have a role to play in protecting the tropical forests of the world? It seems fair to say that only revisions in policies by the forest-owning countries will make a *major* change to the rate of deforestation, together with a recognition on the part of the rich countries that poor countries need to be assisted with the resources to protect their forests. But business is critical to the process. It is the logging companies of the world that are opening up many of the forests, notably in the Far East. It is the demand for fuelwood that causes some deforestation in Africa. Yet, if efficient energy sources not relying on trees could be developed cheaply some of this pressure could be removed. Similarly, some fuelwood plantations could reduce the demand for natural forest timber. In Indonesia and South America there are products from the natural forest that might be developed without destroying the forest. To reduce the agricultural demand for forest land it is important to raise the productivity of existing degraded lands. As productivity rises, there is less incentive to abandon land and clear new forest land, and raising land productivity is very much an activity demanding industrial expertise. What at first sight seems a remote and exotic concern for the corporate sector, is not. For once the causal processes of tropical deforestation are understood, corporations will be seen to play an essential role in reducing the pressures that give rise to deforestation.

Global warming

Chapter 19 looks in more detail at the problem of global warming. While the science remains very uncertain, there is increasing evidence that the rate at which certain 'greenhouse gases' are being emitted to the atmosphere is causing an increase in the average temperature of the earth's surface. The main gases giving rise to this enhanced greenhouse effect are carbon dioxide (from the burning of fossil fuels and from the burning of tropical forests); chlorofluorocarbons (CFCs – used as propellants, refrigerants, solvents and foam blowing agents, among other things); methane (from coal mines, ruminant livestock, rice paddies, gas leakages, and other things); and nitrous oxides (the sources of which are unclear, but do involve fertilizers and fossil fuel combustion). Clearly, then, the greenhouse gases emanate mainly from industrial processes, from electricity generation, and from agriculture. Business is heavily implicated in the generation of the culprit gases.

The policy equation is one of incurring costs now to prevent damage in the future, some of which appears fairly certain, and some of which is very uncertain. A number of countries have already decided that the problem is too important to be left to chance. They have established target reductions for the main greenhouse gas – carbon dioxide. Mostly these centre on the idea of not letting emissions rise above the level at the end of the 1980s. Because energy consumption is likely to increase over time with population pressure and economic growth, some time is needed to implement such a target. Committed countries have generally said they will 'stabilize' emissions of CO_2 at 1990 levels by the year 2000 or 2005. Some, such as Germany, may go further.

Getting a global warming agreement will be difficult. Cutting CO_2 emissions could initially be very cheap – simple energy conservation measures would make a major inroad in CO_2 emissions and they are likely to be very inexpensive. Natural gas has a lower carbon content than oil and coal – substituting gas for coal and oil will therefore lower CO_2 emissions. Later measures could become more expensive – substituting more expensive energy systems for fossil fuel plants, for example. Many countries have no incentive to 'play the game' – they would incur costs that might be incommensurate with the uncertain benefits. That is how the United States tends to view the issue. Some countries may have ambiguous views about the benefits but feel they cannot afford the measures needed to control emissions – China and India, for example. Others, such as the former USSR and Eastern Europe, have other more pressing economic problems to solve.

One of the surest ways to induce energy conservation and encourage low carbon fuels is to introduce a tax on carbon fuels. Coal would attract the highest tax, oil the next highest, natural gas the lowest according to their carbon content. Energy sources such as wind, wave, solar and nuclear would be exempt from the tax. The power of the carbon tax is that it directly affects the price of energy, and the experience from the 1970s and 1980s with energy prices shows us that there is a direct and powerful link between energy prices and conservation of energy (Box 17.3). But however the carbon emissions issue is tackled, there are fairly obvious implications for industry. For even if the CO_2 targets are achieved without taxes, industry will bear the initial cost of the regulations. Moreover, because fossil fuel use is so pervasive to modern industrial economies, few people will escape the burden of controlling CO_2 emissions.

Box 17.4 shows industries in the UK that are heavy energy users relative to their total costs of production, allowing for the energy embodied in the various raw materials they buy as well as for the energy they consume directly. By and large, these are the industries that would bear the *initial* burden of controls on CO_2 emissions. Contrary to what one might expect, an environmental tax such as a carbon tax could work to industry's *benefit*. Unlike other taxes, an environmental tax does not have as its primary purpose the raising of revenue. Its aim is to *change the behaviour* of industry.

Box 17.3 The effect of energy prices on energy conservation in the United Kingdom

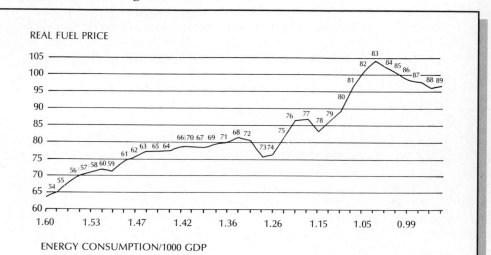

ENERGY CONSUMPTION/1000 GDP

Energy conservation can be broadly measured by the **energy ratio**. The ratio shows the amount of energy needed to produce £1000 of economic activity ('GDP' = gross domestic product) and is measured along the horizontal axis. The lower the ratio the more energy efficiency there is. The price of energy is measured on the vertical axis. While there are other influences on energy conservation, the diagram shows a clear link between higher energy prices and energy conservation.

The tax can be avoided by adopting pollution abatement technology, reducing pollution and therefore reducing the tax payment – as Chapter 11 showed. There are two main reasons why such incentive taxes are beneficial to industry:

1. As Chapters 11 and 13 showed, the cost to industry of complying with the tax-based regulation can actually be *less* than the cost of complying with other forms of regulation. It tends to be overlooked that *all* regulation imposes an initial cost on industry. What is not economically sensible is to impose higher than necessary costs in order to achieve a given environmental quality target.

2. If environmental taxes are not primarily aimed at raising revenues then there is a legitimate case for returning the revenues actually raised back to industry. While taking away with one hand and returning with the other may seem odd, the incentive role of the environmental tax would none the less remain. Industry could still avoid the tax by polluting less. The return

of the tax could take the form of a reduction in corporation taxes, providing a further incentive to enterprise. This is sometimes known as the *double-dividend* feature of an incentive tax.

Motives for industry to exhibit environmental concern

There are at least five reasons why industry can gain from adopting a strong environmental stance.

Environment and efficiency

Anything that can be done to reduce the flow of materials and energy through the economic system will reduce the pollution burden on the environment. But materials and energy are marketed resources. They have prices and therefore their use shows up as a cost in the accounts of the average corporation. Cutting materials and energy costs, then, cuts pollution.

The experience of environmental audits and assessments in the business sector reveals that many businesses have not been paying as much attention to materials and energy costs as they have to labour costs and capital costs.

Box 17.4 Energy intensity of UK industry in the 1980s

Industry	Energy costs as % of total costs (approximate)
Refineries	80 +
Electricity generation	60
Organic chemicals	35
Air transport	25
Cement	22
Coal mining	20
Inorganic chemicals	15 +
Railways	15
Bricks	15
Fertilizers	15 −
Iron and steel	10
Glass	10
Pulp and paper	10

Often, materials and energy costs are a small fraction of overall costs, and where they are not, industry tends to be highly effective in the way it uses energy. But, while the small size of materials and energy costs relative to total costs, or to output, may be an *explanation* for the comparative neglect of energy and materials efficiency in business, it is not a *justification*. Every £1 saved on the materials bill without sacrificing output is an extra £1 in profits. Around 15 per cent of the UK GNP is accounted for by materials costs alone. Some major companies have invented snappy slogans to capture the efficiency–environment linkage: such as 'pollution prevention pays' (PPP), 'save money and reduce toxics' (SMART), 'wipe out waste' (WOW) and 'waste reduction always pays' (WRAP).

Environment as image

Taking a positive stance on the environment can be good for image and therefore for market share. Gaining market share through 'greening' the image of the company will succeed only if consumers themselves think green credentials are important, i.e. if 'green consumerism' persists. Green consumerism has been associated with a confusion about environmental information on products. The establishment of a consistent ecological labelling ('ecolabelling') system, such as those adopted in some European countries, helps consumers sort out true from false claims about the environmental impact of products. No product, for example, can be totally 'environmentally friendly'. In so far as it uses up materials and energy, it will have an impact on the environment, as Chapter 1 demonstrated. Nor are the environmental impacts of may products known with any degree of accuracy – it is not so long ago that CFCs were regarded as safe, efficient and harmless.

Green images may matter for a far less obvious reason than product market share. Getting the best *employees* may also depend on being authentically pro-environment. Some surveys have shown that potential employees think that environmental image is very important to the choice of company to work for. Indeed, many companies cite the 'green employee' as a major force in the reevaluation of corporate image.

Environment and market opportunity

Environmental expenditures must result in income for *someone*: the manufacturer of the pollution abatement equipment, the supplier of a less polluting technology, the recycler, the clean-up industry. The United Kingdom spends at least £6.5 billion every year on pollution control. One report suggests that this market will grow to some £14 billion p.a. over the next ten years, with a European market of £86 billion p.a. and a US market of £100 billion p.a. These are huge market opportunities in technologies ranging from flue gas desulphurization equipment, through to water filters and catalytic converters.

Pollution reduction takes place in two ways: by 'end of pipe' technologies which abate pollution from given technological processes and raw materials, and by 'source reduction', i.e. redesigning the product at source so that it contains less materials and energy that will become waste. By and large, existing environmental policy is based on end-of-pipe technology. In the future it will be source reduction that will matter as it becomes more widely recognized that low-waste designs for products and technologies is more efficient than finding add-on solutions. Indeed, this will be part of the up-and-coming shift in overall policy to anticipation and prevention rather than reaction and clean-up. Terms like the 'precautionary principle' of environmental management will become commonplace.

If this forecast is right there will be a high premium on new designs for vehicles, for containers, for packaging and so on. Only business can make that transition from 'end-of-pipe' solutions to 'waste reduction at source' solutions.

Environmental compliance

The typical industry view of environmental legislation is that it is something with which to comply. This is industry in its reactive mode: government legislates, industry reacts. It does not follow that industry always knows what either the existing or planned legislation is, as a number of surveys show. Non-compliance can be costly, but it can be just as costly to ignore future developments in environmental policy at the national, European and global level. What we might term 'anticipatory compliance' is likely to become vital to industry. There is a need to analyze impending environmental problems and think how governments, international agencies and the world in general will react to them. Those reactions will have implications for the corporate sector. More importantly, by *anticipating* trends business can minimize the disruption from complying with new environmental requirements, and can capture the market opportunities they are likely to generate.

Conclusions

The four preceding business interests in environmental change all have a common feature – *self-interest*. It is in industry's self-interest to cut costs, improve market share, capture new markets and comply with regulation. In all cases, business can escape the 'reactive mode' and enter anticipatory mode; but it can all take place without a genuine concern for environment. After all, the prime motivation for the existence of the corporate sector is to make profit. We have argued that this need not be inconsistent with improving the environment. What is required is careful management to decouple the legitimate pursuit of profit from its impact on the environment. Freely functioning markets will not do that without aid. Wholesale government intervention will almost certainly not achieve it either: governments may set out to be benign but they frequently manage economies and environments no better than free markets.

It is conceivable that the pursuit of self-interest within a regulatory framework will secure sustainable development. But the moral case for the environment remains, and it shows through in business approaches to the environment. It shows as *commitment* – which we might define as a concern for the environment which cannot be explained in terms of the self-interested motives discussed previously. *Proving* and *measuring* commitment are difficult, maybe impossible. But it isn't easy to understand some corporate approaches to the environment unless commitment exists.

Further reading

D. W. Pearce, *Employment and Environmental Policy*, Economic Report, The Employment Institute, London, 1991.

Most large companies issue statements about commitment to environmental policy. Useful illustrations are given in:

T. Burke and J. Hill, *Ethics, Environment and the Company*, Institute of Business Ethics, London, 1990.

Many case studies and useful illustrations are to be found in:

Business International Ltd, *Managing the Environment: The Greening of European Business*, Business International Ltd, London, 1990.

Some sections of this chapter have been taken from:

F. Cairncross, *Costing the Earth: What Governments Must Do; What Consumers Need to Know; How Businesses Can Profit*, The Economist Business Books, London, 1991.

D. W. Pearce, *Corporate Responsibility and the Environment*, British Gas, London, 1991.

The reference to the study on costs and benefits of environmental policy is:

P. Portney, *Public Policies for Environmental Protection*, Resources for the Future, Washington, DC, 1990.

CHAPTER 18

Managing waste

Introduction

The generation and disposal of municipal solid waste (MSW) appears to have become an important policy problem in all industrialized economies. The OECD Member countries produced, according to official statistics, 420 million tonnes of MSW annually in the late 1980s. The precise composition of this waste varied from country to country, but in most countries, packaging, it has been claimed, has become a significant proportion of the total (25–50 per cent). Waste disposal practices also vary between countries and across regions within countries. But with some exceptions (e.g. Japan, Denmark and Switzerland) a majority of industrialized economies dispose of the bulk of their MSW via landfill.

Policy-makers, and to a more limited extent society in general, have become more concerned about MSW, especially in metropolitan areas, as existing landfills have closed or have approached full capacity and resistance (on social acceptability grounds) to siting new disposal facilities has intensified (i.e. the NIMBY syndrome).

Impediments to rational waste management policy

However, although waste management issues have acquired a higher political and social profile in recent years, rational decision making, i.e. the achievement of the least-cost method or combination of methods for managing MSW in a given community, as well as equitable decision-making (i.e. the avoidance of overly regressive policy impacts) has been constrained by a series of 'failures' (Turner, 1991; Turner and Powell, 1991).

At a fundamental level databases on waste generation and disposal are deficient (information failure). While there is a variety of sources of data on MSW and other waste flows, most countries lack a single database that is national, comprehensive and current. Further, few countries have agencies which have taken an overall systems perspective when dealing with waste planning and management, and the lack of economic cost–benefit thinking has also been commonplace (analytical failure).

Even with better data collection and analysis, however, more efficient waste management would still be impeded by market failure. The authorities have failed to correctly price MSW collection and disposal services. The underpricing of MSW services (i.e. failure to reflect the full social costs of collection and disposal) leads to too high an aggregate level of MSW in a market economy and too low a level of recycling or source reduction measures. The causes of the throwaway society lie in the distorted market incentives that affect both consumer and producer behaviour. The result according to some analysts is product design, product choice and disposal decisions that are overly resource intensive (Menell, 1990). Too much waste is produced and additionally, the product-mix will not be optimal. It will not reflect that combination of products with the least-cost net environmental impact.

Box 18.1 illustrates the derivation of the economically optimal level of waste for disposal and why, because of various 'failures', the level of recycling in the absence of government intervention will be too low.

Waste management policy instruments: command-and-control versus economic instruments approaches

Regulatory command-and-control approach

Environment (including waste management) policy has traditionally been secured through the use of the *command-and-control* regulatory standards approach. Under this approach, the regulatory authority sets an environmental standard (target) and the polluter is required to honour the standard, under the threat of some penalty system.

Box 18.2 summarizes some of the waste recycling standards that have recently been adopted, or are under consideration, in industrialized economies.

This targets-setting process is well-meaning but may not always represent a feasible policy objective because of information deficiencies and the lack of a proper 'systems' perspective. In the United States, Alter (1991) has concluded that a proper analysis of the MSW data that are available suggests a future decrease in the amount of recyclable items in MSW, hence a change in the economics of recycling. He further claims that an analysis of the intensity of waste generation (similar to materials intensity of Gross National Product calculations; Evans and Szekeley, 1985) questions whether the generation rate of MSW in the United States is likely to increase as the economy grows. Even

Box 18.1 Economically optimal level of waste for disposal

Panel (a) The optimal levels of waste and disposal and recycling.

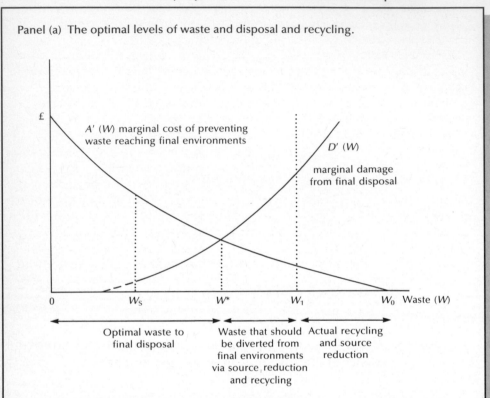

£

$A'(W)$ marginal cost of preventing waste reaching final environments

$D'(W)$

marginal damage from final disposal

0   W_S W^* W_1 W_0 Waste (W)

Optimal waste to final disposal

Waste that should be diverted from final environments via source reduction and recycling

Actual recycling and source reduction

Panel (a) shows stylized costs and benefits of preventing MSW from reaching final disposal. The optimal level of wastage for disposal to final environments is given by W^*, where the marginal benefits of reducing waste (= the marginal damage avoided) are equated with the marginal costs of preventing waste reaching final environments (land, water or air).

More formally, we define

$$NBWR = B(WR) - A(WR)$$

where: NBWR = net benefits of waste reduction
$\quad\quad\quad$ B(WR) = benefits of waste reduction
$\quad\quad\quad$ A(WR) = costs of waste reduction

Thus the optimal waste disposed of to final environments is given by

$$B'(W^*) = A'(W^*)$$

or

$$-D'(W^*) = A'(W^*)$$

where D(W) is damage from final disposal.

Table 1 Comparative recycling tonnages: 1989

	Paper	Glass	Aluminium	Plastics[a]
	(tonnes)			
Belgium	691 000	208 000	n.a.	109 020
Denmark	311 000	58 000	n.a.	55 926
France	2881 000	760 000	233 100	523 800
Germany (FRG)	5627 000	1538 000	527 000	803 980
Great Britain	2975 000	310 000	220 000	102 480
Greece	n.a.	14 000	n.a.	n.a.
Ireland	n.a.	11 000	n.a.	n.a.
Italy	1733 000	670 000	390 000	296 185
Netherlands	1488 000	279 000	129 000	177 215
Portugal	273 000	34 000	n.a.	n.a.
Spain	1591 000	287 000	77 600	64 704
USA	23 500 000	750 000	2600 000[b]	114 000
Japan	13 091 000	1155 000	62 766 000[c]	n.a.
	(tonnes/head)			
Belgium	0.0671	0.021 00	n.a.	
Denmark	0.0610	0.011 40	n.a.	
France	0.0522	0.013 00	0.0040	
Germany (FRG)	0.0922	0.024 70	0.0086	
Great Britain	0.0526	0.005 60	0.0040	
Greece	n.a.	0.001 40	n.a.	
Ireland	n.a.	0.003 10	n.a.	
Italy	0.0304	0.001 75	0.0068	
Netherlands	0.1026	0.018 80	0.0087	
Portugal	0.0268	0.003 30	n.a.	
Spain	0.0412	0.007 40	0.0020	

[a]All plastic waste arisings; average European recovery rate for plastics in MSW = 0.8% (mechanical and thermal recycling).
[b]Includes all metals (ferrous and non-ferrous).
[c]Number of cans recovered.
Source: ENDS Reports (1990, 1991)

Since all (see Tables 1 and 2) industrialized countries are already engaged in some recycling of components of MSW, we show actual recycling and source reduction measures (e.g. product redesign to achieve less resource intensive production) as $W_0 - W_1$, i.e. W_0 would be the amount of waste being disposed of to final environments if there was no recycling or source reduction activity. If actual waste is W_1, then $W_0 - W_1$ is the waste already recycled or subject to source reduction.

Table 2 Comparative recycling rates: components of MSW

	Paper		Glass		Steel cans	Aluminium cans
	1984	1990	1984	1990	1989	1989
Netherlands	46.0	49.0	53.0	66.0	48.0	
Belgium/ Luxembourg	32.8	35.2	42.0	60.0	28.0	
Germany	38.1	43.0	39.0	54.0	58.0	
Austria	n.a.					18.0
Italy	26.1	25.7	25.0	50.0	n.a.	
France	34.1	34.4	26.0	45.0	26.0	
Denmark	29.3	33.2	19.0	40.0	n.a.	
Switzerland	44.0	61.0 (1988)	45.0	56.0 (1989)		38.0 (1990)
Portugal	45.0	39.1	10.0	30.0	n.a.	
Spain	41.0	38.7	13.0	27.0	n.a.	
UK	28.6	30.4	10.0	21.0	n.a.	5.3 (1990)
Eire	n.a.	n.a.	7.0	18.0	n.a.	16.0 (all cans)
Greece	15.1	n.a.	n.a.	16.0	n.a.	20.0
USA	27.3	30.0 (1988)	10.0 (1985)	n.a.	30.0	
Japan	50.1	48.2 (1989)	42.1	47.6 (1989)	43.6	42.5
Australia	22.0	30.0 (1988)	17.0 (1980)	n.a.	n.a.	61.0

In the absence of any government intervention, $W_0 - W_1$ is the financially optimal level of recycling and waste reduction, i.e. the level that will occur because of market forces. But because of the 'failure' phenomena outlined in the text, the economically optimal level of recycling and waste reduction $W_0 - W^*$ is in excess of the current level, $W_0 - W_1$. Intervention policies are required in order to increase recycling and source reduction activity to the level $W_0 - W^*$.

Box 18.2 Examples of the regulatory approach to waste recycling

Country	Regulatory Standard (Target)
Austria	Has passed a regulation which mandates the following refilling/recycling rates for glass and cans: Beer: glass 70% by 1992; cans 90% by 1994 Carbonates: glass 60% by 1992; cans 80% by 1994 Juices: glass 25% by 1992; cans 40% by 1994.
Belgium	Target level of 30% of waste to be recycled by 1995; the balance to be incinerated; landfill to be used only as a last resort.
Canada	National Packaging Protocol adopted in 1990, aims to reduce packaging in the MSW by 20% (from 1989 levels) by 1992 and by 50% by the year 2000.
France	50% recycling target (undated), either involving materials recycling or energy production.
Germany	64% recycling target by 1995, bias towards materials recycling rather than energy production.
Holland	10% reduction in all waste target; 50% minimum reuse/ recycling target for MSW, up to 30% of which could be for energy recovery; landfill to take a maximum of 10% of waste by the year 2000 (intermediate targets to be achieved by 1994).
Italy	Legislation has laid down a 50% recycling target for both glass and cans, to be achieved by the end of 1992. From April 1993, containers which have not met this target will have a penalty tax imposed on them.
Switzerland	Legislation has laid down that the amount of beverage packaging in the waste stream must not exceed 10% by the end of 1993. PVC bottles are banned, and a 50% recycling rate for aluminium beverage cans must be met by the end of 1991.
United Kingdom	50% of recyclables (25% of total MSW) to be recycled by the year 2000.
United States	1988, EPA national goal of reducing waste disposal by 25% by 1992 via recycling and source separation.
EC	Packaging Directive is under consideration; proposals include a packaging waste 'standstill principle' which would operate five years after adoption and be related to a 1990 base level. After five years, materials recycling should encompass 60% of waste, with a maximum of 30% as energy recovery and a maximum landfill requirement of only 10% of total waste.

Source: Pearce and Turner (1992a)

if recycling scheme participation rates and collection system efficiency improve, Alter believes that national recycling targets much in excess of 25 per cent of MSW are unobtainable.

In any case we would argue that neglect of the economics of waste management could lead to the setting of environmental targets that, although feasible possibilities, would still not induce net reductions in total waste flows.

In terms of Figure 18.1 suppose an environmental target W_s is set. The move from W^* to W_s would involve a net loss of economic welfare to society.

Menell (1990) has concluded that although policies such as mandatory separation of household waste and product bans respond to some of the symptoms of the MSW problem, they fail to systematically address the causes of the problem. They do not remedy the distorted incentives that underlie consumer and producer behaviour. Product choice, as well as the disposal decision determines the social costs of MSW. Focusing solely on the separation decision (e.g. via mandatory separation) can lead to perverse results.

Economic instruments approach

The economic approach to environmental policy has now been generally accepted (at least in principle) in most industrialized countries. It stresses the advantages of economic instruments (EIs) which seek to modify human behaviour through the price mechanism. The basic idea is that EIs would be deployed in the economy in order to correct for market failure. EIs have the further advantage that they fit neatly into the cost–benefit approach and principle of management. EIs do not, however, in themselves mitigate the problem of information failure and they will also require careful deployment, with due regard to system-wide effects and the need for integrated management.

A range of different EIs could potentially be deployed (see Box 18.3), including so-called product charges, waste disposal taxes, and deposit–refund systems (in essence a combined tax and subsidy system). Administrative charges (covering among other things disposal site licensing), recycling credits (money paid to agencies responsible for recovering elements of MSW and equal to disposal costs saved by the disposal authority), and material levies, all represent steps in the direction of the EI approach. A system of marketable permits has also been suggested as a mechanism for boosting waste paper and board recycling (Dinan, 1990). EIs are now very much in favour in EC Commission circles and we can expect to see pressure building up in Europe for their more widespread application in the waste management system of the future.

EIs could be applied in the waste management system in order to raise finance and/or stimulate prescribed behaviour via incentives. Financing charges (user charges) have been used to facilitate the collection, processing and storage of waste, or the restoration of old hazardous waste sites. Incentive charges can be used to achieve multiple objectives such as waste minimization, source reduction and increased reuse/recycling. In this chapter only EIs which are *directly* aimed at MSW reduction and/or recycling (reuse) will be covered. We therefore neglect the use of emission charges to air and

Box 18.3   Examples of the use of economic instruments in the management of packaging waste

Country[a]	Type of economic instrument[b]	Application: in use (u); under study/proposed (p)
Austria	deposit–refund	refillable plastic beverage containers subject to mandatory deposit of ÖS 4 (u)
	product charge	non-returnable beverage containers: ÖS 0.5 to 1 per container
Belgium	waste charges (incentives)	MSW (u)
Canada	deposit–refund	beer and soft drinks containers
	waste charge	non-refillable containers
Denmark	deposit–refund	refillable beer and soft drinks containers beverage containers, pesticides in small containers (u)
	product charge	various packaging products
Finland	product charge	non-returnable beverage (carbonated) container (u)
	deposit–refund	refillable beverage (carbonate) containers (u)
France	waste charge (incentive)	MSW (p)
Germany	deposit–refund	plastic beverage containers (u) extension to other packaging[c]
Italy	product charge	non-biodegradable plastic bags (u)
Netherlands	waste charge (incentive)	MSW (p)
	product charge	non-recyclable packaging (p) products with short life PVCs (p)
	deposit–refund	products containing aluminium and long life-cycle PVC (p)
Norway	product charge	disposable carbonate drinks containers (u)
	deposit–refund	refillable beverage containers (u)
Portugal	deposit–refund	metal cans (p)

Sweden	product–charge	beverage containers (u)
	deposit–refund	aluminium cans (u)
	waste charge (incentive)	not specified (p)
Switzerland	product charge	disposable beverage containers (p)
United Kingdom	recycling credits	MSW (u)
USA	deposit–refund	beverage containers (u)
	marketable permits	newsprint (p)
	waste charges	unseparated waste (u)

Source: Pearce and Turner (1993)

[a]Some instruments apply at state, province or regional level only.

[b]User charges for collection and treatment of MSW are applied in almost all industrialized countries; taxes on the use of virgin materials have been implemented in Denmark and have been proposed in the context of sand and gravel resources in Finland.

[c]A 'Dual System' has been introduced (1991), it involves mandatory takeback requirements throughout the supply chain which can only be replaced by industry established separate waste collection and recovery systems (outside of normal municipal system). The Dual System would be financed by 'Green Spot' approval systems, where verification and approval of a package's recyclability will have to be obtained. A payment (user charge) of 0.02DM per package will be imposed, depending on size, to cover the costs of collection and crude separation. A further fee in the form of a recycling subsidy is also being considered.

water, resource extraction taxes and user charges, even though *indirectly* they will serve to reduce the overall generation of waste.

Criteria for choosing between economic instruments

According to OECD Guidelines for the application of EIs (1991), a number of general criteria can be listed against which the various EIs can be evaluated (see Chapter 11):

(a) The chosen EI should be able to mitigate the range of pollution and resource usage impacts associated with packaging. This is the **environmental effectiveness** principle.
(b) The EI should provide a continuous incentive for seeking least-cost solutions. This is the economic *efficiency* (static and dynamic) principle.
(c) The impact of the EI should not be significantly regressive, i.e. should not confer a disproportionate burden on the least well-off in society. This is the *equity* principle.

(d) The EI should have both low bureaucratic and compliance costs (i.e. the practical difficulties of calibration, collection, monitoring and control should be minimized). This is the administrative *cost-effectiveness* principle.

(e) Simple and transparent EIs are more easily internalized by the existing market and institutional system. This is the *acceptability* principle.

Two further criteria can be added:

(f) The chosen EI should be compatible with national, or in Europe, EC regulatory objectives and existing legislation. In the EC, the EI would need to represent minimum requirements for countries newly embarked on a policy course and not in breach of the Treaty of Rome and the Internal Market provisions. Additionally, the EI would have to be recognized as a credible substitute for or supplement to regulatory legislation. This is the principle of **institutional concordance**.

(g) Given that household source separation recycling schemes carry a heavy collection cost burden, the revenue raising properties of a given EI should be considered.

Types of economic instrument

A **materials levy** is an example of an input tax and would be imposed on the raw materials used to manufacture packaging, with due account being taken of existing rates of recycling and reuse. To meet the criterion of economic efficiency and to conform to the Polluter Pays Principle (PPP), accepted by all OECD Member countries, the size of the levy needs to be related directly to the environmental damage done by the production and consumption of the packaging, plus any scarcity premium if relevant. However, where existing legislation covers environmental impacts from earlier stages of the life-cycle, a levy may need to reflect only the MSW environmental costs.

A **product charge** is by contrast an *output* tax, a charge on the packaging end-product itself. The tax would be related to the potential waste disposal and pollution impact. Products made from wholly recycled materials could be exempted and products made partly from recycled materials could carry a reduced charge.

Both the material levy and product charge can, in principle, induce a change in the amount of packaging per product, i.e. a source reduction impact; and a change in the level of recycling that takes place at the point of consumption. The levy stimulates recycling because it raises the price of virgin materials relative to recycled (secondary) materials. It may also stimulate some source reduction if overall net production costs rise and this reduces the demand for packaging. The charge would again penalize products according to their 'embodied' waste and would stimulate a switch in the packaging mix towards lighter packaging. Differential charge rates could be set to allow for recycling performances. Pearce and Turner (1992b) show how a tax can be computed in practice.

Waste disposal charges (*user charges*) should also induce more recycling as disposal becomes more expensive. A system that perfectly charged each consumer all of the social costs of disposal of each item of refuse would require comprehensive monitoring and enforcement and would therefore carry prohibitively high transactions costs. Real world systems (e.g. simple curbside charges based on volume or weight of mixed refuse) represent pragmatic balancing of the efficiency gains of a perfect pricing system and the transactions costs of such a system in practice (Menell, 1990).

Two communities in the United States have implemented (minimum transactions cost) curbside charging schemes, Seattle and Perkasie, Pennsylvania. In Seattle, households are given trash cans with differentiated charges according to the size and number of cans provided. Residents are not charged for the removal of various types of separated wastes. In Perkasie, bags are provided for unseparated waste and aluminium cans, glass, cardboard and newspapers are collected separately. Residents are charged per bag which seems more effective than the can system in which residents are charged on a monthly basis for the use of a specific number of cans per week. Bag users can save money by putting out fewer bags in a given week.

Menell (1990) has further speculated that recent technological advances in scanning technology and the widespread adoption of the product bar code system could lead to the implementation of a fairly low cost yet flexible system of *adjusting relative retail prices* to reflect social costs of disposal.

A *deposit–refund* system (DRS) is essentially a combination of a tax and a subsidy. The consumer of packaging/container materials is given the right to a refund if the waste product is returned to the seller, i.e. to an authorized recycling/reuse point. For this right, the consumer may have had to pay a formal deposit at the time of the purchase or have paid a higher product price. The superficial evidence drawn from schemes that have actually been implemented (most for beverage containers) suggests that DRSs may impose net costs on society. Actual schemes have led to only relatively small reductions in the volume and cost of waste disposal, and litter reduction cost savings have usually been experienced, but their magnitude has varied quite widely. Such schemes have also been expensive to operate and have pushed up product prices.

DRS may be **market-generated systems** or schemes imposed by law. This latter category of **government-initiated systems** can operate with or without the government being financially involved, i.e. owning the deposit. It is also the case that the governments may intervene in existing market-generated systems. Systems (return offers made by firms) that have been generated by market forces have come into existence because the expected costs of handling and reusing the returnable items are lower than the expected overall revenues to the producer. This is usually because the net reuse value of the scrap item is positive, or because the refund stimulates a significant increase in demand, sufficient to offset a negative value of V.

Government initiated DRSs should not be viewed as a simple extension of the systems that would be generated by the market process. The market generated systems will not operate efficiently if refund levels are greater than net reuse value, for a given product. The government has to intervene, and deposits related to the environmental damage caused by the disposal of the product would have to be paid to the government. Refunds equivalent to the damage costs plus the reuse value of the scrap product would also be paid by the government to avoid having the system obstructed by the market. A number of the mandatory beverage container deposit schemes that have been introduced in the real world have, however, been closer in design to the simple market systems than to the government-initiated and economically efficient system proposed by some economists (Bohm, 1981).

An exception is a scheme introduced under Florida's solid waste law of 1988. A deposit of 1 cent per container will be charged from October 1992 on all containers made of materials that are not recycled at a rate of at least 50 per cent. This deposit plus the market value of the recycled container will be redeemable at recycling centres.

A more detailed analysis of the social costs and benefits associated with beverage container DRSs, with special reference to US and Australian experience can be found in Pearce and Turner (1992b).

Marketable permits have been proposed as a means of increasing the recycling of old newspapers, used oil and scrap tyres, in the United States (Dinan, 1990). The EPA has been evaluating a scheme which seeks to establish a minimum recycled content for newsprint. This requirement would not, however, be imposed on a uniform basis, rather a permit market would be set up. The permit market would be designed to achieve an industry-wide recycled content standard, yet still provide flexibility to individual firms responding to the policy. By allowing firms flexibility, those with the lowest cost of increasing their recycling activities are encouraged to do so, whereas firms with high costs are able to purchase virgin material rights.

The full measure of potential cost savings associated with the permit system can be realized only when a market for permits develops and results in an efficient allocation of permits. Four conditions are necessary for this result:

(a) firms comply with the policy;
(b) transactions costs are sufficiently low that they do not prevent efficient permit exchanges from taking place;
(c) there is enough certainty regarding the permit policy that firms are willing to engage in permit transactions;
(d) the market for permits is competitive.

Comparative evaluation of taxes, deposit—refunds and permits

On the basis of the evaluation criteria set out earlier in this paper (i.e. environmental effectiveness; economic efficiency; equity; administrative cost-effectiveness; institutional acceptability; institutional concordance and revenue raising properties), a brief comparative assessment of the different EIs in the context of the packaging waste problem is set out in this subsection.

The *packaging tax* instrument, in principle, scores well on both the environmental effectiveness and economic efficiency criteria. It need not itself involve the calibration of the entire life-cycle (LCA) impacts of a given packaging product, though LCA may be needed anyway in order to determine that such impacts exist. Administration of the tax should be highly cost-effective, especially since it has been demonstrated that in practice it can be computed easily and quickly. The tax fulfils the Polluter Pays Principle and scores well in terms of the principle of institutional concordance. If market/institutional acceptability constraints emerge then the instrument is flexible enough to stand conversion into a materials levy, which might be more attractive to some industrial interests. Finally, the nature of this instrument ensures that a revenue raising capacity is in-built.

Disposal charges (curbside), based on volume or weight of mixed waste, score reasonably well on the environmental effectiveness and economic efficiency criteria. Some US communities seem to be able to operate such simple systems without prohibitive transactions cost penalties (moderate administrative cost-effectiveness).

Deposit—refunds, in principle, score well on environmental effectiveness and equity grounds. DRSs can be aimed at recycling, but also at safe disposal, i.e. an assurance can be given that more material will be disposed of through an authorized outlet, which is important for hazardous material. US beverage container DRSs have been effective in terms of their return rates, which ranged from 72 to 98 per cent in some seven states for which data was available. These container returns account for some 80 and 98 per cent of the total national recycling of glass and PET plastic respectively (and some 64 per cent of aluminium can recycling in the United States). Because DRSs can target specific types of containers, without collecting other materials that might be contaminants, they have an advantage over other recycling collection systems. They may also discourage anti-social littering behaviour. Conversely, targeting means that DRSs do not reduce the overall volume of MSW significantly.

In terms of equity, DRSs may be relatively less regressive depending on whether packaging product prices increase significantly because of extra system costs and on whether less well-off individuals are the main returners. Price increases borne by consumers through the deposit scheme are to some extent offset by securing the refund.

264

Actual DRSs do not appear to be economically efficient in terms of generating net social benefits. Much depends on the prevailing market conditions related to a given packaging product(s), but to date, cost–benefit studies have not indicated that DRSs generate significant net social gains. The administrative cost-effectiveness of these schemes has been open to doubt, at least in the short to medium run, when 'transitional' costs are high.

With the exception of hazardous materials (e.g. batteries, used oil, etc.), the general acceptability of DRSs in industrial and some institutional circles is quite low. There is a risk of competitive distortion particularly within the containers market. Carton and plastics containers manufacturers could impose a deposit for return of materials to an authorized site, but such materials would not be reused because of health regulations covering the use of recycled fibers in liquids containers and sterilization of plastic containers. The carton and plastics container manufacturers would have therefore to bear the cost of the DRS. Other container manufacturers would bear the DRS costs but would gain a supply of directly recyclable secondary material. Some recycled plastics may find a limited end-use in alternative products (indirect recycling).

No significant revenues are generated (unless return rates are low) by a DRS and hence recycling cannot be stimulated by a transfer of funds.

Finally, although the acceptability of DRSs among industrial groups has been low, the general public in the US states that have such schemes seem very supportive of these ventures.

A *Combined Deposit–Refund and Curbside Collection System* has been in operation in California since 1987. Manufacturers of most beverage containers pay a fee of $0.02 per container to a State recycling fund. Returned containers are channelled through recycling centers or curbside collection programmes. The recycling fund pays $0.025 to the recycling center or programme which presents documentation of having handled the container. Small retailers are exempt from handling returned containers, and large retailers may also gain exemption if they can demonstrate that there is a recycling center located within a one mile radius of their store ('convenience zone').

The scheme also requires the State to calculate a 'processing fee' for each type of container. The fee is the difference between the average cost to recyclers of handling returned containers and their scrap value. The container manufacturer must either guarantee a scrap price equal to the cost of processing, or pay the State fund a processing fee equal to the difference between the two. It is also possible for the State to provide subsidies ('convenience incentive payments') to low-volume recyclers to help keep them in business.

The main drawback to this combined system seems to be the high administrative costs that are involved.

Marketable permits depend heavily on the market conditions in a particular industry if they are to generate efficiency gains. The competitive nature and size of the market are critical factors. The market needs to be big enough to allow competition but not so big as to cause significant transactions costs (i.e. low administrative cost-effectiveness). Environmental effectiveness may be a problem if regulatory constraints on permit-trading are required in order to control potential localized pollution 'hot spots'. Acceptability, among industrial interests, will be low unless long-term contractual arrangements or brokering facilities can be established.

Conclusions

Although not a panacea, economic instruments will play a much more significant role in waste management policy in the future. In particular, packaging taxes, disposal charges/levies, recycling credits and selective deposit–refund systems offer many advantages over the alternative inefficient regulatory approach. Such instruments are already in place or are being actively promoted in many countries in Europe and North America.

Further reading

H. Alter, 'The future course of solid waste management in the US', *Waste Management and Research* **9**: 3–20, 1991.

P. Bohm, *Deposit–Refund Systems*, Johns Hopkins University Press, Baltimore, 1981.

T. M. Dinan, 'Increasing the Demand for Old Newspapers through Marketable Permits: Will it Work?', Paper presented at the AERE Workshop, Natural Resource and Market Mechanisms, Waunakee, Wisconsin, 7–8 June, 1990.

ENDS Report 1990, Environmental Data Services, London.

ENDS Report 1991, Environmental Data Services, London.

J. W. Evans and J. Szekely, 'Newer versus traditional industries: A materials perspective', *Journal of Metals* **37**: 12–20, 1985.

P. S. Menell, 'Beyond the throwaway society: An incentive approach to regulating MSW', *Ecology Law Quarterly* **17**: 655–739, 1990.

D. W. Pearce and R. K. Turner, 'Packaging waste and the polluter pays principle: A taxation solution', *Journal of Environmental Management and Planning* **35**: 5–15, 1992a.

D. W. Pearce and R. K. Turner, 'The Economics of Packaging Waste Management: Conceptual Overview', Centre for Social and Economic Research on the Global Environment (CSERGE), Discussion Paper, WM 92-03, University of East Anglia, Norwich and University College London, 1992b.

D. W. Pearce and R. K. Turner, 'Market-based approaches to solid waste management', *Resources, Conservation and Recycling* **8**: 63–90, 1993.

R. K. Turner, 'Municipal solid waste management: An economic perspective', in A. D. Bradshaw, R. Southwood and F. Warner (eds), *The Treatment and Handling of Wastes*, Chapman and Hall, London, 1991, pp. 85–104.

R. K. Turner and J. C. Powell, 'Towards an integrated waste management strategy', *Environmental Management and Health* **2**: 6–12, 1991.

CHAPTER 19

Climate change

Introduction: the greenhouse effect

If the Earth had no atmosphere the average temperature on its surface would be well below freezing (about $-19°C$). A number of gases – water vapour, carbon dioxide (CO_2), chlorofluorocarbons (CFCs), methane (CH_4) and nitrous oxide (N_2O) – in the earth's atmosphere absorb infrared radiation (i.e. long wavelength radiation) and act as a blanket which helps trap the sun's heat absorbed through the atmosphere (because it is short wavelength visible radiation) and reemitted from the earth's surface (as longwave radiation). The consequence is that the total amount of radiation striking the earth's surface is increased, so the average temperature of the surface is increased.

Economic activity (especially over the last few hundred years) is increasing the rate of emission and the concentration of the 'greenhouse' gases in the atmosphere. The 'greenhouse' analogy has been used because like glass, water vapour and CO_2 in the atmosphere is transparent to visible light (from the sun) but relatively opaque to infrared radiation being reemitted by the earth's surface. Hence a greenhouse is a very efficient structure for retaining solar radiation. Industrialization has resulted in the intensive exploitation of fossil fuels (coal, gas and oil) for production and transportation. Burning fossil fuels releases CO_2 into the atmosphere, the concentration of which has risen by 33 per cent since 1800. Agricultural and industrial activity generates other greenhouse gases, methane, nitrous oxide and CFCs. According to the Intergovernmental Panel on Climate Change (IPCC), a body set up in 1988 to investigate global warming, the increases in greenhouse gases in the atmosphere will result on average in an *additional warming* of the earth's surface.

Of the greenhouse gases, CO_2 is probably the most important. It is responsible for around 60 per cent of the human-induced greenhouse effect. Its main source is fossil fuel burning, which, unfortunately, is at present the main means of energy production in industrial economies. Furthermore, energy is essential for the economic development so desperately needed in developing countries. Box 19.1 summarizes the IPCC analysis of greenhouse gas emissions and characteristics. Greenhouse gases already in the atmosphere may have committed the Earth to a temperature rise of 0.9° to 2.6°, only about 0.5° of which has been felt so far. To put this into perspective, the temperature in Europe fell by only 1°C in the past and the result was the Little Ice Age (fourteenth century to seventeenth century).

The actual size of this temperature rise, its rate of increase and its distribution around the globe are subject to considerable *uncertainty*. This is because our climate is controlled by two very complex systems, the atmosphere and the oceans, which themselves are interrelated. But a majority of climatologists now seemed to be agreed that a further increase in the global

Box 19.1   Greenhouse gas emissions and characteristics

			Gases		
	CO_2	CH_4	CFC-11	CFC-12	N_2O
Preindustrial concentration	280 p.p.m.v.	0.8 p.p.m.v.	0	0	288 p.p.b.v.
1990 concentration	353 p.p.m.v.	1.72 p.p.m.v.	280 p.p.t.v.	484 p.p.t.v.	310 p.p.b.v.
Annual rate of accumulation	1.8 p.p.m.v. (0.5%)	0.015 p.p.m.v. (0.9%)	9.5 p.p.t.v. (4%)	17 p.p.t.v. (4%)	0.8 p.p.b.v. (0.25%)
Atmospheric lifetime (yrs)	50–200	10	65	130	150
Global warming potential in terms of CO_2 equivalent	1	63[a]	4500	7100	270
Share of global warming effect	61%	17%	<—12%—>		4%

Notes: [a]i.e. 1 kg of CO_4 emissions is equivalent to 63 kg of CO_2 in terms of the warming effect;

p.p.m.v. = parts per million by volume

p.p.b.v. = parts per billion by volume

p.p.t.v. = parts per trillion by volume

Data in the first three rows of the table are reasonably certain and the opposite is the case for data in the bottom three rows.

Source: Adapted from IPCC (1991a and b) and Howarth and Monahan (1992).

mean surface temperature of the earth of between 2° to 5°C can be expected within the next hundred years if human-produced greenhouse gas emissions double over the same time period. IPCC (1992) has produced a comprehensive review of the most recent information on the greenhouse gas problem. The problem, it seems, is even more complicated than at first thought, but the new information has led to a downward revision of the predictions of temperature rise – mean global warming has now been put at 2.5°C (Wigley and Raper, 1992). Other impact effects may also need to be reassessed, so now we need to know what the effects of increased warming might be.

The effects of global warming

Increased warming has many potential damaging effects and some beneficial ones. The IPCC was not able to reach clear conclusions about the impacts of potential changes in climate. Agricultural impacts could be significant at the regional level, but studies have not yet conclusively determined whether, on average, global agriculture will suffer a decline in productive potential or an increase. Water resources could be altered and relatively small climate changes can cause large water resource problems in drought-prone areas. Disease patterns may be altered and the rise in global mean sea level which will accompany warming could pose a serious risk to low-lying coastal areas. The impact of flooding on the latter would be especially serious if the rise in sea level was accompanied by more frequent storm surges. Millions of 'environmental refugees' being forced to migrate out of vulnerable areas would represent significant human and economic costs.

However, a key feature of the climate change problem, and the *state of transition* it may induce, is the level of uncertainty that surrounds it, in particular, the uncertainty over the *rate of climate change*. Because regardless of whether a warmer world might be better or worse, *rapid change* could disrupt both societies and economies as well as natural ecosystems. When the composition of ecosystems change, some species may benefit but others, unable to migrate or adapt at the rate necessary for survival, face extinction (or, in the case of human populations, very great hardship and stress costs). Damage impacts will probably be most acute in regions already under stress and therefore particularly *vulnerable*, e.g. those exposed to the natural hazards of sea or river flooding and erosion, severe drought, or those located in known storm zones. Hurricane Andrew in the United States offers a recent example of the devastation that can result from extreme weather events. That hurricane probably made 250 000 homeless, destroyed 85 000 homes and cost around $10 billion.

Vulnerability can be defined as the degree to which a system may react adversely to the occurrence of a hazard such as sea level rise. Wigley and Raper (1992) have calculated that the best guess sea level rise is 48 cm by 2100

(19 cm by 2050). This represents a 20–30 per cent reduction from previous estimates (66 cm by 2100), but it is still at a rate roughly four times that experienced in the last century. Conversely, *resilience* in a system is a measure of the system's capacity to absorb, adapt to and recover from the occurrence of a hazardous event. Vulnerability will be determined by both 'environmental' (location, type of local climate and vegetation, altitude above sea level, etc.) and 'economic' factors (income and wealth of the region or nation concerned and its technological capacity). But it is clear that many coastal regions, including major cities, for example, are already facing problems connected with sea level rise. These problems are at their most extreme in developing countries because a combination of 'failures' problems have coalesced with the climate change impact. *Market failure* problems (pollution and resource depletion) have combined with **intervention failures** (poor and uncoordinated government policies in coastal zones) to put some physically vulnerable regions at considerable risk. Typical of these high-risk zones would be the Nile delta, southern Bangladesh, and most low-lying small-island states such as the Maldives. These are all examples drawn from the developing country category, but industrialized nations will not be immune, e.g. the Mississippi delta in the United States, the Po delta in Italy and the eastern coastline of England. Box 19.2 outlines some typical examples of these risk-prone areas.

So the *possible* damage impacts from climate change and the disruption effects of a rapid climate transition would be significant. Yet, the scientists cannot say that so far we have received a definitive signal that global warming is occurring. Uncertainty itself is a key feature, science cannot yet yield concrete facts regarding future impacts. The temperature rise in this century is consistent with, but not definitive in proving climate change theory (Howarth and Monahan, 1992). Climatologists are, however, virtually agreed that greenhouse gases will warm the atmosphere. Economic activity will continue to lead to the emission of such gases through fossil fuel burning, etc. The question then is, how should policy-makers respond to the greenhouse problem?

Policy responses to the greenhouse problem

For many of the pollution problems we have looked at in previous chapters of this book there has *not been a very long time lag* between pollutant emission/discharge and the resulting damage impacts. Further, these problems have stimulated a **reactive policy response** (e.g. stricter regulations and the limited use of economic instruments such as charges and deposit–refunds). It is also the case that the polluters had available, to a greater or lesser extent, **'end-of-pipe' technologies** which were able to reduce the harmful effects of the pollution.

Box 19.2 Vulnerability case-studies

The Nile delta

This area is Egypt's food lifeline since it contains nearly all the country's agriculturally productive land. Because of the Aswan Dam, little sediment reaches the coast and coastal areas have become degraded as the sea enters areas previously taken up by sediment. Large lakes that lie just inland of the coast supply much of the nation's fish. The lakes are protected by dunes, but these may be breached if the sea level rises. In addition, the delta is subject to subsidence, and this may accelerate under the pressure of groundwater extraction.

The effects of different sea level rise scenarios are summarized in Table 1. The *best-case scenario* (BC) assumes a minimal rise in sea level, with natural subsidence being offset by deltaic sedimentation. The *worst-case* (WC) scenario assumes a maximum rise in sea level and uncompensated natural subsidence since the Nile is completely dammed. The *absolute worst-case* (AWS) assume worst-case conditions plus the effect of a market failure, i.e. overutilization of the groundwater reserves which leads to enhanced subsidence of the land.

Table 1 Impact scenarios for sea level rise in the Nile delta, 2050 and 2100

	2050			2100		
	BC	WC	AWC	BC	WC	AWC
Rise in sea level (cm)	13	79	79	28	217	217
Local subsidence	0	22	65	0	40	115
Total	13	101	144	28	257	332
Shoreline erosion (kilometres)	0	1	1	0	2	2
% habitable land lost	—	15	19	—	22	26
% population displaced	—	14	16	—	19	24
% GDP in affected areas (i.e. economic income and wealth)	—	14	17	—	19	24

Note: — means not available.
Source: Milliman *et al.* (1989)

Dhaka, Bangladesh

Dhaka, the capital of Bangladesh lies in the heart of one of the world's great coastal deltas built by the sediments carried by three of the world's largest rivers, the Ganges, Brahmaputra and Meghna. The interaction of these rivers with the tides, waves and storms of the Bay of Bengal has moulded one of the most complex and dynamic physical environments on Earth.

Bangladesh has a total population of 108 million growing at a rate of 2.17 per cent per year. The area of Bangladesh is 144 000 km^2 of which 4470 km^2 is river. The resultant population density is the highest in the world. However, the proportion of rural population is also one of the world's highest. The rich deltaic soils and supply of freshwater during the monsoon period have created a highly adapted traditional agricultural and fishery regime.

Dhaka is situated between the Burhiganga and Lakhya rivers approximately 50 km north of the junction of the Ganges, Brahmaputra and Meghna rivers. The majority of the city is on the southern-most outcrop of the Madhupur Tract of Pleistocene clays. Dhaka is relatively elevated as a result, with the Burhiganga river forming the boundary between the Pleistocene terraces and the younger, lower alluvial deposits of the Ganges–Brahmaputra flood-plain to the south and west of Dhaka. The old city is built next to the Burhiganga river, a location enabling connection by river to the sea and inland to India. The city has grown away from the river.

Dhaka has been an important city since at least the fifteenth century, with a population of close to 1 million by the middle of the seventeenth century. However, the city declined in size during the eighteenth and nineteenth centuries. In 1891 the recorded population was around 100 000. The population of the city increased steadily between 1891 and 1961. Dhaka, like many large cities in the developing world, expanded rapidly during the past thirty years to reach an estimated population of 3.8 million by 1981.

Dhaka was severely flooded in 1988 by a combination of the congestion of its medieval drainage system and by the overflow of river water on the edge of the city. The flooding prompted the Dhaka Flood Protection Project to build a series of embankments, flood walls, sluice gates and pumping stations encircling the city before 1993 at a total cost of US$110 million. However, the construction efforts have not been entirely successful. Some embankments failed in only months after their construction, and their location has deviated from original plans with settlements left outside the flood protection zone. In the old part of the city, the concrete wall is not continuous with frequent gaps. It is unclear if these gaps will be closed, or left open to ease the passage of people and goods. In addition, the concrete flood walls have blocked existing drainage and waste disposal systems. The

➡

problem is complicated by holes in walls made either deliberately by official agencies, or by locals.

The result has been waterlogging in new areas made worse by the city's drainage system. Many of these problems have been blamed on a lack of ministerial cooperation, and a drive to build before the full environmental and social consequences have been assessed.

The coastal zone is also one of the most densely populated zones in the world containing 26 million people in a quarter of the land area of Bangladesh (36 000 km^2). The coastal zone is crucial to the economy of Bangladesh. It contains a third of its cultivable land, and approximately 27 per cent of manufacturing industries, mainly within the Chittagong and Khulna–Khalishpur areas. These areas are also the focus of Bangladesh's exports and imports. In addition, coastal shrimp farming is Bangladesh's fastest growing export industry.

The coastal ecosystems are also a rich resource. The coastal mangroves produce up to 50 per cent of the total forestry income of Bangladesh. The Sundarban, the largest single area of mangroves in the world, contains many rare and endangered species. They also act as nursery grounds for many commercial fish species, and act as a natural sea-defence barrier.

Despite the abundance within the coastal zone, there are a number of chronic problems. As a result, the potential future effects of sea-level rise and climate change on the coastal zone cannot be separated from the existing impacts caused by overpopulation, resource overexploitation, erosion, subsidence and tropical cyclones. These impacts are likely to continue in the future, with or without the greenhouse effect. Instead, sea-level rise and climate change should be viewed as enhancing existing critical coastal zone 'failures' problems, and not as a separate, isolated issue.

Source: Turner *et al.* (1990)

In contrast the global warming problem is different, because:

1. There is a lag between pollutant emission and impact.
2. Damage effects can be anticipated, but their scale and severity is open to great uncertainty, so the policy response might have to be both *anticipatory* of and *responsive* to 'surprise' (i.e. unexpectedly severe effects). Policy actions today will also impact generations far into the future. The uncomfortable message is that by the time we know for certain that global warming is occurring, the warming commitment is already made, and the course of the future impacts may be irreversibly determined.

3. There exists, so far, no end-of-pipe technology to reduce existing stocks of the key greenhouse gas, CO_2 emissions, on a large scale. We are *not* in a position to eliminate in a short time (as is currently being done for CFC production, see Chapter 20) CO_2 emissions on a global scale. Fossil fuel burning is the main source of energy for supporting economic activity in both developed and developing countries.

We cannot be certain then that the impacts of climate change will be gradual and therefore easily managed by **'natural' adaptation** in society and the economy (e.g. changing lifestyles, relocation of people and industry, and a range of technical fixes for specific problems). Therefore a policy aimed at the reduction of greenhouse gas emissions could be said to be an urgent policy priority. On the other hand, we cannot be certain that continued emissions of these gases will stimulate sudden and rapid effects with massive costs (because of the difficulty of adaptation), and therefore a minimal policy response may be the best approach.

Three broad policy approaches may be undertaken to deal with the greenhouse problem. These approaches could be adopted unilaterally (i.e. a single country acting alone) or multilaterally (i.e. a number of countries acting cooperatively). Unilateral action is very unlikely to affect the damage from global warming significantly, but a country might believe that its action is worthwhile as part of a 'political' strategy targeted at some eventual international agreement. The three policy actions are:

1. 'Do nothing' and merely 'wait and see' what happens. No policy steps need to be taken until scientific certainty about the timing, distribution and severity of future climate change has been established. As long as the effects of climate change are gradual then individuals and business will probably adapt without the need for and expense of intervention policies. New research may well, in any case, result in more cost-effective solutions to some of the impact problems. The downside of this policy stance is that the level of committed warming will have been increased and the damage cost burden may be much higher because of the delayed response.

2. Implement 'no regrets' measures which yield net economic benefits even if we ignore climate benefits. Such measures may increase the scope for adaptation and/or reduce greenhouse gas emissions as well as providing other benefits, e.g. energy conservation measures and measures to correct for market failures in fossil fuel pricing and the elimination of other subsidies which play a role in deforestation.

3. Reduce greenhouse gas emissions in order to get climate stabilization at a tolerable and modest level of temperature change, i.e. adopt a precaution-ary approach. The goal of climate stabilization is compatible with the recently signed (1992) Global Warming Convention, as part of the United Nations Conference on Environment and Development (UNCED) process – see Box 19.3. Another perceived benefit of climate stabilization is

balancing the interests of present and future generations and peoples of different world regions in favour of the most vulnerable groups, the poor of today and future generations.

International discussion among members of the OECD (but excluding the United States, which has set an overall target for greenhouse gases but not for CO_2 emissions) has tended to center on trying to stabilize emissions at the 1990 level by the year 2000 or 2005. If no action is taken some models predict that a rate of warming of $0.27°$ C a decade might be expected. The proposed OECD action would only reduce the rate of warming to perhaps $0.25°$ C per decade. Some scientists believe that the ecologically safe limit akin to the safe minimum standard or constant national capital rule (see Chapter 4) is as low as $0.1°$ C per decade.

Other analysts have taken a different approach to try and estimate the acceptable level of warming. One is based on cost–benefit thinking (see Chapter 7), but the degree of uncertainty in climate change forecasting is such that only 'best guess' approaches to scenario formulation are possible. Thus Nordhaus (1991) takes an optimistic scenario approach and models climate change at a slow enough rate to allow for adjustment mechanisms. On this basis he states that climate change is likely to produce a combination of gains and losses with no strong presumption of substantial net economic damages.

Cline (1992) favours a less optimistic scenario, assuming that climate

Box 19.3   Climate Change Convention

The United Nations Framework Convention on Climate Change has as its ultimate objective, the stabilization of greenhouse gas concentrations in the atmosphere to avoid 'dangerous anthropogenic interference with the climate system'. Although the targets for the levels of these emissions are not binding, signatory parties are committed to providing information to the international forum on their strategies to reduce anthropogenic emissions and enhance sinks towards 1990 levels by the year 2000. This will not be a costless exercise for developed or developing countries in terms of forgone development based on greenhouse gas emitting technologies and other familiar costs. The potential damage of climate change and related sea level rise are well-known phenomena.

The costs of sea level rise on the Bengal and Nile delta areas, for example, would be in terms of 13 and 14 per cent of Bangladesh's and Egypt's populations being displaced from present settlements, and the loss of similar percentages of the habitable land in those countries by the year 2050 (as estimated by Milliman *et al.*, 1989). The costs of climate change and related phenomena have the potential to be significant in development terms for developing countries. It is to be stressed that areas vulnerable to increased rates of climate change and its impacts also tend to be vulnerable to other acute hazards. Vulnerability has both a biophysical and a socioeconomic dimension and low lying areas may already be vulnerable to flooding, for example. Existing problems have been made worse by the existence of interrelated economic and institutional failures: information failures, market failures, and past inefficient and uncoordinated strategies in coastal zones. The uncertainty over the regional differences in impacts gives added weight to the argument for precautionary action. Does the Climate Change Convention then set up mechanisms for mitigation of these effects, or for assisting developing countries in reducing emissions to *avoid* these effects?

The Convention does highlight the potential impact of climate change on particular ecosystems, such as montane environments and low-lying states. Within the Convention, there is a commitment to mitigating these effects:

The developed country Parties . . . shall assist the developing country Parties that are particularly vulnerable to the adverse effects of climate change in meeting costs of adaptation to those adverse effects
(Article 2 Para. 4 of United Nations Framework Convention on Climate Change, 1992).

Those countries mentioned as particularly vulnerable include small island states and low-lying areas; countries prone to natural disasters, drought and desertification; and countries with high urban atmospheric pollution. The mechanism for this assistance is to be agreed at a Conference of the Parties signing the agreement. But the interim arrangement is for the Global Environment Facility of the UNDP, UNEP and World Bank, to operate the financial mechanism for up to four years, though this is to be extended to ensure 'equitable and balanced representation of all Parties within a transparent system of governance' (Article 11 Para. 2).

Implicitly then the Climate Change Convention has accepted as inevitable, the damage caused by greenhouse warming – the damage that is already committed to. To reach the stated objectives of the Convention, the stabilization of greenhouse gas concentrations in the atmosphere to avoid 'dangerous anthropogenic interference with the climate system', requires considerable resources and political will. The Convention and the process after UNCED are negotiating other mechanisms for resource transfers, such as emission quotas and related tradeable permits; or agreements by which countries complying with the Convention 'individually or jointly', through bilateral transfers to be set against their own emissions. The equity and political feasibility of any mechanism depends on how the emissions are measured, and how historical responsibility for the present situation is resolved (see, for example, Brown and Adger (1992) and Grubb *et al.* (1992)).

changes will lead to more significant social disruption. Cline's damage estimates are much higher than those of Nordhaus, and he includes in his calculations less easily quantified impacts like species loss, migration and infrastructure degradation.

Box 19.4 compares two damage cost scenario studies which predict quite different results. Because of the uncertainties involved, neither of these studies produce particularly robust results. It is important that damage cost analysis should be made as rigorous as possible, but one should also recognize the inherent limitations of such analysis. Nevertheless, the negotiations over climate change have been overly narrow in their focus. They have concentrated on emission reduction targets only, and are therefore unlikely to represent a very efficient policy response. Cost–benefit analysis could therefore play an important role in determining an acceptable combination of prevention (targets) and adaptation measures.

Box 19.4 Climate change damage cost estimates

The Nordhaus (1991) cost–benefit study can be criticized because it extrapolates damage and abatement functions modelled on US economy conditions across the rest of the world. In this study, sea level rise (SLR) is likely to cost some $50 billion in capital costs (protection costs and losses of low-lying land) to the US economy.

Ayres and Walter (1991) have argued that the Nordhaus analysis significantly underestimates future damage. They produced their own estimate of the costs of sea level rise (this item accounts for 92 per cent of the total costs identified by Nordhaus). Using their assumptions on land values, land losses, refugee resettlement cost and coastal defence costs, total costs come to $18.5–21 trillion. Annualized, this represents 2.1–2.4 per cent of gross world income, nearly ten times higher than Nordhaus's 'central' estimate for total losses and slightly outside his range of error. Ayres and Walter conclude that a cost of $30–35 per tonne of CO_2 (equivalent) is more realistic than Nordhaus's £3.30 ('central' estimate), just to take account of the effects of SLR on 'vulnerable' economies like Egypt and Bangladesh.

However, both studies add the estimated costs of coastal protection to those of the loss of low-lying land, and, in the case of Ayres and Walter, to the cost of resettling refugees. Table 1 summarizes the reported SLR damage estimates from both studies. Although it is logical to include SLR in the damage function, it does not seem obvious why the costs of preventing the major impacts of SLR should be added to the costs when the rise occurs.

Table 1 Estimates of aggregate world costs of climate induced sea level rise

Category of sea level rise impact	Nordhaus (1991)	Ayres and Walter (1991)
Coastal protection	20 000 km coast	0.5–1 m km (world coast) . $5 m/km
Loss of property and land	4000 sq miles	500 m ha . $30 000/ha
Resettlement of refugees	–	100 m refugees . $1000
Total capital cost (world economy)	$405 billion	$18 500–21 000 billion

Policy instruments for achieving global warming targets

In Part IV we examined the two basic approaches to pollution control – command-and-control regulations and economic instruments. If we apply this analysis in the context of internationally agreed global environmental targets, the same general conclusions emerge. These are that regulations (in the form of a protocol on greenhouse gases) run the risk of inefficiency if the protocol requires the same emissions reductions for every country regardless of differences in the costs of achieving it.

Since global warming will not produce uniform effects (gains and losses) across all countries, getting political agreement on targets and the allocation of emissions reductions among countries will also be difficult. Then there is the *free-rider problem*. If global warming is reduced all countries will benefit regardless of whether they participated in the agreement and incurred the abatement costs. The potential existence of free riders means that any protocol must have built-in incentives for cooperation. This involves transferring resources – finance, technology or information – to the countries not cooperating. Given these factors economic incentive instruments – taxes and tradeable permits – need to be considered.

We analyzed the carbon tax instrument in Chapter 12, so we limit our discussion here to the case for permits. As we saw in Chapter 13 the permit solution gives the economic agent (in this context, a country) an incentive to trade permits with other agents and make net gains in the process without breaching the overall emissions target. Countries have an incentive to trade their permits until the marginal costs of abatement are just equal to the price of the permits in the market. If costs exceed price, the countries will try to buy further permits. If abatement costs are lower than the price of permits, they will sell the permits, collect the revenue from their sale and use some of the proceeds to abate emissions.

Any practical permit system for CO_2 emissions would have to address the following problems:

1. Large countries emit large amounts of CO_2 and the sales and purchases of such countries (e.g. the United States, Russia, Germany) may unduly influence price and make the market less competitive.
2. What sanctions could be applied to countries that persistently exceed their permitted emissions?
3. How are the permits to be allocated at the start of the scheme?

Grandfathering of permits (i.e. allocation according to the existing level of emissions) favours the industrialized countries and does not encourage cooperation by developing countries. An allocation based on a per capita (population) basis, on the other hand, would favour developing countries. They could then sell permits to industrial countries at a profit over the cost of abating greenhouse gas emissions. This scheme could be designed so that it does not reward overpopulation by counting only adults in the allocation. Political realities seem to be against an allocation based on population, and grandfathering of some kind is the only allocation that a majority of industrial countries would find acceptable.

Conclusions

The potential effects of global warming and climate change are significant (mostly negative but not uniformly so). But as we have seen the key feature of this set of problems is the great uncertainty that surrounds it. Many regions around the globe are already in a vulnerable state due to some combination of existing physical and socio-economic conditions (e.g. low-lying coastal areas in developing countries). Climate change effects, should they occur, will serve to exacerbate the vulnerability of these regions and their inhabitants. Taking a precautionary approach to policy, what is required is an anticipatory and not a reactive policy response. Such a response would involve measures to reduce greenhouse gas emissions and achieve climate stabilization at a tolerable and modest level of temperature change.

International agreements will be required in order to implement the precautionary approach. However, since global warming will not produce uniform effects – some countries will gain and others will lose – getting political agreement on targets and the allocation of emissions reductions among countries will be far from easy. So-called carbon taxes and emissions permits have been advocated as possible policy instruments for achieving global warming targets. Political acceptability is the most difficult criterion that such instruments will have to satisfy if they are to play a significant role in the mitigation of the climate change problem.

Further reading

R. U. Ayres and J. Walter, 'The greenhouse effect: Damages, costs and abatement', *Environmental and Resource Economics* 1: 237–70, 1991.

K. Brown and N. Adger, 'The Climate Change Convention and the UK: How Large are our Emissions?', Policy Analysis Working Paper 92–08, Centre for Social and Economic Research on the Global Environment, University of East Anglia and University College London, 1992.

W. Cline, *Global Warming: The Economic Stakes*, Institute for International Economics, Washington DC, 1992.

M. Grubb, J. Sebenius, A. Magalhaes and S. Subak, 'Sharing the burden', in A. M. Mintzer (ed.), *Confronting Climate Change: Risks, Implications and Responses*, Cambridge University Press, Cambridge, 1992.

R. B. Howarth and P. A. Monahan, 'Economics, Ethics and Climate Policy', Report LBL-33230, UC-000, Lawrence Berkeley Laboratory, University of California, Berkeley, 1992.

IPCC, *Policymakers Summary*, World Meteorological Organization and UN Development Programme, Geneva, 1990.

IPCC, *Climate Change: The IPCC Scientific Assessment*, Cambridge University Press, Cambridge, 1991a.

IPCC, *Climate Change: The IPCC Response Strategies*, Cambridge University Press, Cambridge, 1991b.

IPCC, *IPCC Supplement*, World Meteorological Organization and UNDP, Geneva, 1992.

J. D. Milliman, J. M. Broadus and F. Gable, 'Environmental and economic implications of rising sea level and subsiding deltas: The Nile and Bengal examples', *Ambio* 18(6): 340–5, 1989.

A. M. Mintzer (ed.), *Confronting Climate Change: Risks, Implications and Responses*, Cambridge University Press, Cambridge, 1992.

W. D. Nordhaus, 'To slow or not to slow: The economics of the greenhouse effect', *Economic Journal* 101: 920–37, 1991.

D. W. Pearce and J. Warford, *World Without End: Economics, Environment and Sustainable Development*, Oxford University Press, Oxford, 1992, Chapter 14.

R. K. Turner, M. Kelly and R. Kay, *Cities at Risk*, BNA International, London, 1990.

R. K. Turner, P. Doktor and N. Adger 'Coastal Wetlands and Sea Level Rise: Mitigation Strategies', CSERGE, GEC Working paper 92–30, University of East Anglia and University College, London, 1992.

UN Conference on Trade and Development, *Combating Global Warming: A Study on a Global System of Tradeable Carbon Emission Entitlements*, UN, New York, 1992.

UN United Nations Framework Convention on Climate Change

T. Wigley and S. Raper, 'Implications for climate and sea level of revised IPCC emissions scenarios', *Nature* 347: 1443–6, 1992.

CHAPTER 20

Economics and the ozone layer

Ozone

The 'ozone problem' can be somewhat confusing since ozone occurs at two levels in the atmosphere: in the **stratosphere** about 15–50 kilometers above the ground, and in the **troposphere**, the lower part of the atmosphere up to 15 kilometers above the ground. Ozone is a naturally occurring gas, and in the stratosphere it is concentrated into what is known as **the ozone layer** which is like a thick belt around the earth. This concentration of ozone is a 'good thing' because it protects the earth from ultraviolet (UV) radiation from the sun, taking out 90 per cent of the UV rays. Ozone concentrated at the lower atmospheric level, the troposphere, can be a 'bad thing' because it is harmful to health, vegetation and is involved in the general process of 'acid rain' formation – see Chapter 22. While tropospheric ozone formation is natural, it can be enhanced by the interaction of nitrogen oxides (NO_x), oxygen (O) and volatile organic compounds (VOCs). So, high ozone levels in the troposphere are bad, high concentrations in the *stratosphere* are good. This chapter is concerned with stratospheric ozone.

CFCs and the depletion of the ozone layer

Regular measurements have been made of the ozone layer. Box 20.1, for example, shows the measurements taken at Arosa, Switzerland since 1926. The vertical axis shows the percentage change in thickness. So, from 1926 up to about 1970 nothing much happens – the 'average' change is zero so the layer was getting neither thicker nor thinner. But the graph shows that after 1970 there was marked downturn: the ozone layer had begun to 'thin'. This thinness matters because it means that the ozone layer would let through more UV radiation. While some extra sunlight on the earth might seem like a good thing, added UV radiation poses all kinds of problems, as we will see shortly. (Strictly, it is one form of UV radiation – UV-B – which is relevant.)

Box 20.1 The depletion of the ozone layer

The diagram records the percentage change in the ozone layer from 1926 to 1988 from readings at Arosa, Switzerland. The trend is steady up to 1970, after which the average change is negative, so that by 1988 the layer had thinned by 6 per cent.

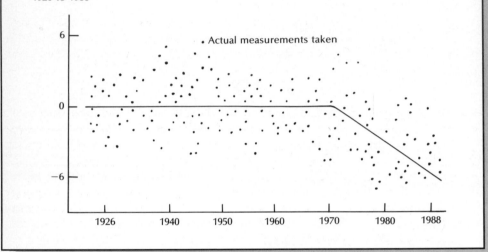

Arosa, Switzerland
1926 to 1988

It was not until the early 1970s that scientists began to investigate the relationship between certain chemicals and the depletion of the ozone layer. Two California scientists, Mario Molina and Sherwood Roland focused on 'chlorofluorocarbons', or CFCs for short, as possible culprits. Normally, most chemicals break down or become dissipated when released into the environment, but CFCs manage to maintain their chemical stability. Moreover, they 'travel' upwards into the atmosphere where the effect of solar radiation does break them down but, in the process, releases large quantities of chlorine. It was already known that chlorine could set off a chain reaction which could destroy ozone molecules at a rapid rate. Moreover, being stable, the CFCs could stay in the atmosphere a long time, continuing to damage the ozone layer long after they had been released on earth. In 1986 a major report was released under the auspices of the World Meteorological Office and the United Nations Environment Programme. This report confirmed the view that CFCs stayed in the atmosphere and damaged the ozone layer through the release of chlorine. It predicted a general trend of depletion worldwide, higher seasonal variations in depletion (i.e. the layer would deplete more in certain seasons), and variations in depletion in certain latitudes. The same report implicated CFCs in the greenhouse warming effects as well (see Chapter 19). At roughly the same time, British scientists made a dramatic discovery in the Antarctic. They estimated that ozone levels between September and November above the Antarctic had fallen by 50 per cent in 1986 compared to the 1960s. The resulting 'hole' was huge, about the size of the land area of the United States. The 'hole' tended to mend itself after this period of depletion, and then reappeared again in later years. Subsequent investigations revealed a similar 'hole' over the Arctic, and thinning over the Northern hemisphere, and even the tropics.

CFCs had been introduced in the 1930s as a 'wonder gas'. CFCs are stable, non-flammable, non-toxic and non-corrosive. Unsurprisingly, they found a great many uses. Box 20.2 shows the uses of CFCs and it will be seen that

Box 20.2   The production and uses of chlorofluorocarbons

Table 1   World output of CFCs

Product	1986 000 tonnes	1991 000 tonnes	1991 Output as % of 1986
CFC-11	415	263	63
CFC-12	441	259	59
CFC-113	241	143	59
CFC-114	18	5	30
CFC-115	13	11	85
Total	1128	681	60

Table 2   Structure of uses of CFCs

Application	% of 1986 use	Reduction by 1991 since 1986 (%)
Propellants	28	58
Cleaning	21	41
Foam blowing	26	35
Refrigerants	23	7
Other	2	–
Total	100	40

Source: Montreal Protocol, 1991 Assessment

they range from refrigeration, aerosol propellants, foam manufacture, solvents and so on. Output and use have been going down since 1986 because, after the scientists' discovery of the link between CFCs and ozone layer depletion, the world acted quickly to control their use. In 1985 the Vienna Convention for the Protection of the Ozone Layer was adopted, and in 1987 twenty-five countries adopted the Montreal Protocol on Substances that Deplete the Ozone Layer. The Montreal Protocol came into force on 1 January, 1989. As scientific knowledge increased, however, the Montreal Protocol had quickly to be revised and made more strict. Box 20.3 outlines the main developments in the international agreements.

Box 20.3 Development of the Montreal Protocol

Measure taken	Target for developed world	Target for developing world
Montreal Protocol 1987–1989	Reduce production and consumption of CFCs by 50% of 1986 levels by 1998	Ten-year grace period allowed before reaching the CFC target
	Freeze production and consumption of halons at 1986 levels	Provision of substitute technology to compensate for going without CFCs
London Meeting of the Protocol Parties June 1990	Reduce production and consumption of CFCs and halons by 50% of 1986 levels by 1995	
	Reduce production and consumption of CFCs by 85% of 1986 levels by 1997	
	Phase out consumption of CFCs and halons by 2000	
	Cut consumption of carbon tetrachloride by 85% by 1995, phase out by 2000	
	Cut consumption of 1,1,1-trichloroethane by 30% by 1995, 70% by 2000 and phase out by 2005	
Actions in 1992	US CFC production to be stopped by 1995	

The damage from ozone layer depletion

Why does increased UV radiation matter?

Human health effects

The most popularized concern has been the effect of additional radiation on sunburn and skin cancer. Skin cancers can be of two kinds: carcinoma and melanoma. Melanomas (cancers of the pigment cells) can be fatal, and all forms of skin cancers are on the increase. How far the increase is due to changes in personal behaviour (the fashion for being 'tanned') and how far to increased UV radiation through ozone layer depletion is not certain, but one estimate has suggested that if nothing was done to reduce ozone layer depletion, skin cancer deaths for the population alive today or born by the year 2075 in the United States could be around 3 million. A rough rule of thumb is that a 1 per cent reduction in ozone produces a 1–2 per cent increase in UV radiation and a 3–4 per cent increase in non-melanoma skin cancers.

Other health effects are less certain. There is some evidence that UV radiation can damage the human immune system, increasing the incidence of infectious diseases and reducing the effectiveness of vaccination programmes. The link to increased cataracts is more direct and a 1 per cent reduction in ozone could give rise to an extra 100 000 to 150 000 cases worldwide.

Ecosystem effects

Perhaps more disturbing than health effects – many of them are avoidable through behavioural change such as increased personal protection against the sun's rays – are the potential ecosystem effects. A major impact is on the single-celled algae – phytoplankton – which produce around half the world's biomass each year and 'fix' (absorb) a large proportion of the world's CO_2 in the oceans. UV radiation affects the phytoplankton by interfering with the process of photosynthesis and it also damages DNA, and hence growth and reproduction. The algae are eaten by krill which are in turn the food of larger ocean species, including the whale, and fish. Some research already suggests that the Antarctic 'hole' is reducing phytoplankton productivity by up to 12 per cent. One study suggests that a 16 per cent reduction in ozone concentration could result in a 5 per cent reduction in primary biomass production and a 6–9 per cent reduction in fish stocks. The science is still uncertain, and it is known that there are some natural defence mechanisms whereby some phytoplankton screen out some of the radiation. These species might end up expanding to compensate for the loss of others, but the effects on complex food chains are still uncertain.

The same potential effects apply to land-based ecosystems since increased UV radiation appears to be correlated with lower photosynthetic activity and reduced growth in vegetation. The impact on crops could therefore be significant.

The costs and benefits of CFC control

Faced with the formidable scientific evidence, the world's governments acted quickly with respect to ozone layer depletion. In little more than ten years from the discovery of the CFC–ozone link, the Montreal Protocol was in place. But the speed with which the Protocol will itself have an effect on ozone layer depletion should not be exaggerated. Box 20.4 shows the effect on concentrations of chlorine if CFC *emissions* are halted in 1995, 2000 or 2005. To get back to the level of concentration of 1975 (around 1.5–2.0 parts per billion by volume (p.p.b.v.)) will take until the end of the next century. The diagram reveals an important point – sometimes it is simply 'too late' to restore situations. This is especially so where pollutants are cumulative, i.e. where they have a long 'residence time' in the environment, as CFCs do.

Apart from the dramatic evidence on ozone layer depletion, there is one other important reason for early international action on CFCs. Basically, they are not very expensive to replace. The cost of compensating the developing world to go without CFC use will be perhaps $2 billion between 1990 and 2010, which is fairly trivial compared to the annual flow of official aid of $45 billion.

The objective of getting back to some original starting point is not, of course, sanctioned by cost–benefit approaches (unless that just happens to be the outcome). This is why adopting certain rules of thumb relating to 'restoring' the environment is not necessarily consistent with the standard economic approach to environmental problems, although such rules may well be consistent with the idea of 'sustainability' and 'constant capital' – see Chapter 4. Thus, achieving 1.5–2 p.p.b.v. of chlorine is analogous to a 'sustainability' criterion, but we do not know if it would be sanctioned by a comparison of costs and benefits.

There is, in fact, only one cost–benefit analysis of CFC control and this was prepared as a 'Regulatory Impact Analysis' by the United States Environmental Protection Agency. Box 20.5 sets out the essential findings of that study but it is important to note that it relates to an evaluation of the *original* Montreal Protocol, i.e. unamended by the later agreements to make the controls more strict. The cost–benefit study shows that there were overwhelmingly substantial benefits to the United States from undertaking the controls formulated in the Montreal Protocol, even if all benefits could not be measured. Recall that perhaps 3 million deaths could be avoided from controlling CFCs. If each 'statistical life' is valued at $3 million, then the

Box 20.4 CFC emission reductions and atmospheric chlorine concentration

The diagram shows the rise of chlorine concentrations in the atmosphere (the rising heavy line) and the effects of stopping all emissions of CFCs if that was done in 1995, 2000 and 2005 (the upper dashed line is for 2005, the middle dashed curve for 2000 and the lower one for 1995). Chlorine concentrations of 1.5–2 parts per billion by volume (p.p.b.v.) are not reestablished until 2100 even with fairly severe, immediate action.

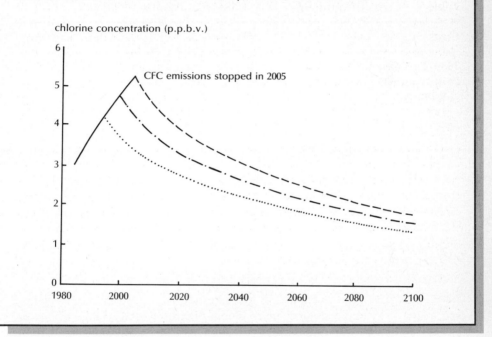

chlorine concentration (p.p.b.v.)

CFC emissions stopped in 2005

economic value of the saved lives alone would be $9 million million, or $9 *trillion*. Even allowing for the effect of 'discounting' – whereby future lives saved are assumed not to be as valuable as current lives saved – the effect is to make the benefits of CFC control absolutely enormous. This shows up in the net benefit calculation in Box 20.5.

Conclusions

The speed with which governments reacted to the challenge of the ozone layer depletion problem and the signing of an international agreement (the Montreal Protocol) to phase out CFCs represent something of a policy success

Box 20.5   Costs and benefits of CFC control in the United States

Table 1 shows that the costs to the United States of reducing CFC emissions by 80 per cent were estimated to be some 22 billion US dollars, but the health and environmental benefits were estimated to be a staggering 3500 billion dollars, or 3.5 trillion dollars. The evaluation of health benefits assumed that a 'value of a statistical life' (often misleadingly called 'the value of human life') is $3 million.

Table 1   Costs of reducing CFC emissions (in billion 1985$)

Costs	No control	80% cut in emissions
1989–2075 discounted at 2%	0	22
Health and environment benefits	0	3553
Net benefit	0	3531

Source: US Environmental Protection Agency (1988)

story. However, international agreements covering other global change effects will require much more protracted negotiations. The CFCs success story was heavily conditioned by the existence of two favourable factors:

1. A significant amount of scientific evidence ('certainty') exists about the cause and effects involved.
2. The replacement of CFCs has proved to be relatively inexpensive.

As we have seen in the context of greenhouse gas reduction and as we will see in the next two chapters, many global environmental change issues are bedevilled by scientific uncertainty and also involve substantial cost burdens which are not equally shared.

Further reading

Montreal Protocol, 1991 Assessment: Report of the Technology and Economic Assessment Panel, United Nations Environment Programme, Nairobi, December 1991.

US Environmental Protection Agency, *Regulatory Impact Analysis – Protection of Stratospheric Ozone*, Vol. 1, US EPA, Washington DC, 1988.

A highly readable account of the 'ozone story' is

R. E. Benedick, *Ozone Diplomacy: New Directions in Safeguarding the Planet*, Harvard University Press, Cambridge, Mass., 1991.

Detailed assessments of the costs of control are to be found in the Montreal Protocol 'Assessments' published regularly through the United Nations Environment Programme in Nairobi. The *Report of the Technology and Economic Assessment Panel* contains the control cost estimates, but says nothing about the benefits of control.

Box 20.4 is taken from

M. Prather and R. Watson, 'Stratospheric ozone depletion and future levels of atmospheric chlorine and bromine', *Nature* **344**: 729–34, 1989.

CHAPTER 21

Conserving biological diversity

What is biological diversity?

Biological diversity, or 'biodiversity' for short, is a general term for the extent of variety in nature. That variety is in terms of:

species of plants
species of animals
species of microorganisms

and the ecosystems and ecological processes of which they are part. Note that diversity refers to *variety* rather than *numbers* of individuals within a species.

Plants, animals and microorganisms have *genes* and the information stored in those genes is *genetic information* or **genetic diversity**. The number of different species gives us a measure of **species diversity**. The variety of habitats, biotic communities and ecological processes is known as **ecosystem diversity**, and this term also embraces the variety within ecosystems and processes. So, biodiversity tends to be analyzed in terms of genetic, species and ecosystem diversity. Box 21.1 indicates what is known about the number of species. Remarkably, the extent of species diversity is not known and estimates range from 5 to 50 million. Of those, perhaps only 1.4 million have been described.

Why is biodiversity important?

The moral argument

For many people the very questioning of the worth of biodiversity is illicit. They would argue that humankind has a *moral obligation* to conserve biodiversity, an obligation that comes with the fact that humans have the capability to destroy much of that biodiversity. With power comes responsi-

Box 21.1   How many species are there?

The true number of species on earth is not known. A great many undescribed ones exist, many of them in tropical forests. The table below describes the identified species. How many are unidentified is not known, but there could be 10, 30 or even 40 times as many as the identified ones.

Group	No. of described species
Bacteria and blue-green algae	4 760
Fungi	46 983
Algae	26 900
Briophytes (mosses and liverworts)	17 000
Gymnosperms (conifers)	750
Angisperms (flowering plants)	250 000
Protozoans	30 800
Sponges	5 000
Corals and jellyfish	9 000
Roundworms and earthworms	24 000
Crustaceans	38 000
Insects	751 000
Other arthropods and minor invertebrates	132 461
Molluscs	50 000
Starfish	6 100
Fishes	19 056
Amphibians	4 184
Reptiles	6 300
Birds	9 198
Mammals	4 170
Total identified	1435 662

Source: J. McNeely *et al.* (1990)

bility. This sense of obligation is often combined with a view that ecosystems and species have *rights*, in much the same way as rights are conferred on some animals, even if it is sometimes only the right to a humane way of dying (think of slaughterhouses and the legislation that surrounds the slaughter of animals for food). Others find a religious support for such a view – there is some *stewardship* responsibility on behalf of some deity.

Such moral views unquestionably exist and are sometimes embodied in religious codes of practice. One problem with the moral view is that it often conflicts with other moral views about, say, the right to earn a living, the right to have access to basic needs such as food and shelter, and so on. If conserving biodiversity conflicts with those rights, then some 'meta-ethical' principle is required for deciding which moral view should prevail. In the economist's language, there is often a *trade-off*. Since moral views tend to be *absolutist* (something is always right, or always wrong), they help determine choices only if we can be sure there is no conflict of absolute views. The fact that there often is such a conflict does much to explain why, for example, some developing countries resent rich countries telling them not to cut down or burn their forests. In the developing countries' view, the loss is justified in the name of economic development and the development is often aimed at the poor in society who have a 'right' to the benefits of development. The 'jobs versus the environment' debate is very much of this kind. It explains why there has been a major effort to look for the other values of biodiversity conservation, values that lie in the human-oriented benefits of conservation.

Economic benefits

Biodiversity conservation can take place in two broad ways. An attempt can be made to *preserve* the biodiversity by placing limits on the use of habitats. This is often done by declaring such areas as 'national parks' or 'heritage sites' and there are many classifications of such sites throughout the world. The other way to conserve biodiversity is to encourage its *sustainable use*. This means looking at the portfolio of natural assets that an area may have and exploiting those assets in such a way that their stock does not diminish. This is akin to the idea of a *sustainable yield* in fishing or forestry. Thus, instead of clear-felling a tropical forest, a sustainable use would involve perhaps taking just a few trees, using selective harvesting methods, and exploiting the area for other products such as fruits, nuts, rattan, honey, and so on.

'Preservationists' tend not to like the idea of sustainable use because they feel it sanctions the idea of human exploitation and conflicts with the moral view outlined above. At the practical level, they feel that any use will eventually lead to destruction of biodiversity because people cannot be trusted with natural resources. Advocates of the sustainable use approach point to the near impossibility of 'sterilizing' any area of the world in the face of population growth and economic development. Their view is that we have to demonstrate that conserving diversity is economically worthwhile, and we have then to design incentives to secure that conservation.

Chapter 8 discussed the concept of *total economic value* and there it was shown that it comprises use and non-use values. In turn, the use values comprised 'direct' and 'indirect' values.

Box 21.2 shows some examples of these values. For example, the direct use values of tropical forests include their role in supplying both the global and

Box 21.2 The economic values of biodiversity

Tables 1, 2 and 3 illustrate some of the economic values that can be derived from using biodiversity as an economic asset. For convenience they have been 'normalized' by expressing them in 'per hectare' terms. This is not

Table 1 Ecosystem: tropical forest (present values US$/ha, $r = 5\%$, $T = 20$)

Benefit	Local	Global	Local + Global
Use value: direct			
Medicinal plants	250–750	12–250	262–1000
Tourism	20–1250		20–1250
Minor products	>0–7000		>0–7000
Use value: indirect			
Carbon fixing	0?	500–1500	500–1500
Flood control	23		23
Non-use value	+	5	5+
Total[a]	>293–9023	517–1755	810–10 778

[a]Aggregation is also hazardous since it assumes that the values are 'transferable' from one site to another.
See text for discussion of items.

Table 2 Ecosystem: wetlands (present values, US$/ha, $r = 5\%$, $T = 20$)

Benefit	Local: LDC	Local: DC	Global	Total
Use Value: Direct				
ag + fish + fuel	23			
for + fish + recr	5200–7155		n.a.	n.a.
fur		90		
recreation		27–1624		
water		38 000		
Use Value: Indirect				
storm protection		1134		
Non-use value		300–350		
Total[a]	23–7155	1600–3200		
		up to c. 40 000	n.a.	n.a.

[a]See text for discussion of items.

Table 3 Ecosystem: rangeland (present values, US$/ha, $r = 5\%$, $T = 20$)

Benefit	Country	Local benefit
Use Value: direct		
wild products	Zimbabwe	7.5
trophies	Zimbabwe	1.2
viewing	Kenya	<40.0
ranching	Zimbabwe	2.0
Use value: indirect	n.a.	n.a.
Non-use value		
elephants	Thailand	22.0
wilderness	Australia	796 800 to 1 907 600

Source: D. W. Pearce *et al.* (1992)
See text for discussion items.

strictly legitimate since it could be taken to imply that if we had just one hectare of tropical forest, for example, it would have these values. There tend to be minimum ecologically viable sizes for tropical forest ecosystems, so it is somewhat misleading to express economic values in per hectare terms. But the importance of expressing value this way is that it enables us to get *some* idea of how biodiversity conservation compares, in purely economic terms, with the alternative uses of land, such as agriculture or forestry or industrial development. The values have been expressed in 'present value' terms, using a 5 per cent discount rate and looking at the benefits over a twenty-year time horizon.

local market with plant genetic material that can be used to make medicines ('medicinal plants'). Tropical forests are also now the focus of much 'ecological tourism'. They supply minor forest products such as nuts and fruits, and so on. Tropical forests also store carbon. This means that if they are cut down and burned, that carbon is released as carbon dioxide, contributing to the global warming effect. There should, therefore, be some 'credit' to habitat conservation because conservation precludes the carbon being released and doing damage. The carbon storage value is an example of an *indirect* use value. The values for wetlands show another example: many wetlands act as storm protection agents. This means that storms are mediated as they travel across the wetland, protecting the inland areas. Wetlands also purify water supplies and, indeed, in some parts of the world, wetlands are artificially created as mechanisms for processing sewage. Ecotourism and medicinal plants are examples of *direct* use values.

Non-use values can also be estimated, although we have much less experience of securing such estimates. One way this might be done is by looking at **debt-for-nature-swaps**. A debt-for-nature swap works in the following way. An interested conservation agency buys up some of the developing country's international debt. This is known as 'secondary' debt and it can be purchased on the world's money markets. It is often priced at less than its face value. For example, if country A owes $1 billion, each $1 of face value can be purchased for a fraction of this price, say 50 cents. The actual value differs from the face value because there is a risk that the indebted country will not pay the debt back. So, secondary debt can often be quite cheap. The conservation agency then promises to dispose of the debt in return for a promise from the indebted country that it will look after a conservation area such as a national park. The swaps often become quite complex and are always associated with some kind of management plan and the conversion of the foreign debt (which is denominated in international currencies) for domestic currency bonds. There have been quite a few debt-for-nature swaps so far, ranging from Bolivia to the Philippines and Zambia. The sums are modest by comparison with the indebtedness of the countries (although quite big in the case of Costa Rica) but often enable conservation of very large areas. By looking at what the conservation agency actually pays and the areas conserved, a 'per hectare' value can be derived. This is one way in which a very approximate non-use value can be estimated and that is how the figure for non-use value in Table 1 of Box 21.2 has been obtained.

Non-use value for wilderness is shown in Box 21.2 for Thailand and Australia. These values were obtained through 'contingent valuation', i.e. by asking people questions about their willingness to pay to conserve these areas (see Chapter 8). The Thailand example involved asking people in Thailand and the Australian example involved asking people in Australia. The very large differences are not just a matter of differences in income, but reflect the perceived uniqueness of the region in Australia that was the subject of the valuation experiment (the 'Kakadu' area in North Australia) and made famous in a film.

Notice that the economic values listed in Box 21.2 are separated into 'local and global' categories. This is important because many sustainable uses of habitat will benefit the local people, but some of the values benefit the world as a whole – carbon storage, for example, means less global warming and that means a benefit for all countries (in general, anyway). Similarly, the non-use, or 'existence' values often accrue to the rich nations. But some of these values have associated cash flows and some do not. The global existence values, for example, do not have a cash flow: no-one pays Brazil, say, not to set fire to its rainforests. One way to encourage less biodiversity loss, then, is for the countries possessing the biodiversity to *appropriate* the benefits they are providing for the rest of the world. This is no more than a simple application of the idea of *external benefits*. Just as we argue that the creator of pollution should pay a tax or penalty of some kind (the Polluter Pays Principle), so it is justified for the creator of an external benefit to extract a price from the beneficiaries.

This idea of appropriating the global benefits is exactly what was discussed at the 'Earth Summit' in Rio in 1992. There it was agreed that the rich countries should pay more to the poor countries to encourage them to conserve their biodiversity. The mechanism for this is the Global Environment Facility (the GEF) which transfers funds from rich to poor countries in return for conservation of biodiversity, reduced pollution in international waters, control of carbon dioxide emissions and measures to combat deforestation and desertification.

The opportunity cost of biodiversity conservation: why biodiversity is disappearing

In themselves, the economic values of conservation are not particularly interesting. They must be related to the alternative land use that 'competes' with biodiversity conservation. For example, if it can be shown that biodiversity conservation can yield $X per hectare and agriculture only $0.5X then we have a powerful argument for conservation. It does not mean it will take place – not many land use decisions are based on a careful comparison of costs and benefits of alternative uses. But it is part of the economic argument for protecting more of the environment. The basic rule, then, is that for conservation to be economically justified:

$$[B_c - C_c] > [B_d - C_d]$$

where B_c is the benefit of conservation, C_c is the cost of conservation, B_d is the benefit of 'development' and C_d is the cost of development. Here the term 'development' is being used to describe the non-conservation use of the land, but strictly, conservation should be thought of as another form of development. The expression $B_d - C_d$ is the *opportunity cost* of conservation, i.e. it is what has to be surrendered if conservation takes place.

Box 21.3 shows some rough estimates of the economic value of using land for development purposes. Once again, these are indicative only, because the development value will vary country by country and place by place; but they reveal an important fact. What the landowner or land use receives by way of development benefits may bear very little relationship to the benefits of that development to the nation in question. The reason for this is that many developments are subsidized or encouraged in some way by governments. Measures include subsidies to output, tax breaks, cheap credit, subsidies on machinery, fertilizers, irrigation water and so on. We could argue that these subsidies reflect the development priorities of the countries in question. In that case, they would have some economic justification. But in practice, they tend to have far more to do with the political lobbying power of the groups who benefit, whether they are farmers or logging companies. Nor is this economic distortion confined to the developing world – the European Common Agricultural Policy is a good example of a special and expensive level of financial protection for one group in society (farmers). Subsidies in other countries are often even more dramatic, as in Japan, for example.

Box 21.3 therefore shows that the economic return to development is higher for the individual landowner than it is for the nation generally (the value to the nation is measured net of the various financial distortions). This means that biodiversity conservation begins with a disadvantage. Conservation is not subsidized (generally) but the alternative land uses are. Therefore, biodiversity conservation has to face unfair competition, and that unfair competition goes a long way to explaining why biodiversity is disappearing at an alarming rate.

Of course, there are other reasons for this disappearance or 'erosion of diversity'. Apart from the economic distortions in the alternative land uses, we have seen that biodiversity values often have no market – the watershed protection values of the tropical forest, for example, or the water cleansing values of the wetland. And where the benefits can be estimated, they are

Box 21.3 Present values of 'development' options
(US\$/ha, $r = 5\%$, $T = 20$)

	Private	National
Forestry	200–500 (sustainable 1000–2500 (unsustainable)	n.a.
Crops		
General LDC, USA	2700–4630	1660–2320
Japan, NICs	up to 100 000	5800
Livestock	large	negative to small

The 'private' values are the financial returns secured by the owner or user of the land. These differ, often substantially, from the returns to the nation because the owner often obtains subsidies of various kinds. The table shows that this 'distortion' of the economic returns to agriculture and forestry is not confined to developing countries. Biodiversity conservation has to compete not with the 'national' returns but with the financial returns to private individuals. It therefore does not secure what the businessman would call a 'level playing field'.

often global in nature and can be realized only if some new institution enables the relevant country to appropriate the global benefits.

So, environmental economics sheds a great deal of light on why biodiversity is disappearing. The main reasons lie in the 'public good' nature of biodiversity and the economic distortions in the market-place. A public good is one that, when it is provided, benefits a lot of people at the same time and the benefit to any one person is in no way affected by the benefit to another person ('joint consumption'). In addition, it is difficult to prevent anyone from enjoying the benefit once it is provided – this is the problem of 'appropriation'.

- The alternative land uses are often subsidized, explicitly or implicitly.
- The local benefits of biodiversity often have no market. This is especially true of indirect use values such as watershed protection. We say they are **local public goods**.
- Some of the benefits of biodiversity are global in nature, making it difficult for countries to appropriate the benefits. We say the benefits have the characteristics of a **global public good**.

Conclusions

Biological diversity is important for both moral and economic reasons. But if the morality of conservation can be disputed, the economic case for conservation is becoming increasingly powerful. This means investigating the economic values of conservation and, above all, the economic factors that create diversity erosion.

Further reading

D. W. Pearce, D. Moran and E. Fripp, *The Economic Value of Conserving Biological and Cultural Diversity*, Centre for Social and Economic Research on the Global Environment, University College London, 1992.

The economics of biodiversity conservation is a rapidly evolving subject. There are few detailed books on it but readers will find it useful to consult:

J. McNeely, *Economics and Biological Diversity*, International Union for the Conservation of Nature, Gland, Switzerland, 1988.

J. McNeely, K. Miller, W. Reid, R. Mittermeier and T. Werner, *Conserving the World's Biological Diversity*, International Union for the Conservation of Nature and World Bank, Washington DC, 1990.

T. Swanson and E. Barbier, *Economics for the Wilds: Wildlife, Wildlands, Diversity and Development*, Earthscan, London, 1992.

On the writings of ecologists in this area see:

P. Ehrlich and A. Ehrlich, 'The value of biodiversity', *Ambio* **21**(3): 219–26, 1992.

(This whole issue of *Ambio* is excellent and is devoted to the biodiversity issue.)

E. O. Wilson (ed.), *Biodiversity*, National Academy Press, Washington DC, 1988.

CHAPTER 22

International environmental policy: acid rain

Introduction

Increasingly, environmental policy has taken on an international dimension. The two reasons for this are:

(a) that many of the world's threatened natural resources are shared resources, or 'common property', as with the oceans and the atmosphere; and

(b) because actions in one part of the world affect the quality of life of another part of the world. This may be because pollution 'travels' and is no respector of political boundaries, or because individuals' psychic wellbeing in one country is affected by loss of environmental assets in another country (as with the loss of tropical forests, for example).

The 'internationality' of environmental problems poses many special challenges for environmental economics. For example, imposing a tax on a polluter in one country is one thing, but what happens when the pollution is international? There may not be a transnational authority with the power to impose the tax. The same is true if we wish to establish a tradeable permits system: it may be that countries will have to trade with other countries and that means setting up some transnational institution to monitor the trades and ensure compliance. Because we do not have 'world government', the application of any measure of environmental policy becomes more complex in the international arena.

Acid rain is one such example of an international pollutant. Acid rain is a generic term for the deposition (in wet or dry form, hence the somewhat misleading name) of the pollutants sulphur dioxide (SO_2), nitrogen oxides (NO_x) and chloride (Cl^-) in their acidic form. The conversion to acids occurs in the atmosphere. Acid rain does damage to buildings and materials (through its corrosive properties), to trees (through leaf damage and perhaps impairment of growth), to crops, to water resources through acidification which reduces the capability of rivers and lakes to support aquatic life, and probably to human health as well. These acidic pollutants 'travel' because they become airborne at the point of emission and can be deposited several hundred kilometres from the source. In this sense they are 'transboundary' pollutants, crossing national boundaries. This is why the control of acid rain has become an international issue (see Box 20.1).

International action on acid rain

In the United States, the 1990 Clean Air Act calls for a reduction of 10 million tons of sulphur emissions. Despite an exhaustive research programme which found comparatively small *national* damage impacts from acid rain (the National Acid Precipitation Assessment Programme – NAPAP), political pressures, including those from neighbouring Canada which receives some of America's acid emissions, forced the measure through. The Clean Air Act is also notable for its use of *tradeable pollution credits* (see Chapter 13) as the mechanism for achieving the reduction target efficiently.

European nations, including the East European 'economies in transition' and the ex-Soviet Union are now (1992) negotiating a Second Sulphur Protocol. The First Protocol (following the Convention on Long-Range Transboundary Air Pollution) called for all signatories to reduce SO_2 emissions by 30 per cent by 1993 compared to 1980. The United Kingdom and United States did not sign the first Protocol, but all nations will come under pressure to sign the second one. The long-term targets are likely to be dramatic, since they are couched in terms of 'critical loads'. A critical load is a level of pollutant deposition below which no significant damage can be discerned. Put another way, achieving critical loads means aiming for *zero ecological damage*. To gauge some idea of what this means in practice, achieving critical loads in Europe will require reductions in SO_2 of over 80 per cent, making the first Protocol modest by comparison. Box 22.1 illustrates the idea of a critical load by showing how it relates to the economic concept of environmental damage.

Critical loads may not be achievable for at least two reasons. They may not be *technically* achievable, i.e. they may require reductions beyond the capability of current technology. They may also be economically unfeasible, imposing unacceptably high costs on industry. The issue is further complicated by the fact that East European and ex-Soviet Union countries will not be able to bear the cost of their own clean-up. The rest of Europe will have to pay their own clean-up costs and those of the East as well. That it is in their own interest to do so can be seen from Box 22.2 which shows the matrix of emitters and receivers of sulphur oxide emissions in Europe. Since emissions from the East pollute the West, there are gains to be had from helping the East clean up.

Box 22.1   Critical loads and economic concepts

The diagram shows the total damage done by acid rain and the total cost of abating that damage. The total damage curve (TDC) is read from left to right: as pollution increases so does damage. The total abatement cost curve (TAC) rises from right to left, this is because the cost of reducing pollution rises as the amount of pollution is reduced. The economic optimum is where the sum of total damage costs and total abatement costs is at a minimum (not where the curves cross – that would be correct if the curves were *marginal* damages and marginal abatement costs). That is, the aim is to minimize the total costs to society whether they are environmental costs or the monetary costs of abatement. But the critical load concept refers to a situation in which no damage is done. So CL marks the critical load point. Clearly, the economic approach and the critical load approach are inconsistent. The only way that critical loads and the economic optimum could be close is if the damage curve rose very sharply indeed after point CL, or if the TAC curve was very flat, i.e. it is cheap to control pollution.

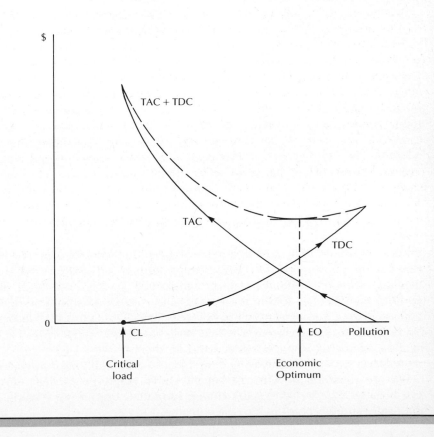

How big is this cost? No-one knows for sure. The mathematical models used to simulate various policy measures suggest that 'maximum feasible reductions' by 2000 could cost up to £30 billion per year. In practice, more moderate targets can be expected. Existing country reduction plans are expected to cost perhaps £5 billion per year, but these would leave 20 per cent of ecosystems above critical loads, i.e. with damage still occurring.

Moreover, there are other factors likely to make the 80 per cent reduction targets appear unnecessarily demanding. As East European industry is restructured, energy intensive industries will give way to less energy intensive industries, efficiency of energy use will increase, and acid pollution will fall 'naturally'. Additionally, some countries, including the European Community countries are considering the introduction of a *carbon tax*, a tax on the carbon content of fossil fuels, in order to achieve targets of getting back to 1990 emission levels of CO_2 by 2000, a commitment confirmed at Rio. But the policies that reduce CO_2 emissions tend also to reduce sulphur oxide (SO_x) and nitrogen oxide (NO_x) emissions. Energy conservation and fuel substitution are the most obvious examples. If the carbon tax goes ahead then SO_x and NO_x reductions can be secured as 'free goods'.

Finally, the cost estimates relates to 'add on' technology such as flue gas desulphurization (FGD). This is technology which is added to, say, a power plant and which captures nearly all of the sulphur in the chimney stack. In practice, many other cheaper measures are likely to be justified before these technologies are introduced, especially energy conservation measures. And even where add-on technology is required, the US example of tradeable pollution permits is worth taking note of. Anyone achieving pollution reductions below the target set, secures a credit. This credit can then be sold to others, as in the US Clean Air Act provisions. The relevance is that such schemes are very likely to save compliance costs relative to traditional 'command and control' measures, as Chapter 13 showed.

The costs and benefits of acid rain control

Whether it is *worthwhile* spending money on acid rain control depends on the benefits Europe can expect to receive in the form of reduced forest and crop damage, reduced buildings damage, improved health and lower water acidification. The data to compare benefits and costs do exist, but no rigorous exercise making the comparison has yet been done. Getting to critical loads may or may not make sense on economic cost–benefit grounds. However, the analysis in Box 22.2 suggests that acid rain damage would have to be very severe indeed to justify achieving critical loads, even as a long-run objective.

We can illustrate how a cost–benefit study might be carried out. The numbers used here relate to the United Kingdom, but are very crude. The interest is in the procedure, not the outcome.

302

Box 22.2 Acid rain in Europe: who pollutes whom (million tonnes sulphur, S)

Receivers			Emitters				
	East Europe	East Germany	ex-USSR	EC	Scandinavia	Other	Total
East Europe	2.2	0.5	0.1	0.3	0.0	0.2	3.3
East Germany	0.1	0.6	0.0	0.1	0.0	0.0	0.8
ex-USSR	0.5	0.2	2.2	0.1	0.0	0.5	3.5
EC	0.2	0.2	0.0	2.3	0.0	0.4	3.1
Scandinavia	0.1	0.1	0.1	0.1	0.1	0.1	0.6
Other	0.5	0.3	0.3	1.7	0.1	1.5	4.4
Total	3.6	1.9	2.7	4.6	0.2	2.7	15.7

To read the matrix, select a country in the first row, say EC. This gives the *emitter*. Read down the relevant column and select the country or area of *receipt* of the pollution. For example, EC emissions result in 0.1 million tonnes of sulphur deposition in Scandinavia. Notice that the largest amount of pollution is accounted for by 'self-pollution', i.e. emissions in a region tend to land in that region.

First, we have some idea of what it costs to install flue gas desulphurization equipment. The costs for varying degrees of pollution reduction are shown in diagrammatic terms in Box 22.3. As noted above, these costs will typically *exaggerate* the true costs because there will be significant scope for switching to cleaner fuels (such as natural gas) and energy conservation, both of which are cheaper than installing add-on equipment. So, we might think of the cost curve 'MAC' (marginal abatement costs per kilogram of SO_x removed) as being some kind of upper bound to the true cost curve, although the shape of the curve is likely to be altered only at the lower end since this is where fuel switching and energy conservation will tend to apply.

Various estimates exist of the damage done by acid rain in the United Kingdom. Some very preliminary results suggest that the cost of repairing and maintaining buildings is higher by some £400 million every year in the United Kingdom because of acid rain deposition. Now, the United Kingdom receives some 1 million tonnes of SO_2 each year as depositions. So, very crudely, the damage is some £400 per tonne of SO_2, or £0.4 per kilogram. Health costs from SO_2 are thought to be very low at perhaps only £0.007 per kilogram, but health damage from other pollutants could be much more significant, an issue we return to below. Damage to forests could amount to as much as £0.6 per kilogram, although there are reasons for thinking this is

303

Box 22.3 The costs and benefits of SO₂ control in the United Kingdom

The diagram shows the marginal cost of abatement based on the assumption that all control costs involve add-on desulphurization equipment. On to this curve is superimposed the marginal benefit value of £0.375 per kilogram of SO₂ derived in the text. Where marginal benefits equal marginal costs is the economic optimum, and this suggests a 74 per cent reduction in SO₂ compared to 1980 levels based on the view that the United Kingdom is

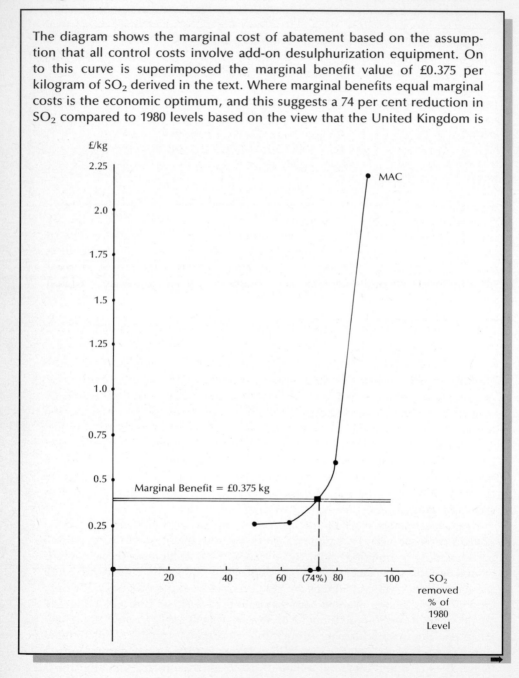

concerned only with its own damages and not with those imposed on other countries through the export of pollutants. This is clearly simplistic given the international nature of acid rain and the obligations that exist toward other countries. None the less, the analysis suggests that even with a UK 'selfish' perspective only, there are some grounds for thinking that significant acid rain control is economically justified.

too high an estimate since it involves an arbitrary adjustment for the recreational value of forests. Crop damage has been estimated at £0.11 and damage to water is certainly positive. So, adding up the damages from SO_2 for which we have estimates we obtain:

buildings	£0.400
health	£0.007
forests	<£0.600
crops	£0.110
	————
	<£1.117
	————

say £1 per kilogram of SO_2. All of these estimates are obtained by using various 'dose–response' functions. However, if we are considering policies to remove SO_2, those policies will also remove some NO_x and some particulate matter ('dust' or 'smoke'). We cannot say exactly how much, as this would involve an extensive analysis, but estimates suggest that 1 kilogram of NO_x removal could produce £0.8 of benefit, and 1 kilogram of particulate removal would yield £10. There will also be an associated benefit from the fact that the same policies may help to control carbon dioxide, but this is not so straightforward as equipment to reduce SO_2 can actually *increase* CO_2 emissions.

Now, the value of £1 per kilogram of SO_2 is for SO_2 *deposited*. But we have already seen that what is deposited is not what is emitted. The United Kingdom in fact emits around 3.8 million tonnes of SO_2 every year, but its depositions are just 1 million tonnes. The United Kingdom also 'imports' comparatively small amounts of SO_2, so we might adopt a rule of thumb that says that for every tonne of SO_2 emitted, something like 25 per cent stays in the United Kingdom and 75 per cent is exported. Assuming that the United Kingdom is mainly concerned with damage in its own country, it follows that the policy of controlling SO_2 *emissions* will yield a benefit *in the United Kingdom* of about 25 per cent of the total economic benefit of some £1 per kilogram. Thus the UK component becomes £0.25 per kilogram for SO_2 damage. In the same way, the NO_x figure has to be reduced if the focus is UK benefits only.

The UK emits about 2.7 million tonnes of NO_x every year but has depositions of only about 0.3 million tonnes. So, the damage done by 1 kilogram of NO_x emissions is reduced to about one tenth, or £0.08. The final adjustment allows for the fact that removing one tonne of SO_2 will not remove 1 tonne of NO_x and particulate matter. In the UK power sector, for example, which is the focus of much acid rain control, every tonne of SO_2 is associated with about 0.3 tonnes of NO_x and 0.01 tonnes of particulates. So, every tonne of SO_2 removed would yield:

£0.25 SO_2 benefit + (0.3 × £0.08) NO_x benefit + (0.01 × £10) particulate benefit

or some £0.37 per tonne SO_2 removed.

Box 22.3 shows what happens if we superimpose the average benefit of £0.37 per kilogram on the marginal abatement cost curve. We see that the lower estimate would justify around 74 per cent pollution reduction relative to the levels in 1980. Although very crude and simplistic, the approach suggests that stringent controls on acid rain would be justified. By 1990 the United Kingdom had already achieved around a 25 per cent reduction in SO_2 emissions compared to 1980. Clearly, the extra 50 per cent would be difficult.

Conclusions

The cost–benefit procedure can play a valuable role in any assessment of acid rain pollution control. But some do not believe that the cost–benefit comparisons matter anyway. They argue that our understanding of the consequences of ecosystem damage is so poor, and if we do nothing or too little the costs of being wrong are so high that action is justified on the 'precautionary principle'. The precautionary principle declares that it is worthwhile to *prevent* pollution even in circumstances where we have no firm knowledge that significant damage will be done. The principle reflects the state of uncertainty about our knowledge of ecosystems, but it also reflects environmentalist pressure to keep pollution emissions down to 'zero damage' levels, i.e. in terms of Box 22.2, to what we are calling critical loads.

CHAPTER 23

Environment in the developing world

Introduction

What role can environmental economics play in the developing world? While the application of environmental economics post-dates the development of the subject in the developed world, a decade or so of research has shown that the issues are similar in the developing world, and the solutions are generically the same. When looking at an environmental issue, a useful sequence to remember is:

scale
cause
incentives

By scale we mean, how big is the environmental problem? How serious is it? By cause we mean what should now be familiar from the earlier sections of this book, namely, that the cause of so much environmental degradation lies in the workings of the economy. So we should look to how the economy is managed (or mismanaged) for the clues to environmental degradation. The reference to incentives is the obverse of the analysis of causes: if we are to conserve environmental assets people must have incentives to conserve. Environmental economics argues that people have to have a *stake* in the environment if the environment is to be conserved.

We will follow this sequence of scale, cause, incentive in this chapter and illustrate each with some empirical material. But a few preliminary observations are in order.

Property rights, environment and development

It is widely argued that the environment would be better protected if the political system is based on one or other form of property rights. The idea of *open access* has already been discussed (see Chapters 5, 6 and 15) and there it was made clear that if *no-one* owns a resource, the environment is indeed likely to be at risk. Some people argue that *common property* – where the resource is owned or is subject to rights of use by a fairly well defined community – also risks environmental degradation. The evidence does not support this blanket view: some common property regimes 'fail', many succeed. The cause of failure is often some external event which causes the internal rules and regulations about the use of resources to break down. Central government may interfere, population growth may simply strain the common property management system to breaking point. This tends to leave **private property**, with rights vested in a single individual or household units or corporations, and **state property** as the final options. While there is no absolutely necessary linkage, state property tends to be associated with regulation of the market-place. Private property systems tend to veer more towards the 'free market' with less government intervention. In the developed world, most property systems are based on regulated private property, with the degree of regulation varying quite substantially. In the developing world there has been an historical tendency for property to be vested in the state, and for it gradually to be 'privatized', a process that is still going on. It is important to understand that neither private property nor state property guarantees environmental conservation. Some of the worst environmental degradation occurs in countries where the state has traditionally owned and controlled the environment (the ex-USSR, for example, or central Europe – see Chapter 6). Unrestrained market systems also tend to degrade the environment because of 'market failure' (see Chapter 5).

These observations are worth repeating because there is a temptation to think that the developing world would develop better and conserve its environments, if it pursued a different path of development based on a different structure of property rights to the developed world. We have no evidence to suggest this would be true, if by this is meant that they should pursue unrestricted market systems or state control. But it is an appealing idea if the focus is put on a regulated market system. Environmental economists tend to support the idea that market systems backed by interventions which themselves are based on market incentives are likely to be the best way forward. In the developing world, that view is complicated by the often absent institutions to manage such a regulated system – markets are often controlled, regulatory agencies are poorly staffed and informed, and often non-existent. The debate about the best way forward is therefore a continuing one.

Are developing countries different?

Poverty and the environment

There are obvious senses in which developing countries differ from developed countries. Their level of development, as measured by incomes, for example, is very much lower. Box 23.1 shows some selected countries' **Human Development Index**, a measure of development based on relative achievement in economic growth, education and health status. Our picture of developing countries tends to be one of poverty and ill-health and that is indeed true of the poorest countries. But it may come as a surprise to find that, say, Uruguay is ranked higher than Singapore on the Human Development Index (because of its educational attainment), and Mexico above Saudi Arabia (educational attainment and life expectancy). Nor is the United States the 'most developed' economy on this basis.

By and large, however, the poorer countries are also the least developed countries. From an environmental standpoint does this difference in wealth create different problems? It is widely thought that poverty is the greatest 'cause' of environmental degradation. The intuitive rationale for this view is appealing. The poorer one is, the less likely one is to worry about tomorrow. The immediate concern is for food today. This suggests that poorer communities will show little concern for 'sustainability' and will not undertake conservation practices to prevent soil erosion, or plant trees. It is true that poor people are often trapped in just such situations. But it is not so much that they do not care about tomorrow, as that they have limited ability to do anything about conservation if it diverts resources from the process of meeting today's needs. Nor, indeed, is it universally true that poor communities fail to conserve resources. Many have fairly elaborate structures of rules and regulations which are aimed at conserving resources.

Box 23.2 shows some possible links between income and environmental degradation. These indicators suggest that some indicators improve as income grows – population with access to safe water and sanitation, for example, and some measures of air pollution once certain minimum levels of income have been exceeded. This pattern is echoed for deforestation (not shown here). But others get worse as income grows, as with solid waste and carbon dioxide. If poverty and environmental degradation were always associated with each other we would expect the curves all to look like the ones for sanitation and safe water. The fact that they do not shows that there is no simple correlation between poverty and environmental degradation. Box 23.3 shows that the richer countries are responsible for using up more of the world's resources than the poor countries, but, as Box 23.2 shows, rising incomes often create the means for reducing environmental problems.

Box 23.1 The Human Development Index

The Human Development index (HDI) is published annually by the United Nations Development Programme (UNDP, based in New York). It is a fairly sophisticated average of educational attainment – measured by the degree of adult literacy in the population and the average number of years at school – a measure of income – which gives a lower weight to an extra $1 of income to a rich compared to a poor country – and life expectancy, a surrogate for health status. Each measure is reexpressed as a measure of 'deprivation'. For example, if Singapore has a life expectancy of 74 years, if the maximum life expectancy in any country is 78.6 years, and if the minimum life expectancy in any country is 42 years, then Singapore's health status measured as deprivation is:

$$(78.6 - 74.0)/(78.6 - 42.0) = 0.126$$

This deprivation index will be smaller the higher is Singapore's life expectancy relative to the maximum life expectancy. It will also be influenced by the minimum life expectancy in other countries – the higher that is, the higher will be Singapore's deprivation index. Converting a deprivation index to an achievement index simply means subtracting it from 1, e.g. health achievement in Singapore would be $1 - 0.126$.

A similar process is used to obtain measures of income and educational deprivation and achievement, and the three indicators are then simply averaged. The table below shows the ten 'most developed' economies and a selection from the remaining 150 countries listed in the HDI.

	Country	HDI		Country	HDI
1	Canada	0.982	29	Uruguay	0.880
2	Japan	0.981	33	USSR	0.873
3	Norway	0.978	40	Singapore	0.848
4	Switzerland	0.977	46	Mexico	0.804
5	Sweden	0.976	67	Saudia Arabia	0.687
6	USA	0.976	79	China	0.612
7	Australia	0.971	135	Indonesia	0.491
8	France	0.969	160	Bangladesh	0.185
9	Netherlands	0.968		Guinea	0.052
10	UK	0.962			

Source: UNDP (1992)

Box 23.2 Income and environmental quality

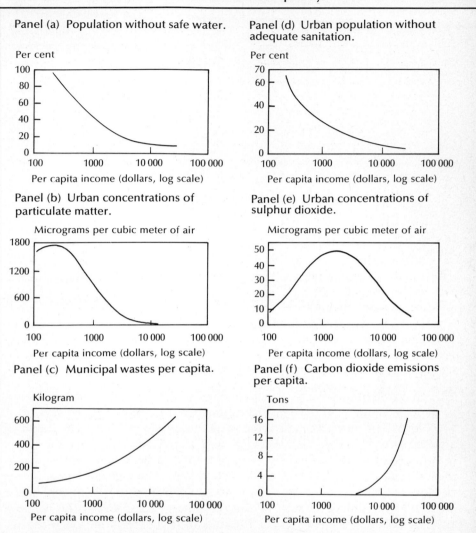

Panel (a) Population without safe water.

Panel (d) Urban population without adequate sanitation.

Panel (b) Urban concentrations of particulate matter.

Panel (e) Urban concentrations of sulphur dioxide.

Panel (c) Municipal wastes per capita.

Panel (f) Carbon dioxide emissions per capita.

Panels (a) to (f) show the possible links between the level of income in a country and selected environmental indicators. The data are very imperfect and not too much should be read into the diagrams at this stage. But they suggest that there is no simple blanket relationship between income and environmental quality as we would expect if, for example, poverty was always associated with environmental deterioration, or 'richness' was likewise associated.

Source: World Bank (1992)

Box 23.3 'Overconsumption' in the North. Comparative
resource consumption in North and South

	Developed	Developing	Ratio (kg or square metres per cap)
Food: cereals	717	247	2.9
milk	320	39	8.2
meat	61	11	5.5
Wood: roundwood	388	339	1.1
sawnwood	213	19	11.2
paper	148	11	13.5
Fertilizers	70	15	4.7
Cement	451	130	3.5
Iron + steel	469	36	13.0
Aluminium	16	1	16.0
Cars	0.28	0.01	28.0

The scale of the problem

We can now return to the issue of scale. How big are environmental problems
in the developing world? There are various ways of indicating the scale of a
problem. The environmental economist tends to prefer the idea of showing
scale in terms of the *economic losses* involved. Box 23.4 shows some measures
of economic damage done by environmental degradation and resource
depletion in various countries in the world. The estimates are obtained by
looking at how economic production – e.g. crop output – is influenced by
environmental indicators such as soil erosion. In some cases, the damage
done by pollution is included. The data are once again very imperfect (this is
both the problem and the challenge of applying environmental economics in
the developing world), but they suggest perhaps that developing countries
stand to lose a large percentage of their economic output through environmental degradation. If this is right it casts an interesting light on the
environment and development debate. For it is widely argued that developing countries *ought* to sacrifice their environments in the interest of economic
development. After all, this is how the currently rich world developed. The
United Kingdom, for example, was once richly forested and now has only a
tiny proportion of its land covered in trees. Arguably, deforestation in the
United Kingdom was one of the *means* by which it developed. The estimates

Box 23.4   The economic cost of environmental degradation

Country	Environmental damage	Year	% GNP
Burkina Faso	Crop, livestock and fuelwood losses due to land degradation	1988	8.8
Costa Rica	Coastal fisheries destruction, deforestation, soil erosion	1989	7.7
Ethiopia	Effects of deforestation on fuelwood supply and crop output	1983	6.0–9.0
Indonesia	Soil erosion and deforestation	1984	4.0
Madagascar	Land burning and soil erosion	1988	5.0–15.0
Malawi	Soil erosion and deforestation	1988	2.8–15.2
Mali	Effects of soil erosion on crop output	1988	0.9–12.5
Nigeria	Soil degradation, deforestation, water pollution, other erosion	1989	17.4
Philippines	Coastal fisheries destruction, deforestation, soil erosion	198–	4.0

Source: D. W. Pearce and J. Warford (1992)

in Box 23.4 could be telling a different story, for they suggest that environmental degradation may be costing 10 per cent or more of a country's gross national product. Put another way, those countries could be 10 per cent better off without the degradation than with it. But this is still consistent with a view that says the degradation is a necessary evil in order to develop, for it could be that the GNP would be lower without the environmental losses. The next section reviews why this is unlikely to be the case.

The economic causes of environmental degradation

Chapters 5 and 6 have already indicated why environmental degradation occurs, and Chapter 21 discussed the issue in more detail in the context of the erosion of biological diversity. Both freely functioning markets and governments 'fail' to secure the right ('optimal') amount of environmental quality. Unfettered markets often fail to account for the full cost of using natural resources. Public policy can alleviate such failings, by ensuring that markets reflect environmental values. On the other hand, inadequate policies may of themselves create environmental problems. Appropriate institutions and incentives are required to encourage producers and consumers, including government, to be prudent users of natural resources.

Inefficient use of natural resources arises for a number of reasons, including:

- when positive or negative external impacts resulting from production and consumption are not compensated: this is the traditional case of market failure (see Chapter 5);
- ambiguity or insecurity of tenure and use rights, resulting in excessive exploitation of resources. Basically, the more secure the right is to land or natural resources, the more incentive the individual has to look after the resource. If there is insecure tenure, the individual will not invest in conservation because the fruits of that investment may be lost when others seek to take over the land.

A form of market failure prevalent in many developing countries is the lack of clearly defined and secure tenure over renewable resources, such as forests, fisheries and arable land. Growing populations and economies place even greater demands on such resources. Weak or ill-defined tenure systems can break down under the pressure, leading to excessive exploitation and rapid degradation of valuable resources. A study of the causes of deforestation in Ecuador, for example, indicates that demographic pressure is only partly to blame. Land-clearing on the agricultural 'frontier' reflects efforts by farmers to secure economic rents and stake a claim to forest land. Open access situations are often exploited by powerful economic interests, creating entrenched resistance to restraints on the use of resources. In other cases, anarchic use of natural resources may be condoned by political authorities as a short-term expedient to relieve rural unemployment and poverty.

Public policy can alleviate or exacerbate environmental market failures by modifying incentives governing the use of resources. In addition, policies designed to stimulate economic growth and promote social welfare may have positive or negative environmental impacts. The environmental impact of economic policies is often ambiguous, because links are indirect or the causes of resource degradation are not clearly understood. Studies of fertilizer pricing policy in some developing countries reveal both positive and negative environmental impacts. Evidence from Indonesia, for example, indicates that price subsidies encourage excessive and inefficient use of fertilizer on lowland farms. Subsidies also discourage soil conservation in upland areas, by lowering the perceived cost of erosive farming practices.

314

On the other hand, research in Malawi and Nepal suggests that fertilizer subsidies can have a positive environmental impact, by alleviating rural poverty. Poor farmers are often caught in a vicious circle; they lack the means to undertake conservation investments, while the gradual degradation of resources leads to declining yields and income, and ever deeper poverty. Cuts in farm subsidies may be counter-productive. Lower farm incomes will depress investment further, and can induce more desperate attempts by farmers to extract the maximum current revenue from limited resources.

Reform of price incentives must be combined with an appropriate regulatory and institutional framework. Resource users will not respond to price-based instruments, if they perceive that rights of access to resources are not secure or that regulations are inconsistent. A high priority, especially in many developing countries, is to define and enforce clear rights of access and use, to private individuals and firms or to entire communities.

If they are devised carefully, policies can ensure that everyone benefits from the resolution of environmental problems. In the United States, for example, subsidies on water for irrigated agriculture in arid western lands have led to misallocation and inefficient use of scarce water resources. Farmers pay less than 20 per cent of the supply cost of the water they consume. While these subsidies ensure large profits for farmers, in most cases the economic value of irrigation water does not cover the cost of its supply. Water users in urban and suburban areas pay far higher prices for the water they consume, but rural and farm interests have consistently fought efforts to reallocate water rights in order to protect their subsidized profits. A potential solution is to assign water rights to rural residents, but let them trade with each other and with the cities. This would ensure that water is put to the most profitable uses, while protecting the economic interests of rural communities.

Incentives

The discussion of causes helps to define the nature of economic solutions to environmental problems in the developing world. First and foremost, rights to land and resources must be clearly defined. This can be done through land registration procedures whereby land rights are recorded and exchanges of land are monitored and regulated. Second, price signals need to be corrected. As Chapter 6 showed, the pricing of irrigation water, pesticides, fertilizers tends to be controlled at below market levels. This encourages wasteful use. The control of agricultural output prices means that farmers get less income than they would if market prices ruled, and hence have less surplus resources to invest in resource conservation measures such as building up bunds and terraces, conserving water and planting shelterbelts of trees. Box 23.5 shows the simple analytics of why this effect takes place.

Box 23.5 How agricultural price controls harm the environment

The diagram shows a simple supply and demand graph. Instead of the price being P^*, however, it is controlled at P_c through government regulation. The resulting quantity supplied is Q_c, whereas the quantity that consumers would like to buy is Q_d. The important point, however, is that the price control markedly reduces the farmer's income. In this case, the farmer receives income of $P_c \cdot Q_c$, shown by the heavy shaded area. If the market was allowed to operate he would receive $P^* \cdot Q^*$, or the heavy shaded area plus the light shaded area. The price control has therefore lowered his income and hence the ability to invest in longer term conservation measures such as terracing, bunding, water harvesting and tree planting.

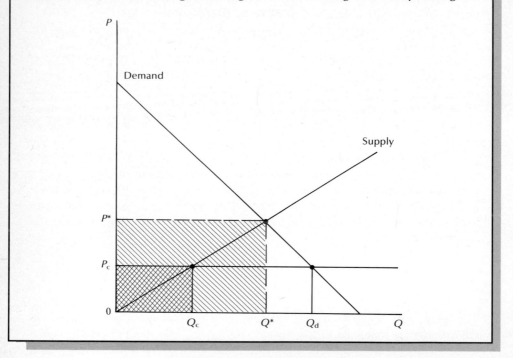

Conclusions

Overall, then, the application of environmental economics to developing country problems reveals many of the same issues as arise in the developed country context. In the developing world, the major distinguishing factors are:

(a) the extent to which individuals' rights to resources and environmental assets are not well defined. In the developed world, those rights tend to

316

be better defined through the private property system and through the system of government regulation;

(b) institutional weakness: where there are environmental policies, e.g. with respect to national parks, there frequently are limited resources available to monitor and implement regulations. This is why 'institutional strengthening' is a major feature of much international aid, especially in the environmental area;

(c) intervention in the market-place with consequent 'government failure'. This feature is not as marked as the first two because developed economies also engage in substantial market distortions. None the less, it is important.

Further reading

There are several popular introductions to the issue of acid rain – see for example,

Fred Pearce, *Acid Rain: What It Is, What Is It Doing to Us?*, Penguin, Harmondsworth, 1987. A balanced account of the science and policy is Chris Park's, *Acid Rain: Rhetoric and Reality*, Methuen, London, 1987. For an economic perspective, see David Newbery, 'Acid Rain', *Economic Policy*, October 1990.

D. W. Pearce and J. Warford, *World Without End: Economics, Environment and Sustainable Development*, Oxford University Press, Oxford, 1992.

D. W. Pearce, E. Barbier and A. Markandya, *Sustainable Development: Economics and Environment in the Third World*, Earthscan, London, 1990.

UNDP, *Human Development Report 1992*, Oxford University Press, Oxford, 1992.

World Bank, *World Development Report 1992*, Oxford University Press, Oxford, 1992.

INDEX

324 *Index*